THE
TOXIC
EXECUTIVE

THE
TOXIC
EXECUTIVE

STANLEY FOSTER REED

HarperBusiness
A Division of HarperCollinsPublishers

HarperCollins books may be purchased for educational, business, or sales promotional use. For information write: Special Markets Department, HarperCollins Publishers, Inc., 10 East 53rd Street, New York, NY 10022.

FIRST EDITION

Designed by George J. McKeon

Library of Congress Cataloging-in-Publication Data

Reed, Stanley Foster.
   The toxic executive : A step-by-step guide for turning your boss (or yourself)
   from noxious to nurturing / by Stanley Foster Reed.
      p.   cm.
   Includes index.
   ISBN 0-88730-562-8
   1. Managing your boss. 2. Executives. 3. Problem employees.
I. Title.
HF5548.83.R44 1993
650.1'—dc20   91-58509

93 94 95 96 97 ❖/RRD 10 9 8 7 6 5 4 3 2 1

To Shirley
Who taught me what caring was really about

CONTENTS

ACKNOWLEDGMENTS

I could not have written this book if I, myself, were not a toxic executive for a large part of my working life. I believed that most people were out to exploit *me* as I repeated the operations research mantra that "large groups of people and large groups of machines act in a consistent and therefore a predictable manner." My mistake: I applied it not only to individuals but to small groups.

In my drive to succeed, to become important in the eyes of others, to grow in wealth and influence, I needed help. At times I made demands on people who loved and respected me, but were too shy or frightened or inhibited to tell me when *my* reach exceeded *their* grasp. I judged them as I judged myself. Critically. And that is wrong, for no two people have the same skills, knowledges, ambitions, hopes, yearnings, and satisfactions.

While this book is to some extent a *mea culpa*, I take comfort in the words of one long-time employee, who, at a retirement party, said, "Stanley Foster Reed certainly was not the easiest person to work for, but there's one thing that was certain: He made you learn something new every day."

I owe special thanks to editors at HarperBusiness. First to Jim Childs, my editor at Dow Jones-Irwin who dragged me with him when he left DJI and went to HarperBusiness. Thanks also to Eamon Dolan, who inherited me from Jim. And to my agent, the accomplished Fifi Oscard, who is not only expert at handling prima donnas but *primo signori* as well.

I owe special thanks to my daughter, Alexandra Reed Lajoux, who edited the first two drafts of the manuscript, tore much of it apart, and forced me to think more about the reader and less about myself. And many thanks to Lura Dillard, whose double-masters—in library science and human behavior—helped immeasurably in bringing not only order but breadth and learning to the project.

Many thanks to my brother, Preston Turner Reed, psychologist, teacher, and strict constructionist, who made me concentrate on executives' *behaviors* rather than their words. And to my sister, Beryl Reed Clegg, whose wisdom, gained from a lifetime of dealing with recalcitrant students and brothers, gave me much insight into some of my own behaviors that might have brought out toxic behaviors in others, but never in her.

Finally, I thank Elina Sternik, recent émigré from Leningrad (now St. Petersburg), through whose widened eyes I saw America, Russia, and the USSR in a new light, and whose high-level computer skills sped this slow courier on his appointed round.

Stanley Foster Reed
McLean, Virginia,
1993

SECTION ONE

INTRODUCING THE **TOXIC** EXECUTIVE

1

TYPICAL **TOXIC** EXECUTIVE BEHAVIORS

The typical toxic executive (T.E.) locks his or her desk every night and then goes through everyone else's!

"I know someone just like that" responded most of the people I interviewed in writing this book.

Toxic executives are those who abuse the power they wield—particularly over subordinates—to serve and satisfy both economic and emotional personal ends. These personal ends are usually inconsistent with the institutional ends, whether church, state, labor, or business. And especially business.

Toxic executives range from the super-toxics, who get up every morning mistrusting everyone in their ambit, to the career toxics, who hate and mistrust only those people they must work with, to the subtoxics, who are understudying full-fledged career toxics, to the tyro-toxics, who are just beginning to learn how to be mean, rotten, mistrustful, deceitful, and noncaring.

If you yourself believe you are, have been told you are, or might be on the way to becoming an inherently mistrusting, suspicious, hostile, and uncaring toxic executive, before reading this book, take the Test for Executive Toxicity in the last chapter. (Since you'll probably take it several times, use the office copier.) Take the test again when you finish the book and compare the two. Take it again a few months later, after you've had a chance to apply what you've learned, and again compare. How toxic are you?

Based on my research, and backed by my forty years either as executive-in-charge, corporate CEO, or consultant, there appears to be much more T.E. behavior in business today than in the past. Being more toxic and less caring than others in the executive marketplace seems to have become a career objective. If there is a kinder and a gentler nation out there, it is certainly not in business.

As proof, look at the increasing level of lawsuits by employees against their companies and their bosses. Look at the increasing number of physical attacks and even murders of bosses by disgruntled employees who feel that they have been mistreated.

Just as the executive corps of the nation has *chemically* polluted and toxified our rivers, our harbors, and tens of millions of acres of our land, so that same executive corps is polluting and toxifying the interpersonal relationships in the workplace as well.

Further, it appears to me that there is a new exploitiveness in business. Subordinates, customers, and suppliers are all there to be exploited, not served and developed. People in their executive lives lie and cheat as if it were expected of them. Lecturing at graduate-school level, I have found that most executives are disdainful of ethics, citing the ancient line "If *I* don't do it, someone else will!"

It is also my belief, based on hundreds of interviews with executives while carrying out my consulting assignments, that subordinates who are compliant and worshipful are rewarded over those who have the courage of their convictions, are independent-minded, and express their opinions. Independent and creative thought has historically been a high-value attribute in a subordinate, something to be sought out and encouraged. But no longer. In this age of workforce reduction it's often an invitation to a pink slip.

I believe the subject of T.E. behavior is vital to the very survival of American business. If America's executive corps continues its toxic ways, it will be isolating itself from the worldstream of participative management—the engine that has driven Japan, Inc., to world leadership.

The United States, with only 4 percent of the world's landmass and only 5 percent of its population, at its peak in pre–World War II supplied 43 percent of the world's goods and services. Today that number is down to 31 percent and dropping. Something is terribly wrong.

Is it that toxic rather than caring behaviors have become the norm in the United States? This contrasts with what I believe was the partnership of capital, management, and labor that built the great businesses of America.

Based on the evidence I've seen, it is my opinion that toxic rather than caring behavior *has* become the nation's executive norm and has become the common denominator in executive advancement.

After forty years in business, I have come to the conclusion that making the working environment as soul-satisfying as possible—satisfying people's inner needs as well as their economic needs—is the only way to long-term resultful operations. Trite? Of course. Wishful thinking? Maybe.

In my research I seem to be dealing more and more with people who have lived out their entire business lives in a humorless atmosphere of mistrust and conflict. Many cannot conceive of a business milieu where progress and profits are created in an atmosphere of goodwill, where interpersonal conflict is the exception and not the norm, where a sense of humor is looked on not as an aberration in an executive but, as David Campbell of the Center for Creative Leadership sees it, as an entirely necessary ingredient in what is an essentially stressful environment.[1]

Campbell's view is reinforced by that of James Autry in his *Love & Profit*,[2] another delightful book whose thematic material is laced with poetry. In contrast to the views of Campbell and Autry, many executives appear to me to positively *enjoy* being mean and rotten to other people! They seem to believe that's how successful executives are *supposed* to act!

Being mean and rotten, however, I'm told by behaviorists, is "learned" behavior—they had to be taught by someone to be toxic rather than nurturing. They probably learned it either from their parents or their bosses or in school—even in B-School!

Today, as never before, the executive reward system, whether monetary or psychological or both, has many built-in elements to reward short-term executive toxicity. The restructuring process that is taking place all over America today involves hard decisions and sometimes harsh measures. The everyday caring executive is not given the task to effect a workplace transformation that is nontraumatic for most employees. The job goes to the T.E. who is near-totally unconscious of the damage that he or she is capable of inflicting on the ego and personality of someone who is to be fired or transferred to a business Siberia. But toxic behavior it is not confined to the restructuring process.

For instance, top management will recruit "genius" or "star-quality" executives, cash in on their early efforts, but eventually inherit the wind of massive discontent. Why? Because modern, star-quality executives seem to thrive on conflict and this builds resentments in the work force, which shows up in poor products and poor performance. Further, many of the brightest and most immediately productive executives, in the long run, prove difficult to manage. In spite of their talent, their overt and covert toxicity drives good people away, sometimes with massive resentments. Many flee to the competition, taking company secrets. That shows up in the bottom line. Like a virus that runs wild through a group of close-working people, one toxic executive in a key position in a business can infect an entire organization and its stakeholders—the executive corps, staff and line people, suppliers, customers, the community, and, of course, the stockholders.

It was in my twentieth year of experience in running business operations and as a consultant that I came to the conclusion that, *long-term*, the nicer, less intense, nurturing executives—the ones who cared about people, the ones who were sensitive to the inner wants and needs of their subordinates, peers, and superiors—were the most productive. They were successful because they made their fellow employees feel better about themselves and they all became more productive both as individuals and as a group.

Being caring and nurturing is not a sign of weakness, it's a sign of strength. It takes *strength* to be nice to others. Being rotten is much easier. A caring person is a principle-centered person. This theme is developed in two books by Stephen R. Covey, *Principle-Centered Leadership* and *The Habits of Highly Successful People*.[3] Read them.

Many American companies are just now discovering how positively nurturing, caring executive behavior boosts the bottom line.

One of those companies is the General Electric Company.

THE GE 1991 ANNUAL REPORT AND VALUE SYSTEMS

In GE's 1991 Annual Report, Chairman and CEO John F. Welch, Jr., had this to say in his letter to shareholders:

Over the past several years we've wrestled at all levels of this company with the question of what we are and what we want to be. Out of these discussions, and through our experiences, we've agreed upon a set of values we believe we will need to take this company forward, rapidly, through the 1990s and beyond.

In our view, leaders, whether on the shop floor or at the tops of our businesses, can be characterized in at least four ways:

The first is one who delivers on commitments—financial or otherwise—and shares the values of our company. His or her future is an easy call. Onward and upward.

The second type of leader is one who does not meet commitments and does not share our values. Not as pleasant a call, but equally easy.

The third is one who misses commitments but shares the values. He or she usually gets a second chance, preferably in a different environment.

Then there's the fourth type—the most difficult for us to deal with. That leader delivers on commitments, makes all the numbers, but doesn't share the values we must have. This is the individual who typically forces performance out of people rather than inspires it: the autocrat, the big shot, the tyrant. Too often all of us have looked the other way—tolerated these "Type 4" managers because "they always deliver"—at least in the short term.

And perhaps this type was more acceptable in easier times, but in an environment where we must have every good idea from every man and woman in the organization, we cannot afford management styles that suppress and intimidate. Whether we can convince and help these managers to change—recognizing how difficult that can be—or part company with them if they cannot will be the ultimate test of our commitment to the transformation of this company and will determine the future of the mutual trust and respect we are building. In 1991, we continued to improve our personnel management to achieve much better values and "numbers." That balance will change further in '92 and beyond, because we know that without leaders that "walk the talk," all of our plans, promises and dreams for the future are just that—talk.

Welch called on his managers to adopt a set of "soft concepts" having the "self-confidence to empower others and behave in a boundaryless fashion." This CEO, believing in "empowerment," describes how teams of hourly workers in the company's Schenectady, New York, plant now run, without supervision, $20 million worth of new milling machines that they specified, tested, and approved for purchase. Wrote Welch, "It is embarrassing to reflect that for probably 80 or 90 years, we've been dictating equipment needs and managing people who knew how to do things much better and faster than we did."

Welch inferred that GE's strong performance in 1991—when many companies in similar businesses posted losses or sharply lower earnings—was driven by "sensitivity to human factors."[4]

From my own experience, companies that wish to compete effectively in the global marketplaces, in the long run must learn to recognize and eliminate (or at least retrain) the toxic executive, whose iron fist in an iron glove wins a battle but loses a war. The toxic executive's targets for destruction are often the most productive people, the ones with ideas. Other targets of the T.E. are those with a "sense of future," those who think of the long-term effects of a course of action rather than short-term profits.

Welch has long been an advocate of inspiring every GE-person to contribute to modernizing management methodologies. GE has long been known as an experimenter in management methods and Jack Welch, as CEO, is accelerating the process. One of GE's most successful innovations is something called the "Workout," where groups of up to fifty meet with facilitators—usually business school professors—to tear apart the management structure without their managers present. Managers come in at the end of the three-day sessions to listen, to implement those things that make immediate sense, and to take under advisement the other recommendations.[5]

Welch's strong current drive for values might have been influenced by GE's history of criminal fraudulent activity by its executive corps, going back many years. GE is one of the nation's most frequently indicted companies for criminal activity, highlighted by the circuit-breaker price-fixing scandal of the 1950s, when fifteen of its sixteen vice presidents went to jail. That shook up the whole company, and elaborate measures were taken to ensure that there was no recurrence. But it hasn't worked and there have been continual problems right up to today.

In June 1992, GE was suspended by the Defense Logistics Agency from bidding on further government contracts for its jet engine division. The suspension grew out of the alleged activity of GE executive Herbert Steindler and his subordinates in conspiring with Israeli General Rami Dotan to bilk the U.S. military aid program of $42 million, of which some $12 million was to have been diverted to a private bank account in Switzerland that was supposedly set up by Harold Katz, a U.S. lawyer and Israeli citizen, for Dotan and Steindler. The balance was either spent on unauthorized programs for the Israelis or on Israeli espionage programs operating in the United States. GE was suspended more for failure to punish the executives involved than for the theft.

GE has been thwarted in its pursuit of the facts in the case due to Israel's blanket refusal to allow Dotan—who is serving a fifteen-year Israeli-imposed jail sentence for his part in the fraud—and Katz to be questioned by U.S. authorities. According to the *Wall Street Journal*, former Boston lawyer Katz had been involved in the Jonathon Pollard spy case and his Washington apartment used by Israeli agents in 1985 to copy thousands of classified documents supplied by Pollard. Mark Richard, the deputy assistant attorney general, wrote to the Pentagon that Mr. Katz "was essentially Dotan's money launderer." Israel's refusal to allow Katz to be quizzed was because of his involvement with the Pollard espionage affair and not necessarily the Dotan scam.

A whistle-blower broke the fraud wide open. Chester Walsh, a GE employee, working in Israel, blew the whistle on them.[6] Walsh did not report his suspicions to the elaborate internal investigative system installed by Welch after a major 1985 scandal. (In 1985, GE was convicted of bilking the Defense Department of many millions of dollars by altering the timecards of its Philadelphia Aerospace employees. CEO Welch personally promised the Pentagon that there would not be a repetition, even as another division was accused of tampering with invoices to bump the profit on a government contract from the negotiated 8 percent to 15.) Walsh said he did not complain internally because his investigations showed that whistle-blowers at GE were always fired.[7] Walsh claimed this was the reason he waited for four years to report the fraud, and not so his whistle-blower fee—up to 25 percent of the recovery under the Federal False Claims Act—would be larger as the fraud expanded.[8] GE agreed to plead guilty and to pay a fine of $69 million.[9] (Israel recently eased its stance against questioning of Dotan and Katz, as it rightly feared that this would hold up the approval of a $10 billion U.S. loan guarantee and wanted to allay the growing impression that the government of Israel was involved in the fraud.[10])

A GE spokesman told the *Washington Post* that already some of Welch's "Type 4" executives had been fired because they fell into Welch's category of "tyrants and corner-cutters." And during a retreat in January 1992, Welch also hammered home that point, reminding his top executives that "we will not shoot Indians and let the chiefs who turn the other way, who ignore the issues, who were too busy to see it, go free." But Bruce Drucker of the Pentagon's criminal investigative unit says that it is difficult to change the corporate culture in any large corporation—it probably takes a generation. Drucker said that "middle managers throughout the defense industry grew to maturity at a time when the commitment to integrity may have been given along with a wink of the eye."

Welch gets high praise from many people for his internal program to detect fraudulent activity in a company with $60 billion in sales. GE vigorously polices the activities of its 275,000 employees and vigorously investigates its own wrongdoings—it now leads the defense industry in the number of voluntary disclosures it has made about its own violations.[11] Recently, before a congressional committee, Welch testified that GE's investigative unit "missed the boat" and should have uncovered the Israeli fraud.[12]

But detection of "Type 4" executives—who will perpetrate a fraud to make their targets, who will run roughshod over people to attain their ends—appears to be difficult. Unfortunately, most detection must occur after hiring— after toxic behavior has reared its ugly head on the job, sometimes after severe damage has already been done.

Following are some keys to toxic conduct that can be used to identify the employed T.E.

SOME **TOXIC** EXECUTIVE BEHAVIORS

1. Toxic Executives Invade the Privacy and Space of Others

One of the principal behavioral traits of a toxic executive is the invasion of the privacy of others. Social scientists are saying that the advent of the computer and electronic surveillance equipment of all kinds in business has created the "Surveillance Society." (The Privacy Act of 1974 applies only to federal government employees.) Meanwhile, six European countries have made personal privacy a constitutional right. Harvard Law School's Laurence H. Tribe, a constitutional scholar, has suggested a Twenty-seventh Amendment to protect the privacy of the individual not only at home, but at business—in fact, anywhere.[13]

I, myself have had problems with overenergetic executives who were more interested in the private affairs of their subordinates, peers, and superiors than they were in making money for the company.

Building my *Mergers & Acquisitions* magazine, I started to run M&A seminars as well. They were very profitable, but took a lot of my time to plan, organize, promote, and run. While off to a good start, I needed someone other than me to run the seminar division. After some years, I found a well-educated, highly energetic and ambitious chap, who took over very effectively.

But one day I saw him searching his lead subordinate's desk while she was out to lunch. I thought it strange, but I said and did nothing. Later, I caught him going through my own desk when I returned unexpectedly from an aborted plane trip. He gave a lame excuse.

He should have been released, but I needed him. While I did not understand his actions, I thought them not particularly harmful behavioral anomalies, and not part of a larger toxic behavior pattern. I was wrong.

I discovered first that toxic executives rarely have only one fault. His next-favorite aberrant activity, after desk searching, was as a *frotteur*. One day he rearranged the furniture so he could brush against a row of female typists on his way to the john.

We could see the annoyance on the women's faces, and one of them left. But, like Anita Hill working as a subordinate under Clarence Thomas, none of them ever made a complaint, not about him or the weird arrangement of the furniture. Not being into either desk searching or *frotteurism*, I couldn't understand his behavior. Nor did I confront him with it. When my seminar program was finished, I had the furniture moved back where it had been and he quietly resigned shortly afterward.

Like my desk searching *frotteur* T.E., the typical toxic executive has no regard for the property, feelings, dignity, or privacy of others. T.E.s like to read other people's mail— even private mail. They listen in on phone calls. They believe it is their right to monitor and invade the privacy of subordinates, peers, and even superiors.

This kind of mild toxic behavior is quite common. The determinants of these particular behaviors are shrouded in mystery, but one thing is sure: T.E.s believe that *everyone* is interested in everyone else's private affairs. That's why they lock their own desks, are astonished when you don't, and are shocked when you say you don't really care who opens your mail, since you have no secrets.

But mild can turn to malignant, as it did for me when working in New York City at Moran Towing Company, whose big white *M* against a red background graces the stacks of one of the largest fleet of tugs in the world.

I worked in operations at Moran during World War II, acting as liaison for an oceangoing, tug-barge fleet I had helped design and some of whose construction I had supervised. Frank Belford, who had married into the Moran family, was the CEO.

I counted various members of the Moran family among my friends and pleasant acquaintances: Joe Moran, grandson of the founder; Commodore Moran, then of the U.S. Maritime Commission; and Brooklyn's Monsignor Moran.

All of them were very pleasant people. All but Belford. Belford was a toxic executive of substantial proportions. He was ignorant, rude, secretive, demanding, and suspicious. No one liked him, least of all me.

During one morning-long session with Fractious Frank, in which he rudely questioned my design of a towing rig which had been working very well, it was hard to keep my temper, but I managed. Why? Because I loved my job!

At lunchtime, I worked out my frustration by writing a description of the meeting in my diary. I closed with the observation, "Gentlemen are as scarce as Protestants at Moran." I put the diary safely back in its home, the bottom drawer of my unlocked desk.

The next day I was called into Belford's office. He shook the diary at me, read me that last line, immediately fired me, and refused to return my diary. Evidence!

Now, *that's* toxic!

Ray Fox, a Moran V.P., couldn't get Belford to change his mind. Nor could my immediate boss, Captain Earl Palmer. I stayed fired.

But Ray Fox did advise me to lock my desk in the future.

2. Toxic Executives Have Secrets to Protect

Most desk searchers are projecting their own mistrust on their subordinates. Some project it onto their superiors as well. They are thus more concerned with protection of their secrets than they are with their job.

George Cooke was of that kind.

An extremely competent engineer, he headed advanced geophysical instrumentation projects at my company, Reed Research. But George quit in the middle of a major project for the National Academy of Sciences—a project designed to discover why highways deteriorate so that the $40 billion the nation was about to spend on highways would be properly spent. His leaving left Reed Research in a terrible fix. His reason: The front office, which daily opened and logged in all the mail for our sixty professionals, could not physically comply with his demand to separate out his mail, both personal and project-related, and deliver it to him before it got to the automatic letter opener.

When mail volume was low, we tried to separate out anything that looked personal or was marked as such. But we were under severe time constraints to get the mail to all the project managers as soon as possible. Many days it was physically and economically impossible to take the time to search through the mail and seek out George's mail. Furthermore, we were under security and all the project-related mail, both incoming and outgoing, had to be logged.

My good friend George, it turned out, was a toxic executive. Why? Because he objected to his mail being opened? In part, yes. But the fact that he quit in the middle of a job that he had promised to finish, that he did not find us a successor that was trained in the special electronic circuitry he had designed, made him a T.E. It hurt Reed Research, him, the National Academy of Sciences, and the nation.

3. T.E.s Are Changeable and Unpredictable

Next to the T.E. privacy invasion trait and its derivative, super-secrecy, changeability is the most recognizable characteristic of a T.E. Yo-yo behavior is particularly demoralizing to subordinates. Listen to this secretary:

He may be brilliant, but he makes my life miserable. One day it's a pleasant "good morning" and the next day a growl. The next, no return greeting at all, just a stare. The next, a going-over before I've even had my morning coffee. I don't give a damn if he never smiles, or never says anything, and even growls every morning. I can handle that. What I can't handle is never knowing what to expect. Never knowing what kind of a day I'm going to have. I think I hate him.

A related type is what some behaviorists call an exploder. Exploders suddenly explode into wrath without warning. This can have a demoralizing effect on everyone around.

I remember that one of my top engineers, the head of the

design division, ordinarily one of the mildest and the nicest of people, was given to sudden but infrequent rages. One day he kicked a great big hole in his office wall, no less. Why? Because one of the missile transport systems we had designed for the Navy had collapsed at a sea trial. That could happen to anyone. But the unexpectedness of that sudden rage and the vision of that demolished wall colored our relationship from then on. He eventually went elsewhere. We both lost out. Was he a T.E. based on only a few such incidents over a five-year period? Unfortunately, yes, because it was so intense, so unpredictable, so graphic, we could not avoid the memory.

4. T.E.s Are Abrasion Junkies

A T.E. is often an abrasion junkie who gets a druglike "rush" from conflict and must have an "abrasion fix" at least daily and sometimes hourly. He or she thrives on conflict. But the company or operation does not.

Admiral Hyman Rickover, reputed father of the nuclear submarine, was of this nature. President Jimmy Carter described his old mentor as having absolutely no tact. "As a matter of fact, all the time I worked for him [Rickover] he never said a decent word to me…. If I made the slightest mistake, in the loudest and most obnoxious [of] voices I ever heard, he would turn around and tell the other people in the area what a horrible disgrace I was to the Navy and that I ought to go back to the oldest and slowest and smallest submarine."

Rickover never made any pretense of affability. Once, in line for a seat on a fully booked plane, Rickover and I stood shoulder to shoulder. As a member of the American Airline's Admiral's Club (of which I was the youngest member and sometimes temporarily refused admission because of it), I had a priority. I asked Rickover if I could help. His answer: "No. They all know me!" We left without him.

The Congress loved Rickover and disliked the Navy. But he played politics well, and a succession of Congresses insisted that he be preserved as an admiral of the line.

It brings to mind the dead Lord Nelson, preserved in a barrel of brandy for the long trip home from the victory at Trafalgar. Shot to death by a French sniper, he was entombed in a cask of the best French brandy and, burbling all the way home to England as his stomach turned to gas, he rose and fell in the cask, scaring the watch half to death. So too did Rickover burble his way along to a ripe old age, scaring the Navy into expensive and some say unwise atomic action.

Nelson lies in London's Trafalgar Square, and Rickover in Arlington National Cemetery. The one revered, the other already half forgotten.

(While Rickover was indeed brilliant, and prescient, he was *not* the inventor of the nuclear submarine. But he exploited the myth that he was and accepted the accolades. He was indeed a gifted engineer, but everyone in the Navy disliked him. No matter—a continuum of abrasion kept him alive even if heartily disliked by everyone else in the Navy. A succession of recalcitrant congressmen kept him appointedly alive unto his seventy-ninth year, which generated huge resentments in the Navy establishment. Like J. Edgar Hoover, he far outlasted his useful life.)

There is quite some literature about the abrasive personality. "Keenly analytical and capable of cutting to the core of a problem, the abrasive executive also has a knack for jabbing others in an irritating and often a painful way. Abrasive executives are alert to the faults of others, and are unhappy when things turn out to be well done and there's no hope of conflict and confrontation." [14]

It is my conviction that T.E.s do not differentiate between mistakes of *commission*, which normally are forgiven, and mistakes of *omission*, which usually are not. Rather, they have a craving for conflict. Anything for a fight and the resulting abrasion fix. In the long run, they will not make it to the top, regardless of how smart they are or how hard they work. In the meantime, they can make life miserable for many very nice people. But what about Rickover? Didn't *he* make it to the top? Yes. But only through the intervention of the Congress, which had a bone to pick with the elitist Navy.

5. T.E.s Are Non-, Under-, and Half-Instructors

T.E.s often create the conditions which call for an abrasive confrontation. The precipitating cause is often a lack of instruction. One T.E. I know gets an abrasion fix by consistently failing to inform his secretary where he can be reached on a trip. Once, for instance, he switched from his usual hotel in Milwaukee (which he'd been using for some twenty years) to a private club. There was an emergency and his secretary frantically tried to find him. She failed. On his return he tore into her, saying it was *her* fault because she didn't ask him where he was going to stay! He is happy. He's had his abrasion fix. His secretary is miserable.

T.E. underinstructors are even worse than noninstructors.

They rush out the door leaving half-instructed people in their wake. They target the unskilled and the unprepared, the unknowledgeable and the frightened, all under the pretense of delegation. This way they ensure that a series of mistakes will be made. Upon return they raise hell about all the bad things that happened. But the T.E.s are happy. *They* haven't made any mistakes; everyone else has. They've had their abrasion fix, but everyone else is miserable.

Under- or noninstruction can be active or passive. It is active and highly identifiable in the T.E.'s own ambit. It is passive and difficult to identify when it occurs in peer administrators.

6. T.E.s Are "Trappists"

Even if things are going well in their own shop, T.E.s will create the conditions for a continuum of failure for peers. I call this the "Trappist" syndrome for two reasons. First, because the executive tries to ensnare or "trap" his or her victims. Second, because he or she uses silence to accomplish this, as if taking the same vow as Trappist monks.

These T.E.s are far from saintly, however. Like watchmen setting fires in order to get kudos and credit for putting them out, they engage in complicated, destructive behavior for a range of reasons—from egoistic attention seeking to financial rewards.

A typical passive case: Two salesmen are taking phone orders. Each makes a separate promise to a different valued customer for the last lot of special parts in inventory. The head of the computer section hears the orders being taken and knows there's a problem, because the first salesman delayed keying in the order. But the computer head says and does nothing. Why?

It's not her job. *She* isn't in sales! "The salesmen are always giving me problems. They're overpaid, and don't understand computers," she insists.

Mistakes like this make this witch feel superior. She has effectively trapped them, because she could have easily prevented a major glitch.

The trappist syndrome is omnipresent in business at nearly every level and can tear an organization apart. From my experience, it is rare in Japan, where this kind of jealous behavior does not get in the way of serving the customer and the company. The Trappist T.E. serves neither.

7. T.E.s Have Bad Manners

T.E.s have really bad manners. A thank-you from one of them is as rare as palm trees in the Arctic. A thank-you is a piece of flesh torn from a T.E.'s body, for it means he or she now "owes" something to another. The T.E. has lost control of the other person. And that hurts.

Please always seems to come in italics. "Will you *please* get that report to me by five o'clock?" infers that the chance is very low that it will be there.

Giving compliments is like giving up an arm or a leg.

And a T.E.'s handshakes are like holding a bunch of cold, wet noodles, *if* he or she is inclined to shake hands at all.

Bad manners are bad business. There are many "charm schools" around the country where the T.E. can learn some manners.[15]

8. T.E.s Are Late for Appointments

T.E.s love to keep people with appointments waiting. It's part of what I call the "New York Treatment" (because it happens more frequently there than in any other major city). Keeping people waiting gives the T.E. power—especially over supplicants: salesmen, job seekers, unhappy employees. Apologies for keeping someone waiting are rare. Apologies also *hurt!*

On one occasion with one of my lawyers, we had just barely made the shuttle from Washington to New York and had missed breakfast. We had an appointment with a lawyer who left us unfed from nine to three. No coffee. No snack. No nothing. He sat at the head of the table in his library and was really difficult to deal with. He disappeared from time to time to "take a phone call." Later that day I looked in his office only to find the remains of his lunch and several coffee containers from the downstairs snack bar. This was all part of the "New York Treatment."

It's taken me a long time to get over my intense dislike for this guy. Only when I substituted my dislike of his *behavior* for my dislike of his *person* did I get over my resentments. I wonder what demons are eating at *his* soul to treat us so rudely. In later meetings I looked at his face. It was always gray. In spite of that, I learned. In subsequent meetings, to save him from himself, *I* sat down at the head of the table. And that was the end of the New York Treatment.

Once you're inside a T.E.'s office, if the sun is shining, know you'll have it in your eyes. This way you can't see the T.E.'s eyes or facial expressions. Know that the T.E.'s chair will be bigger than yours. And higher than yours. And more comfortable than yours.

The T.E. will call you by your first name but will not offer a reciprocal privilege.

And some T.E.s graduate to super-T.E.s when they get their own (or a bigger) office. Once in that great big ego chair, and behind a monster desk, they undergo a strange metamorphosis. They might not even come forward to greet you or get up from their chair to shake hands. They might not even look up when you enter. Real sickos.

A New York T.E. has called you for an appointment in his office. He needs your help. You agree, *but no phone calls!* He promises.

You arrive on time. You get the New York Treatment and are forced to wait. Finally you're in. The T.E. immediately reneges, taking call after call. Worse, you might even be asked to leave the room while he talks on the phone!

If it's cold, the rugged, he-man T.E. will have on a sweater and a jacket *and* an open window. You're freezing. He does nothing unless you complain. Your "whining" puts him in control, as *you* are the complainer. Drop him. Fast.

9. T.E.s Are Late for Meetings—And Ruin Them

Meetings are even worse than appointments, because more people are inconvenienced by late arrivals. T.E.s have many troubles with meetings.

It starts with introductions. I've been in a dozen meetings run by T.E.s who never took the trouble to introduce attendees to each other. It gives the T.E. power to know all the names and have you struggle. "Those names are *mine!*"

T.E.s are usually late for meetings—mostly with subordinates, but occasionally with superiors, as it makes them look busy. Often they arrive, staging a look-at-how-busy-I-am entrance, and then ask questions about agenda items already covered. They seldom apologize for their lateness. If they do, it's mumbled.

And T.E.s break the first commandment of social congress: *Thou shalt not interrupt.* They frequently cut in— especially on subordinates, who then lose their train of thought. This makes the T.E. happy, as it makes him or her feel superior. (Further, interrupting is typical of a "Type A" personality described in Chapter 5 of this section.) Professors Bruce H. Mayhew and Roger L. Levinger state, "The one universal social norm in all human society—interrupting an ongoing conversation—is taboo. In casual groups it is merely impolite, in task-oriented groups it may be strictly forbidden."[16]

Further, T.E.s are often unprepared for meetings. They try to wing it. They've not read the agenda, the minutes of the last meeting, or the premeeting memos. Instead of a meaningful hour, it's a wasted two.

Even further, if not running the meeting, they often sit outside the group and, carping from behind, effectively gain control. If the rules or setup do not allow such arrangements, the T.E. will be sure to sit himself or herself down in a confrontational position. This way the T.E. is happiest.

10. T.E.s Use "Avoidance English"

T.E.s don't like to use the words *you* and *me,* much preferring one of the "self" words. This is only partly because they vaguely remember the difference between the nominative and the objective cases.

You'll hear "people like myself" rather than the proper "people like me." You'll also hear the tortured "people such as yourself" rather than the simple and correct "people like you," because they avoid the word *like.* I've heard a T.E. change "tell it *like* it is" to "Tell it *as* it is" because in the dim, dark recesses of the T.E.'s mind the *like* versus *as* problem still exists, unsolved, and the modern phrase "tell it *like* it is," which is an attempt to bring reality to a relationship, is anathema to a T.E. On January 1, 1993, Donald Trump, in an interview with John McLaughlin on CNBC cable used the word "myself" twenty times including "I'm working on a book that will be written 'only by myself'"

You'll also hear avoidance English: "at the present time" or "in a very short time frame"—or "at the current time" instead of "right now," because facing up to what's happening right now gives T.E.s problems. They slide away from the here and now.

T.E.s like to use the word *lady*, as in, "There was this drunken *lady* lying on the sidewalk, who'd wet her pants." This kind of false egalitarianism, elevating street people to the nobility, stems from the T.E.'s own inner feelings of inadequacy. *Ladies* don't get falling-down drunk in public and certainly never wet their pants (at least not in public).

In another kind of avoidance English, T.E.s also like to slur words. One of their favorite slur words is *probably*, which they pronounce to rhyme with *trolley*. It probably means that they don't like to think about probabilities!

If the T.E. is running a formal meeting, the parliamentary rules are sure to be trashed. T.E.s hear what they want to hear, and then dictate minutes that seem to come from Oz. Put-down language is also practiced by the T.E. Many follow the pattern of political speech promulgated by politicians like "bare majority" Newt Gingrich, the Republican from Georgia who suggested that, in speaking of themselves, candidates use words like "environment, peace, freedom, fair, flag, we-us-our, family and humane." When speaking of opponents, Gingrich recommends using words like "betray, sick, pathetic, lie, liberal, hypocrisy, permissive attitude and self-serving."[17]

T.E.s will insist on finishing sentences for you. They'll also finish jokes you're telling or will tell you they have heard that one before. They destroy humor. Jokes are like songs. Certainly you would not stop someone from playing Beethoven's Fifth because you'd heard it before—there is a world of difference between the New York Philharmonic's rendition of the Fifth and the Washington Symphony's, just as there is between Sid Caesar's and Milton Berle's rendition of a traveling salesman joke. I could listen a hundred times to each rendition of the Fifth and at each telling of the same traveling salesman joke. There would be something new and different at each rendition.

11. T.E.s Are Control Freaks

Many T.E.s may never have really experienced a sunset or felt a dawn because sunsets and dawns belong to every-body, and not just to the T.E. Not owning them, they can't control them, and they don't like the neighbor's kids either.

12. T.E.s Are Cosmeticians

The typical T.E. is a cover-up artist. He or she is into the appearances of things rather than the real values, into images instead of issues, into finding out what is currently fashionable rather than real. Really phony companies have beautifully and expensively printed annual reports, gold plumbing fixtures in the executive bathroom, knockout receptionists, and knee-deep carpets and golden-toned cork on the walls, none of which help the bottom line.

The typical cosmetician T.E. might even prefer one of those very expensive fake convertibles that have a top that doesn't go down! That there are a lot of phonys in the United States is proved by GM Cadillac Division's current promotional program for their latest fake convertible, which they even miscall a "cabriolet," which the dictionary says is an automobile where the "top folds down." In addition, that new fake is called the "Liberty" Edition.[18] (Sirs, have you no shame?) "Buy one and win a free trip to the fabulous Greenbrier Hotel!" No way! I assure the reader that the doorman would probably turn you away if you drove up in one of those desperate excretions. No wonder GM lost $8.5 *billion* on their automobile business last year.

13. T.E.s Are Highly Competitive

You must always be slower and dumber than the T.E. or you're a threat. T.E.s *hate* to lose. *Hate* to be wrong. *Hate* to be bettered at anything.

14. T.E.s Abuse Both People and Things

The T.E.'s attack priority is ideas first, people second, and things third. You'd think that T.E.s, who so mistreat ideas and people, would not abuse things. But they do. Very often their own cars are unpolished and filthy. And they mistreat company property. They borrow books from the library and mark them up. They drive nails in expensive walnut walls to hang up pictures of their dopey kids.

15. T.E.s Hate Others' Ideas

The NIBM (not invented by me) syndrome and related to the more common NIH (not invented here) syndrome has been adopted by most T.E.s as policy to reject anything not conceived in-house. As the *Wall Street Journal* philosophized, "Build a better mousetrap and . . . corporate America might just slam a door in your face."[19]

Be careful with ideas. Buckminster Fuller and I long ago decided that a good idea is generally met with immediate discouragement, a really good idea with outright rejection, and a blockbuster idea with "malevolent obstructionism"![20]

T.E.s simply hate *inside* people with ideas because the ideas aren't their own. Thus, T.E.s will drag in *outside* consultants and spend millions of dollars of their company's money while the outsiders learn the business and extract all of the good ideas lying around. Now the T.E. can bring those ideas into the company as his or her own without being reduced to the expedient of "stealing" the ideas.

So, Mr. Junior Executive, be careful with ideas. NIBM is the T.E.'s first criterion for getting rid of troublemakers. To the T.E., people with ideas—especially good ones—are a threat. They are troublemakers. Away with them!

If it is mandated that ideas be handled in an enlightened and perhaps a more formal manner, the T.E. will attack the person rather than the idea. This is very easy for the T.E. to accomplish, since everyone has something wrong with him or her that can be capitalized on to support an attack.

16. T.E.s Are Credit-Snatchers

T.E.s don't share. Not experiences, not possessions, and especially not credit. You won't get credit for your successes, the T.E. will! It goes on *his* or *her* record, not yours.

This can quickly tear a business apart. In the deals business—setting up mergers, acquisitions, joint ventures, and the like—this is quite common. Credit snatching is dramatized in the film *Working Girl,* in which Sigourney Weaver, playing a deals person, takes credit for some cogent merger analysis by her secretary, played by Melanie Griffith. Unlike the real-life situation on Wall Street, where credit snatching is universal but seldom condemned, Weaver loses out.

This same theme dominates the film *Nine to Five* in which the super-T.E. boss, played by Dabney Coleman, takes all the credit for the good ideas of his office staff, played by Lily Tomlin, Dolly Parton, and Jane Fonda.

Both films are set in New York City. Natch. But if this were not a reflection of real life, one would not get the head nods: "I know people exactly like that!"

Ray Kroc did not found McDonald's. That's a crock. Richard McDonald and his brother, Maurice, did in 1948 with the world's first "fast-food" restaurant, in San Bernardino, California. They hired Ray Kroc to sell franchises. Yet last year McDonald's celebrated "Founder's Day" for Ray Kroc, who bought out the fabulously successful McDonald's chain from Richard and Maurice, golden arches and all, in 1961 for $2.5 million. Richard, who has the engraved, gold-plated spatula that flipped the fifty billionth hamburger, says it "really burns the hell out of me. Ray Kroc was the founder of the McDonald's *corporation,* not the chain which already had 200 McDonald's stores when we sold to Kroc."[21]

17. T.E.s Play the Blame Game

But for all the credit that T.E.s don't share, they will spread around the blame when things go wrong. They are only too eager to share the responsibility for their own mistakes and might have *your* record debited for their mistakes.

(By 37 to 29 percent, staff employees are more willing to admit mistakes than are managers.[22] "Men often deflect what doesn't go well, contending it wasn't their fault, but women take more of the blame for things," says management consultant Richard Hallstein.[23])

John F. Akers, CEO of IBM, blew up at his executive corps. They had been making too many excuses for poor performance, blaming, for instance, the market or organizational change. "But the fact of the matter is, they are all excuses,"[24] said Akers.

"Whose fault was it?" is still one of the most important questions ever asked in business. "Who did it?" and "What happened?" according to writer Charles I. Cragg, "are simple straightforward questions to which correct answers usually can be found. But, 'whose fault was it' is a profoundly disturbing question, one that is essentially unanswerable, and one that cannot be asked safely."[25] T.E.s are driven to seek out others to affix blame to when things go wrong.

David Rieff's seminal article in *Harper's*[26] reviews the latest rage in self-analysis, the so-called "Recovery Movement," which is sucking up millions of dollars in fees from confused and unhappy people all over the United States. In an adaptation of the Alcoholics Anonymous twelve-step program to sobriety, the Recovery Movement, in an attempt to make you feel better about yourself, blames parents, in-laws, society—just about everybody and everything—for your problems as you "get in touch with your inner child" and zero in on the people who were responsible for your present unhappiness, which the movement assembles as "codependency." This is supposed to effect a sea change in your personality.

Rieff was quite critical of the Recovery Movement, and the article evoked a storm of reaction from its progenitors and votaries, including a long and prolix condemnation of the piece by John Bradshaw, author of *Homecoming: Reclaim-*

ing and Championing Your Inner Child[27] and the guru of the Recovery Movement.[28] Rieff's view is supported by Wendy Kaminer in her book *I'm Dysfunctional, You're Dysfunctional*,[29] in which she points out that the entire country seems entrapped by the self-help movement with groups such as Dual Disorders Anonymous, Youth Emotions Anonymous, Love Addicts Anonymous, and even Children of Bisexual Parents Who Smoke Anonymous! Maybe this book about toxic executives will result in a movement called Toxic Executives Anonymous, or Rotten, Mean, and Devious Executives Anonymous. More likely will be a group called Victims of Toxic Executives Who Are Not Anonymous: We're Telling Everybody How Rotten You Are!

Suzanne Slesin, writing in the *New York Times*, quotes a riddle going around at meetings where codependency is discussed. "What is a co-dependent? Someone who, when hit by a bus, sees someone else's life flash by!" While women predominate at Recovery Movement meetings (and little wonder, the way they have been abused in society), the Recovery Movement offers some relief. Marilly White, the director of the Realization Center, an alcohol and substance-abuse center in New York City, says that "the next step is to change behavior."[30] But there are really no weekend-wonders! Habits are ingrained along with prejudices and compulsions. Effecting behavioral change is something that neither the teacher nor pupil should expect to take place over a weekend. Further, all such attempts to effect behavioral changes are fraught with dangers in the hands of unskilled people. Recently the founder of est, Werner Erhard, was ordered to pay $380,000 in compensatory and punitive damages to a Silver Spring, Maryland, woman, Stephanie Ney, who had sued Erhard for $5 million, claiming she suffered a mental breakdown after attending a self-help program established by Erhard.[31]

Far better are long-term programs setting up systems of values and standards of conduct for concomitant rewards/punishments for successes/failures in meeting standards and objectives in human relationships. This, in effect, is what John Welch has been trying to do at General Electric with only meager success, but he and GE are certainly on the right track.

18. T.E.s Are Criticophiliacs

Most T.E.s are *criticophiliacs*. (Don't try to look the word up; it's not in any of my dictionaries and probably not in any of yours. I invented it for this book.) It means someone who *enjoys* being critical! Criticophiliacs love finding fault. And they do the unpardonable: They give criticisms *in front of others.*

I've never found anyone who could stand very much criticism, especially in front of peers and subordinates. A criticophiliac can destroy the strongest and the most talented of people. It is something that the sadist T.E.s do because they know how much pain criticism can visit on *them*. For them, it's turnabout time! They practice not the Golden Rule, but the Leaden Rule: *Do unto others as you were done to!* (There's another rule—*You're a fool unless you do unto others before they do unto you*—but I've not run into that in business.[32])

Sometimes criticism may be the only way to surface inner fears. Many a criticophiliac is a frustrated mentor. He or she simply has a problem in conveying the reasons for the criticism. The toxic executive will seldom invite criticism, while the successful, nurturing executive will. Many women executives are so much on the defensive that they see all criticism as personal attack. It destroys them and their potential.[33]

19. T.E.s Isolate Special Targets

The criticophiliacs gain super-T.E. status when they graduate to what I call the T.E. Target Stage. Here they're bucking for a Master's in Mean. They daily, or even hourly, concentrate their toxicity on one person, usually some young, talented, but inexperienced person who lacks the power of position or the necessary retaliatory skills. The daily T.E.-torment tears at the target's guts. The T.E. should beware. In Vietnam it often resulted in "fragging," tossing a live grenade into a T.E. officer's bunk. And every so often, in civilian life, a long-suffering T.E.-Target goes nuts and buys an automatic or semiautomatic assault rifle or pistol, using it to redress real or fancied wrongs. It is of considerable concern to the U.S. Postal Service that just in the past ten years there have been thirty-two such incidents among their workers. One incident, in which two people were killed, was set off by a new rule forbidding employees to smoke while sitting in their Jeeps. And fourteen people were killed by about-to-be fired letter carrier Patrick Sherrill before taking his own life. In one post office, a worker was disciplined for whistling while he worked!

In a recent piece in the *Wall Street Journal*, the sharply increasing rate of in-office homicides was detailed at length. At a General Dynamics plant in San Diego, at the end of a termination hearing for a discharged worker in which he lost his case, he pulled out a gun, shot his supervisor, killed another manager, and then calmly surrendered. Incidents like this are what criminologists call the fastest-growing form of murder in America: workplace homicide. Of some 7,000 fatal injuries that occur in the workplace, 12 percent are homicides. From January 1, 1980, to December 31, 1988, a total of 6,956 cases were identified as work-related homicides. Arthur D. Seale, who recently pleaded guilty to federal charges in connection with the kidnapping of Exxon executive Sidney J. Reso, seems to have been "obsessed with retaliating against Exxon for his firing."

And it's not only men. In Bennington, Vermont, an unhappy woman shot and killed her boss and then set fire to the plant. In Woodlawn, Maryland, a fired auto mechanic killed two bosses and wounded a third.[34]

To someone whose life is his job, firing itself is an attempt at murder. The fired worker responds in kind. A career T.E., one who might even *enjoy* firing people, evidently faces increasing risks as the National Rifle Association defeats all attempts at local and national legislation to keep guns, including rapid-fire military assault weapons, out of the hands of criminals, nuts, and disgruntled employees.

And even if T.E. targets don't go completely nuts, they may subscribe to the admonition "Don't get mad, get even" and buy the nightmare book, *The Art of Getting Even*, subtitled, *The Do-It-Yourself Justice Manual*, which lists hundreds of ways to make life miserable for someone. A sample: "Put any of the commercial hair removal products into the person's shampoo bottles. It won't knock out all of the person's hair, but it sure will leave a few bald spots, the size of silver dollars. The victim will look like a refugee from the bowels of Chernobyl."

That's one of the milder suggestions!

20. T.E.s Are Super-Simplist/Reductionists

T.E.s are creatures of absolutes. Life for them is a series of step-functions. There is no sliding or easing to an opinion. A glissando of discussion is not for them. You want an opinion? Bang! There it is.

T.E.s are generally super-simplist/reductionists. The most complex of situations, the most involved of human actions and reactions, must be reduced to a simple formulaic statement. Typically: "All lawyers are crooks," "All women have a jealous streak," "No one from a church-connected college is educated," "Psychoanalysis is all junk." Not understanding the societal universe, possibly afraid to, T.E.s must create their own. And the simpler the better. T.E.s would much rather deal with these simplisms than think or talk things out. This trait taints all decision-making by an executive corps and can establish the "persona" of the organization. In extreme cases, it can destroy it.

These T.E.s live a life of invariant aphorizing. They are the heroes of half-knowledge—exploiting their listeners' ignorance. One sure sign of the simplist/reductionist is repetition. It is not unusual for such a person to repeat something twenty or thirty times in a two-hour meeting.

This may be to convince the T.E. or the audience or both of the truth of some ridiculous simplism. (Next meeting, keep track and show him or her the number of repetitions. Do it with humor and you may not lose your job.)

21. T.E.s Have Secret Agendas

T.E.s seem always to have secret agendas. They're never daydreaming, they're day-scheming. Always using sleight-of-mind to twist things to their own advantage.

Most people with secret agendas are definitely not "company-men" or "company-women." They're the ones that always lock their desks and seldom let you into their homes—too many office files squirreled away against the day when they're going to be fired.

They are also *camouflageurs* (male) or *camouflageures* (female), who guard their eyes with glasses they don't need—especially dark sunglasses so you can't see into their soul. (There is some strong evidence that the habitual wearing of dark or tinted glasses is associated with emotional disturbance.[35])

Connivers are a special class of those T.E.s who have secret agendas. They schedule their vacations for times of intense activity so that someone else has to take the load. They're the ones who wait until you're rushing out the door to catch a plane to L.A. to tell you they want you to stop in Milwaukee on the way back to take care of a long-smoldering business problem.

They're the ones who wait until there are twenty inches of new powder at Aspen to visit a long-unhappy customer in Denver. They're also the ones who wait until 5:00 P.M. on Friday, or just before the start of your vacation, or both, to tell you you're fired so they won't have to look you in the eye either the next day or even for two weeks. They're the ones who arrange it so that *their* name goes on a report and a subsequent technical paper and *yours* is left off even though you (a) dreamed up the project, (b) wrote the proposal, (c) negotiated the contract, (d) did half the research, and (e) edited the final report.

22. T.E.s Have Problems With the Truth

T.E.s have terrible problems with the truth. They *prefer* to lie! The socioeconomic imperative to tell a straight story has passed them by, and the worst of them find their way into activities where truth is anathema, like politics, real estate, advertising, used-car sales, stock and bond brokerage, or investment banking. As with desk searching, these T.E.s believe everyone does it, everyone lies. Therefore it's okay. In the congressional investigation of fraud in the conduct of game shows including the *Sixty-four Thousand Dollar Question*, hundreds of contestants, producers, and sponsors lied to Congress. One producer's excuse: "It was a lie that no one was supposed to believe!"

23. T.E.s Zealously Protect Their Power Positions

Because T.E.s usually operate from positions of power, it is often difficult to pinpoint exactly what interpersonal relationships are dictating their behavior. T.E.s are experts at protecting themselves with cover-ups, some quite elaborate.

The effects are evident in excessive turnover of personnel and in poor financial performance. But, accounting being an inexact science and often controlled by the T.E., poor financial performance can be covered up, sometimes for years, by manipulation of transfer costs (costs absorbed by other intracompany operations). In larger companies, these costs are not accurately tracked by outside auditors.

Because they must operate from power positions, T.E.s must rid themselves of challengers to their authority. One of the most common and most vicious methods is to give the challenger nothing to do. The best of men or women will quit under those conditions, giving the T.E. "evidence" that the challenger was not doing his or her job. Additionally, firing of challengers can be covered up under the guise of "cost cutting" or its euphemism, "profit improvement." And many a challenger has been "reorganized" out of his or her job.

24. T.E.s Have Aggressive Possessions

Many T.E.s have guns. Sometimes lots of them. Their guns go off as sexual surrogates because *they* can't. If they have dogs, you can bet on it, they have long pointy snouts, are aggressive, and bite. Again, sexual surrogates.

25. T.E.s' Clothes Can Give Them Away

Once, with my wife, I visited a Dr. Murdock Head, who ran Airlie House, a conference center just outside of Washington, D.C. I was considering booking the place for a meeting of the Young Presidents Organization. Head wore a black handkerchief in the breast pocket of a black suit and claimed that at Airlie House they "dealt in ideas"—but when asked to name one, he couldn't. This, with the black handkerchief, made me think he simply had to be a crook. I pulled out of the deal mostly because of the black handkerchief and fear of the YPO name being exploited. Shortly thereafter, Head was off to the federal penitentiary for a nice long stay for longtime income tax evasion.

26. T.E.s Have Little or No "Sense of Future"

Cause and effect are not tied together in the now-oriented executive. Long-range planning is for academics. The workplace is problem-filled and success requires instant action. Recently, these instant-action executives have attained high places in organizations, especially under the influence of a large number of books which encourage instant decisionmaking. One of those books, *In Search of Excellence*[36] mistakenly celebrated a "fire, aim, ready" philosophy. The rest of the book is great. But a dedication to instant action can result in instant bankruptcy. Strictly now-oriented businesses usually fail. Long-term success in business is based on a blend of not only a sense of now, but a sense of future as well.

The commercial bankers are a perfect example. The Federal Deposit Insurance Corporation insured depositors for a minuscule premium, paid by the banks, of 12 cents for each $100 of deposits. From the 1950s through the 1980s, the FDIC built up a comfortable surplus. But the go-go banks agitated for the return of a large part of the accumulated presumed surplus premium. And, unfortunately, they got it back.

But now, due to go-go loans in the real estate and international area, the go-go banks are in trouble and the FDIC cannot cover their expected losses even at the new rate of 23 cents for every $100 of covered deposits. After the last few years of more pay-out than pay-in, the FDIC must raise rates even higher and charge the higher-risk, go-go banks a minuscule surcharge over the stronger, historically more cautious banks. And, of course, the go-go bankers, who as a class decimated the fund, are screaming!

2

THE DETERMINANTS OF **TOXIC** BEHAVIOR

Often the persona of a company or an operation is derived from the persona of the top executives. If you're insensitive to employee problems, you may be insensitive to customer problems as well. Manfred F. R. Kets de Vries has done extensive research on the persona of the neurotic organization.[1] But we're more interested in the *individual!*

Many T.E.s are very smart people who have some nasty compulsions. They hurt their subordinates, peers, and even superiors. In business, the company is the loser. Can they be cured? In most cases, yes. By directly and continuously confronting the T.E. with the effect that his or her toxic behaviors and actions have on fellow employees, the T.E.'s behavior can be changed for the better.

In the more severe cases, personality assessments supported by tests may be used to create awareness of personality strengths and weaknesses, perhaps as a first step in effecting a behavioral change.

Most large companies today have a V.P. for human relations (VPHR) or someone with an equivalent title. These people set up standards for hiring, firing, and promotion, not of top-of-the-line executives, but generally of executives' subordinates. They spend a major part of their time counseling employees as to how best to get along with their bosses. They try to get disaffected employees to "surface" their feelings and then review what kinds of interventions, if any, they should take to make things better for both.

The behaviorists' solution to the T.E. problem is to make the T.E. aware of the deleterious effects of his or her toxic actions on job satisfaction and thus the productivity of subordinates. The VPHR has the difficult job of convincing the T.E., who may be paid at five to ten times the VPHR's rate, that nurturing behavior is not only better, it can be learned. Making the T.E. aware of the deleterious effects of his or her toxicity on his or her *personal* bottom line may be all the "therapy" needed.

GROWTH OF THE TWO-CLASS INDUSTRIAL SOCIETY

Business in the United States is fighting what is perceived as "middle management bloat." It is operating with increasingly more flattened organizational structures. As a result, mass layoffs in the middle management area are happening all over America. Is it only a coincidence that the United States' shrinking share of world markets has paralleled the shrinking of middle management?

No. It is not a coincidence. The squeeze-out of middle management has meant the elimination of their historical role as the communication bridge between top management and the shop floor. As the middle management bodies disappear, top management, through good times and bad, is diverting much of middle management's former compensation to themselves, constantly raising their own pay and privileges and substituting computer-based cold-think for the human-based warm-think of departed middle managers.

The Pulitzer Prize–winning series by Donald L. Bartlett and James B. Steele about basic changes in American society—especially its business and political society—that appeared in the *Philadelphia Inquirer* in 1991 is now in book form. The very first chapter of Bartlett's and Steele's *Amer-*

ica: What Went Wrong? is entitled, "Dismantling the Middle Class."[2]

Bartlett and Steele point out that total salaries of people earning more than $1 million per year went up 2,184 percent in the decade of the 1980s, as compared to those of the middle class, which increased by only 44 percent, "a phenomenon unlike any America had seen in this century."

Tax reform through the minimum tax provisions of the 1986 Act was supposed to bump up the tax payments of the very rich. But their payments dropped from $6.7 billion down to $0.7 billion. Whose taxes got bumped up to compensate? Those of the middle class.

Bartlett and Steele wrote of happier times when there were "owners and managers who had known the employees by name, who had known their families, who had known the equipment on the floor, who had walked through the plants and offices and stopped to chat. They talked about working with—and for—people who were members of an extended corporate family."

One squeezed-out worker said that "everybody knew everybody. Everybody was friendly. The supervisors were all nice. The owner would come in and talk to you. It was just a nice place to work. It was a nice family, you know. I loved to go to work." But he went on to say that after some Wall Street operators bought the company, "It just became so competitive and things just started getting nasty and out of hand. It just seemed like they didn't care what you did to get the numbers . . . they'd expect you to get on somebody about a problem that wasn't their fault to start with."

The elimination of middle management in business necessarily means the creation of a new elite. The new elite is not those who have inherited wealth, but those who have gotten it by manipulation of markets in Wall Street and by taxing businesses with exorbitant salaries, fees, and perks. The *Washington Post* reports that "middle management isn't what it used to be."[3]

Fewer and fewer business executives do their jobs in a

caring and nurturing way. For them, conspiration has replaced inspiration. Industry produces less and less with more and more assets, supporting a trillion-dollar annual bill for the services of drones—lawyers, investment bankers, government employees, insurance salesmen—who make an insignificant contribution to the general welfare of the nation or its citizens, at a significant cost.

The work forces of the more successful nations—led by Japan and Germany, under the guidance of nurturing executives—have learned to care about the people and the products or services into which they have invested themselves. That investment yields a continuum of pride of product or pride of service that reaches from the CEO down through the executive corps, through middle management, and right on down to the lowest-level employee.

A Toyota executive, walking down a street in Kyoto, passing a new Toyota with a bent windshield wiper, will straighten it. That's pride of product. The Japanese executive doesn't think that such an act is demeaning.

In contrast, the typical American executive sees the bent windshield wiper as sloppy workmanship on the part of labor. He will not straighten it.

The elimination of middle managers as a class may well be raising the current level of discontent in business because it is helping to create a two-class society. Historically, the creation of elites has been responsible for much of societies' troubles. It was certainly a major source of difficulty in the Soviet Union—the executive corps or *nomenclatura* didn't do any work, and in reaction, neither did the lower levels. My research assistant, who is a Russian émigré, tells me that she left Russia, among other things, because "nobody did any work anymore." The trouble might well have been the drift of the Soviet industrial society from classless to multiclass to duoclass—an elitist, perk-exploitive executive corps and a disaffected, non-working work force *including* much of the white-collar work force. In America, with the decimation of middle management ranks, we may be headed the same way.

PRIDE OF PRODUCT

Pride of product requires long-term commitments to innovative cooperation of all of the elements of entrepreneurship: management, labor, and capital providers. We will never lick the quality problem without maintaining a familial atmosphere in our business institutions. And that means the elimination of toxic me-first executive behavior.

Consider the huge differences between management tenure in Japan and in the United States. It takes many years of product championship to develop something truly new, useful, and lasting, to get it to the market and maintain market share afterward. As a longtime adviser to the late Ichiro Hattori, managing director of Seiko Watch, I know personally the dedication to quality of the Seiko people. They have a long-term view of their jobs. They can plan because they have management continuity, something that has been lost in the United States over the last fifty years.

Institutional memory, the main source of pride of product, under the assault of the merger and buyout movements and institutionalized executive job-hopping, hardly exists anymore in the American company.

It seems that in all sectors of our society we have lost efficiency because of tensions between executives, top management, what remains of middle management, and blue-collar working men and women. The lack of productivity in both the private and public sectors and the lack of real growth in industry have yielded increasingly depressing national statistics. Pride in the "American system" seems to have gone the way of eatable apple pie.

Everybody seems to be out of money. Government at every level is broke because it is confused, resentful, and vastly overstaffed. In only a dozen years, the United States has gone from the world's leading creditor nation to its leading debtor nation. Why?

Because a toxic attitude has been adopted not only by industry, but by government and by all of our institutions and their executive corps. No one in a line or staff position really cares about doing a job anymore because no one else seems to. All of the workers take their cue from the nation's executive corps, who themselves are short-term thinkers only worried about their perks and pay today! *I want what I want when I want it, and* when is *today!*

Look around you. Except in a few small businesses, everybody seems sullen and cynical as they see the executive corps reward itself with huge salaries and salary boosts even as profits slip down and down. The U.S. Congress, one of the most screwed-up institutions in the country, is in shambles as the PACs pay for favorable legislation, and 355 present and past members of Congress abuse their house bank accounts with penaltyless overdrafts. This even after a 40 percent pay raise, conspiratorily passed without debate in the middle of the night.

As a result of vicious exploitation, the American people seem to be fed up not only with their congressional representatives, but with their local legislators, their lawyers, doctors, businesspeople, investment bankers, and college professors, to say nothing of plumbers, electricians, auto mechanics—whatever. From a nation of trusting neighbors, we've become a nation brimming with suspicions, dislikes, and mistrusts. Looking over our shoulder has replaced looking ahead. We are rapidly losing carefully wrought skills at participatory management and replacing them with a superabundance of pure, unadulterated, shameless, resultless greed.

From 1980 to 1990 the number of millionaires in the United States increased fourteenfold, from 4,414 to 63,642.[4] Much of this was due to huge tax reductions pushed by the Reagan and Bush administrations, whose purpose was to "stimulate investment" by the rich now made richer. But the tax breaks have not done so. Rather, those huge tax breaks are helping to create the two-class American society.

The remnants of our national engineering, production, and participatory skills show up in strange ways. In Desert Storm we knew how to come together to kill great masses of ignorant people and not get killed ourselves. In the process we have become the world's major supplier of arms to the world, with the Pentagon today spending real money funding glowing exhibits on the performance of U.S. weaponry in the Persian Gulf War. In addition, the Pentagon has ordered hundreds of Desert Storm veterans to attend the shows "to bear witness to the impressive role U.S. armaments played in the war."[5] And in the 1992 presidential election year, the White House geared up to sell arms to help close the budget gap.[6] Further, the Bush administration, to win votes, was upsetting the balance of power in the Middle East by handing out what the *New York Times* called "other people's pork: $9 billion in warplane sales and 10,000 jobs in Missouri, thanks to the Saudis, and $5 billion in sales and 6,000 jobs at the General Dynamics F-16 assembly line in Texas, courtesy of Taiwan." The Saudi deal has upset Israel and the Taiwan deal contravenes the 1982 U.S.-China agreement "to do no such thing." In the words of Morton Abramowitz, president of the Carnegie Endowment for International Peace, "For a President who was establishing a new world order to massively violate a written agreement is hardly conducive to world order."[7]

Now, *there's* pride of product for you! We can't build automobiles that are safe, comfortable, beautiful, economical, and serviceable, but *can* build machines that kill and maim. Hey! Just like our automobiles!

We are now by far the largest and most successful supplier of armed mercenaries in the world. We proved it when we rented out our armed forces for some $60 billion in Desert Storm. Together with the mass marketing of our killing machinery, it's a sorry way to make the national living!

Universities, historically the womb of philosophical thought, have become nearly completely dependent on government. The very biggest, and supposedly best, have been stealing huge sums from the government for many, many years.[8] Pride of product has moved from skills at scientific and technical innovation to skills at accounting tricks that swindle the government. While historically there has been no question that the work of our universities was of world renown, some of us are beginning to wonder if the fudging of expense reporting has not led to the fudging of research results as well. It begins with plagiarism.

At the National Institutes of Health, a research team has built a computerized text-scanning system that can check an entire article against another in the same field and in twenty seconds tell the investigator whether or not it contains plagiarized material. A copying of one whole paper substituting only the plagiarist's name for the author is rated at "one freeman," named after an alleged notorious plagiarist. One "millifreeman" would mean that only a tenth of one percent of the piece was stolen.[9]

Brilliant and highly creative and analytical people, such as W. Edwards Deming, must go to Japan to get an audience and to establish quality control mechanisms and methodologies that are whipping the tar out of the American automobile business.

And how can workers on the assembly line at Chrysler get excited about putting out a good product when they see little or no return from the substantial wage cuts they took when Chrysler got into serious trouble? With a voluntary ceiling on Japanese auto imports, Chrysler's sales boomed in the mid to late eighties. Together with the wage give-backs, sliding down the experience curve bumped Chrysler's earnings and cash flows 1,000 percent. But instead of consolidating their new market share gains by cutting prices, Chrysler executives *raised* them, and Chrysler cashed in short-term!

But what happened to the money? It did not go to labor as a partner. It did not go to research and new product development. It did not go to capital improvements to reduce costs. Instead, it went for obscenely large bonuses to management and to a string of dopey, nonautomotive, ego-driven, unstudied acquisitions foisted on them by fee-happy, uncaring, greedy Wall Street investment bankers. Now you can understand why a Chrysler *worker* won't straighten a bent windshield wiper!

And business, it seems, believes it must steal to stay in business. For example, Chrysler turned back odometers on used demonstrator cars, selling them as new. That decision was made by Chrysler *executives!* And Chrysler was recently told to pay Robert W. Kearns—inventor of the intermittent windshield wiper which Chrysler swiped from Kearns by using four of his patents—$11.3 million. They got off cheap. That's only 90 cents each for twelve million-plus vehicles and the company luckily escaped triple damages.[10] Yet Chrysler spent *millions* in law fees fighting Kearns. Stories in the press about both of these incidents must have turned many people away from buying Chrysler products.

In April 1990, some five hundred coal companies were cited for nearly five thousand violations in 847 mines. The companies' executive corps of super-toxics, subtoxics and tyro-toxics jiggered the detectors *that protect their own miners* from the horrors of black lung disease. Why? To save a few bucks in safety equipment.[11]

And Rockwell International "intimidated" and "belittled" employees into filling out false time cards while working on the space shuttle even as it was on probation for overbilling on a satellite contract.[12]

Wall Street is stealing at a constantly increasing pace. And they've moved from the ancient practice of stealing from widows and orphans to stealing from each other, as in the recent Salomon Brothers scandal.

Business is thinking only from quarter to quarter. Everybody seems to be lying and stealing. Why? What in the world is going on?

The answer is found in our business culture: The exploitive executive is believed to be superior to the caring executive. And because executives run businesses, governments, universities, investment banks, S&Ls etc., most of them have been trained in the modern mold, exploitive and toxic! That's what's going on, and it's killing the country.

My good friend the late writer, novelist, critic, and TV personality Marya Mannes pointed out in a piece in the *Saturday Evening Post* some years ago that, beginning a few years after the end of World War II, we began "exalting jerks" in our literature, beginning with *The Carpetbaggers*, in which the protagonist, Jonas Cord, "bludgeons his way through more than 600 pages of fornication, sadism and multimillion dollar deals to become—essentially—an object of admiration." Mannes went on with this: "The same reader who clucks at his [Cord's] shocking ways is invited to envy him."[13] Mannes expanded on the theme at one of the seminars I organized for Aspen East. She pointed out that the exaltation of jerks was a growing phenomenon. The theater was especially guilty of exalting jerks with its *I Can Get It for You Wholesale* and *How to Succeed in Business Without Really Trying*.

Mannes went on to note that in music, Frank Sinatra, one of the people who habitually dumped on waiters, women, and just about everybody but his gangster friends, was looked up to and admired, as was husband-hopping Elizabeth Taylor. "Success excuses, applause condones, money rationalizes," deplored Mannes.

But we have more troubles than just the jerks. The social Balkanization of America has begun as the gap between the haves and the have-nots widens. Study after study shows that the rich are getting richer and the poor are getting poorer under the assault of the know-nothing Reagan Bush White House, with the cooperation of a venal national legislature whose votes can be bought for cash money thinly disguised as campaign contributions.

Trying to understand the behaviors of our executive corps gives one the brain-shudders. But psychologist Abraham Maslow had some ideas as to why many people act the way they do and ascribed at least some of their actions to a "heirarchy of needs." This in turn led to the development of McGregor's "Y Theory," which did much to explain executive behavior. But one must also be conscious of the powerful role that institutions play in molding the life and the persona of the typical executive.

3

THE NEEDS HIERARCHY

What drives the T.E.? I believe at least part of the answer can be found in the theories of the noted psychologist Abraham Maslow and his Hierarchy of Needs.

Maslow posited in his book, *Motivation and Personality*, that human beings have developed a series of levels of needs and that the next-higher level of need cannot be attempted until a lower-level need has been substantially satisfied.

PHYSIOLOGICAL NEEDS

The first level of need is physiological. Food, shelter, clothing, and health needs are necessary to sustain life itself. It is unlikely that a hungry man will seek fulfillment of the four higher-level needs of safety, belonging, self-esteem, and self-fulfillment if his stomach is empty.

Monsignor Rice, the "labor priest" of Pittsburgh, observed, after I said in a speech at Penn State that I would rather die than accept welfare, that "self respect begins with a full stomach." I'm sure he was right and was not overlooking the biblical "Man doth not live by bread only." Emerson's line "He thought it happier to be dead. To die for Beauty, than live for bread" was, most likely, written on a full stomach.

Once the food-shelter-clothing-health continuum has been relatively well gratified, there then emerges a new set of needs.

SAFETY AND SECURITY NEEDS

With their physiological needs met, human beings next look for stability, for protection against danger and deprivation, and for structure, law and order, and freedom from unjust and uncontrolled retribution.

It is often true that toxic behavior stems from unmet safety needs of individuals, perhaps those who have been physically, mentally, or sexually abused and harassed. Classical behavioral theory says that abused children abuse their own children in retribution. They never gained the freedom-from-safety needs and are unable to pursue the higher needs of belonging, self-esteem, and self-actualization. They are stuck in a rut of fear-based resentments that they take out against their fellows in the work environment, usually targeting the less-advantaged.

And the toxic executive can be either male or female. Though these abused abusers are often classified as "bullies," are thought of as male, there are many female "bullies" in the T.E. category.

Many a T.E. is cowering permanently in a trench of fear, acting aggressively in a compulsive-possessive fashion. T.E.s try frantically to order and stabilize the world around them by creating simplistic and authoritarian criteria to govern the behavior of others. That which is a mild preference in the nurturing executive (for example, preference for the familiar) becomes a life-and-death necessity in the T.E. "They hedge themselves about with all sorts of ceremonials, rules, and formulae so that every possible danger contingency is provided for," writes Maslow.[1] For T.E.s, threats to their authority seem to invite the very dangers they have worked so hard to exclude. But once his or her safety and security needs have been met, even the T.E. moves on to the next level.

THE NEED TO BELONG

After fulfilling basic physiological and safety needs, every human being seeks to be accepted by his or her fellow humans. People need to belong. It could be to their own family, to a group of friends, or to some social institution such as a church, a country club, a trade union, a trade association, a service club, a Boy Scout troop, or a bridge club. Even a bar!

Listen to the first line of the chorus of the song that introduces the television program *Cheers*, which is set in a neighborhood bar in Boston: "Sometimes you wanna go/where everybody knows your name,/and they're always glad you came."[2] The words evoke the importance of belonging, even if it's only to a neighborhood saloon.

The first of the higher-order needs, "belongingness," the need to be loved and treasured, is recognized and felt more keenly in its absence than in its presence. One may forget that, when one was hungry and frightened, one scorned love and belongingness and now without it, again in Maslow's words, "feel[s] sharply the pangs of loneliness, of ostracism, of rejection, of friendlessness, or rootlessness."

A true feeling of belonging is a rare achievement. I have met thousands of executives both on-site and in my seminars who may never feel as though they belong, at least in their executive life. It may well be that the only way that an Ivan Boesky, the convicted felon, could ever feel that he belonged was to join that congress of crooks that set the social and ethical mores and behaviors of that special society that was Wall Street in the 1980s. Even then, did he ever really belong? Perhaps not.

This herd instinct of being with one's own kind, one's class, one's gang—this tendency to herd, to flock, to join with others—is explained in Robert Ardrey's book *The Territorial Imperative*.[3] Lack of a feeling of belonging is probably responsible for much if not most toxic behavior, not only in executives but in families and other social institutions. Read the books *Toxic Parents*[4] and *Toxic Faith*[5] to discover how universal this syndrome is.

This understanding of the group imperative is being exploited by thousands of institutions worldwide. For those who never felt they belonged, we now have the booming business of group therapy. It even has its own television program, *Dear John*, in which the therapy group is called the "One on One Club." Is it more than a coincidence that it is, like *Cheers*, also one of the top five TV programs for the past five years?

Many people have only so much love in their love-bank and are constantly overdrawn into hate, dislike, and distrust. Thus, even the most hated male T.E. at work might have a loving, supportive, nurturing relationship in his family life, but is in overdraft in business life. Because peers and superiors see the T.E.'s family life as loving and stable, they fail to detect the misery he is capable of inflicting on his subordinates in his business life, refusing to believe the complaints that arise. This is one of the reasons that sexual harassment charges are seldom believed and rectified by higher-ups: "But he has such a nice family!"

Simply stated, the typical toxic executive is two different people: one at work and another at home. This can also work conversely—the executive is kind at work but a tyrant at home. Consider the case of the highly regarded Securities and Exchange Commission enforcement chief John Fedders, who at home was a notorious wife beater.

THE NEED FOR SELF-ESTEEM

Mark Twain wrote, that "Deep down in his heart no man much respects himself."

Once an individual achieves a sense of true belonging,

that person moves on to the next higher level in Maslow's need-achievement hierarchy, that of self-esteem, perhaps the most difficult of the five to attain. For women, this is much more of a problem than it is for men in our Western society. Gloria Steinem, in her seminal book *Revolution From Within: A Book of Self-Esteem*, writes that for years she had assumed that "concern for inner change was secondary to societal change, the examined life is not worth living." But she continued to encounter women with too little self-esteem to take advantage of hard-won opportunities and too many men who were addicted to authority and control as the only proof of their value. "Both lack faith in a unique self: that 'core' self-esteem without which no amount of 'situational' self-esteem can be enough,"[6] writes Steinem.

For many, simple adequacy, such as the completion of high school or college, may be enough to attain a sense of self-worth. The joy in the faces of those receiving their high school equivalency certificates shows how difficult it is to establish generally accepted criteria for establishing where one is in the needs achievement hierarchy.

For many executives, the prime needs criterion is the opinion of others. This has been imprinted on them by half-educated parents: "Who wants to be bothered waiting for a child to do something right when it's so much simpler just to praise him all the time?"

I always objected when, in contests among children, there would be a "first winner," a "second winner," and even a "third winner." They weren't all winners, and I'm sure some of them knew it. You gain self-esteem by coming in first, *really* first. In California, the San Diego school system voted to abolish failing grades, a move that was "widely misconstrued as an effort to legislate failure out of existence. An outraged public rescued the 'F' before the plan could take effect." A University of Michigan psychologist discovered that "American schoolchildren rank far ahead of students in Japan, Taiwan and China in self-confidence about their abilities in math." Unfortunately, this achievement was not matched by their actual performance. "Japanese parents don't lavish praise on their children—they're concerned they will end up thinking too much about themselves and not enough about the group," says Michael Lewis, author of the book *Shame: The Exposed Self.*[7]

In academe, mastery and competence, and thus self-esteem, is evidenced by honors accorded, papers published, or positions attained. Tenure, by a vote of fellow faculty members, may suffice. But in business, where there are few defined "values," and especially in Wall Street, feelings of self-worth are equated only to net worth. And it's never enough. As author John Updike recently said in an interview in the *Wall Street Journal*, "The number of already very rich men who were willing to commit crimes during the 1980s to get even richer proved there was not enough." Mr. Updike reflects, "Maybe that's one of the words Americans have a hard time learning: The word enough."[8]

Reputation, prestige, and high net worth attained by sleazeball methods will never generate permanent self-esteem. Further, many will never feel comfortable no matter what the acclaim of the crowd, if that acclaim has been attained by treachery or by the cheating of others. This acclaim can be easily taken away, as Messrs. Levine, Siegel, Boesky, and Milken discovered.

Few of us remember or even know about the "Couéism" movement of the first half of the twentieth century. In this early embodiment of the self-motivation movements, French pharmacist-turned-hypnotist Émile Coué invented the phrase *"Tous les jours, à tous les points de vue, je vais de mieux en mieux,"* and insisted that it be repeated daily and in front of a mirror.

It soon caught on in the United States and millions of people were soon involved in the rigor of its daily repetition in English: "Every day, in every way, I am getting better and better."

Coué claimed to have effected organic change through such methods, as did my late friend Norman Cousins. After being told he had only a short time to live, Cousins reported that he watched Marx Brothers and Laurel and Hardy films and played the organ to cure himself of a dreadful illness. He described the transformation in a book.[9]

Coué's technique was also responsible in large measure for the success of L. Ron Hubbard's Dianetics or "Scientology" movement, based on the use of biofeedback techniques to recall and thus cure early trauma, including birth-trauma.

Other biofeedback behaviorists are worth a look. Read *New Mind, New Body* by Dr. Barbara B. Brown,[10] an extremely well written and well documented account of how to reduce stress. Dr. David Harold Fink's engaging and highly useful *Release from Nervous Tension*, published in 1943, is still good today.[11] (I lend it to nervous nerve specialists and I still use some of the techniques described to release tension; using them, I can often fall asleep on a plane in five minutes.)

All of us need to feel good about ourselves if we are to advance to the highest and final stage of the needs hierarchy.

THE NEED FOR SELF-FULFILLMENT

Also referred to as "self-actualization," the striving for "self-fulfillment" is present in artists, writers, doctors, lawyers, bakers, and even tank-drivers. (Think of the U.S. Army's TV recruitment "Be all that you can be" commercial.) This is the highest level in the needs hierarchy.

While rarely attained in life, some say that they know they have attained this level by the transcendental peace that comes over them when they attain some goal utilizing the full range of their talents. At that rare moment, they become one with the universe.

One can easily see that all of this makes heavy going for those anxious to discover what level they have or have not risen to. It is nearly impossible for anyone—even the most trained and experienced psychologist or psychoanalyst, or the wisest of men or women—to sit outside another's being and make a judgment about which of the higher levels of the needs hierarchy that person has attained—though I understand that some have tried.

The first level can probably be measured fairly accurately; the second less so, as "*security*" and "*safety*" are relative terms that depend nearly as much on human perception as on actuality.

Though one can conjecture, from observations of behavior, which need level one has achieved—as I do in assessing the aberrant behavior of Washington, D.C.'s former mayor Marion Barry—who's to certify that one has a feeling of "belonging" except the individual?

Barry named himself "the night owl" and spent the major part of his mayorality in frequenting the topless bars of the city where drugs were readily available and where he was accepted and felt at home. He "belonged." No, where we are in the needs hierarchy is a truth to be found only within each of us.

During our tour through the world of the toxic executive, we will refer frequently to Maslow's hierarchy of needs, because the failure to attain a certain level may induce toxic behavior.

Certain kinds of aberrant, neurotic behavior and their origins are well-described in the literature of abnormal psychology. Some executives are really nuts. They do very irrational things. Reading this book alone will not change their behavior because they don't know it's nutty and irrational. With therapy, some will learn how to modify their toxic behavior or at least learn to live with it.

But for those T.E.s who can see the pain in the eyes of their victims, for those who "just don't understand" how hurtful their behavior is—and for their victims, who also "just don't understand" why they are treated so shabbily, and would like it to stop—this book may help.

4

INSTITUTIONAL DARWINISM

While the Maslow Needs Hierarchy helps us trace the wellsprings of toxicity, by examining human institutions we may better understand how this toxicity takes its various *executive* forms.

Executives do things and get things done *ex officio*, as agents of institutions.

There are forces working on the executive psyche that are derived from the institutions that mankind has created to serve itself. And in that societal universe, within and among and between those institutions that make it up, there is an "institutional Darwinism." It parallels the biological Darwinism of the biological universe. The fittest but not necessarily the best, institutions survive, because institutions are run by the product of two billion years of evolution: people.

Institutions are made up of people. People not only created them, they must also run them to satisfy that hierarchy of social and economic needs we just explored.

In this societal, rather than physical, model of the universe, man operates as both risen ape and fallen angel. And there's the rub. The two are often in conflict.

But first we must look at the role that institutions play in the life of man.

THE INSTITUTIONS OF MAN

The primary social institutions are Family, Church, State, School, and Theater. The economic institutions, known collectively as Commerce or Business, for the purposes of this disquisition, have subinstitutions such as Bank, Labor Union, and Insurance. All institutions, created by man as he came down out of the trees, follow certain laws of survival.

The Family is a collective. It also has specialists. Not each one hunts, cooks, sews, grows, reaps, or earns money. Rather, each does what he or she is best suited for, for the family's common good.

The Church was born out of people's need for explication of mysteries and the special rituals of propitiation believed to be required.

The State was born out of the need for a common defense and the need to right complex wrongs between individuals, families, and the other institutions. The protections that mankind won from the State under the Social Contract were large compared to the freedom given up—the private right of retribution for actual or perceived wrongs.

The School was born out of the need for the collective storage of knowledge and ritual and its dissemination using the special talents of memorization, recording, and recitation.

The Theater and the Arts were born out of the need for relief from the state of nature in which the life of man was "solitary, poor, nasty, brutish, and short."

The Economic Institutions were born out of the need for the sharing of economic risk and the focusing of economic wealth to fulfill the lower-level needs of people.

THE FIRST LAW OF INSTITUTIONS IS THIS:
Institutions are formed to derive the benefits of human collectivization and specialization.

But the creation of institutions was not without danger for the individual. This gives rise to the Second Law.

THE SECOND LAW OF INSTITUTIONS IS THIS:
Institutions have a life of their own, independent of the constituency that created them.

All institutions, both generic and specific, must be run by people. Personal *economic* survival depends on the survival of one's institution. This creates a drive in the individual to ensure that the institution survives, independent of the benefits that might or might not derive to the constituency served by that institution.

Thus the generic institution of the State will take on the form of a dictatorship to preserve the role of the stewards. Marx, Engels, and Lenin were quite sure that under communism the better nature of man, released from his chains, would assert itself, and the State would wither away. The history of the USSR and its creators and rulers shows that they knew nothing of the workings of the Second Law, as the institution of the Soviet State grew ever-larger and eventually suffocated and collapsed under the weight of its own super-bureaucracy.

And the institution of the Church, now that explanation of the supernatural has moved to the province of the natural sciences, runs bingo games and therapy sessions and fulfills peoples' need for social congress.

THE THIRD LAW OF INSTITUTIONS IS THIS:
Institutions expand into the space available to them.

Each of the generic institutions seek to become dominant. They expand until they run into the turf of another institution. The State is always trying to expand its power into the entire domain of human endeavor and has had territorial disputes with the Church since the beginnings of history. Both State and Church are still fighting over the

School. And that contest is getting more and more nasty.

The invasion of the School by the Church has its parallel in the State/Business relationship. In many countries, such as Egypt, 90 percent of industry (Business) is owned by the State, much to its sorrow. Only at the end of the twentieth century has the State across the world learned that it will never learn to run businesses, and some fifty thousand government-owned businesses (not including some fifty thousand to one hundred thousand in the nations that were formerly the USSR, and some one hundred thousand each in India and China) are currently up for sale in the booming world "privatization" market.

This infighting of institutions is known as pluralism and is supposed to be good for the country, its citizenry, and society at large. It leads us to the Fourth Law.

THE FOURTH LAW OF INSTITUTIONS IS THIS:
Institutions faced with severe competition join forces.

The oldest joining was that between Church and State. "You make them come to our church and we'll see that they vote [in more primitive societies, fight] for you." As for the State/Business joinder, most Americans know the words of the retiree who raised his head from his putter long enough to warn the citizenry in his 1961 Farewell Address:

In the councils of government, we must guard against the acquisition of unwarranted influence, whether sought or unsought, by the military-industrial complex. The potential for the disastrous rise of misplaced power exists and will persist.

It was a fair warning from Dwight David Eisenhower, a five-star general who was made president of these United States of America for two successive terms. No one ever claimed that Ike knew very much, but he knew the military and how they brown-nosed industry to get jobs when they retired. Eisenhower got a top job, but thousands of his fellow officers from the "factories" on the Hudson and the Severn rivers found their way into industry and cut up a government so grateful to industry for its win in World War II that it had no resistive resources. Billions of dollars went for useless projects, and still do.

We are now in an era of big institutions. Big Government, Big Business, Big Church, Big Labor, Big School, and so on. And they're always making deals with each other to slice up the other institutions *and* the individual. Much toxic executive behavior can be traced to the instinctive drives of the executive corps in many of our institutions to ensure their survival and growth in accordance with the above-outlined laws of institutions.

THE AXES OF ACTION, REACTION, AND CHANGE

A Prudential-Bache commercial of a few years ago showed a Bache broker getting up in the dark, phoning London for the price of gold at the morning fixing, and catching the milk train to the city while it was still dark. This is not the kind of person we want to be, but is the kind we want working for us.

One of the unsolved problems in management is this conflict.

This Bache person is assumed to have a "Type A" personality and is a poor insurance risk because of a tendency to heart attack. But Bache wants you to let him use up his energy bank for you even if he might have a heart attack in the process. As the *Boston Globe's* Ellen Goodman wrote, "For all the talk about stress, for all the talk about leading a full life, there is still a real tension between the life we want for ourselves and the work we want out of others." She goes on to point out that "we admire the well-rounded, and then hire the single-minded."

As a result of this ambivalence, managers agonize over this great dilemma: whether to have a happy, relaxed work atmosphere where it's fun to come to work and just get by, or whether to create a hard-driving, frenetic pace that makes money, is only borderline honest, and isn't much fun. They weigh both sides of the issue and choose—almost invariably—the latter. Why?

One clear cause for the Type A bent of our business culture is revealed by Robert Levine, chairman of the psychology department at California State University at Fresno. Levine studied the pace of business and businesspeople in many different cities. He measured speed of walking, accuracy of timepieces, and transactional time—how long it takes to buy some stamps. He then looked for correlations of pace with coronary heart disease and found a high degree of correlation between pace and heart disease *except* in Japan. Levine could not explain this, but I can. It lies in the greater participation in decisionmaking enjoyed by the Japanese executive.

From my experiences with Seiko Watch, where I was a consultant for some time, just about everybody is brought into the decisionmaking process. Contrary to common belief, decisionmaking in the Japanese company is not by autocratic or even normal statistically consensual methods such as by majority vote. Decisions are made by strongly encouraging unanimity of decisionmaking in a large group, perhaps as many as fifteen people. Even if only one objects, the project will not be undertaken if that one person cannot be persuaded to change. And the objector does not seem to lose face.

This is also the reason for some of the success of the Japanese production system. Everyone feels a part of it. Though there are many ostensibly Type A people in the Japanese system, their energy is directed toward benefiting the company they work for—usually for life. There is also massive nationalism in Japan in spite of their enthusiastic adoption of American language and habits—such as our music. Unlike much of the world, there is not only a Japan, Inc., vector to the work ethic, but a company man vector as well—employers are looked on as kind of second parents. In addition, Japanese are very group-oriented. Thus, their

effort is not solely in their own self-interest but acts holisti-
cally in service of Japan, Inc., their group, their company,
and themselves.

It is only with this work philosophy on the part of the
individual that the fabled process of Kaizen, of "gradual,
unending improvement, doing little things better; setting—and achieving—ever-higher standards," will work.
There is a book by my old friend Masaaki Imai, with whom
I ran a series of corporate planning seminars in Japan in the
seventies, by that same title, Kaizen.[1]

While the work on Type A and Type B individuals (the
Type A individual is intensely ambitious, competitive,
preoccupied, and deadline-driven. Type B is the con-
verse) of the sixties was somewhat simplistic, later work
has shown that the epidemiology of hostility, suspicious-
ness, aggressiveness, and volatile tempers not only
threaten the executive's own life, but the life of the organization itself.

Redford Williams, M.D., of Duke University, author of
The Trusting Heart: Great News About Type A Behavior,[2]
reports that not all elements of Type A behavior are bad for
your health. He claims his research shows that hostility,
only one of the many behavioral characteristics of the Type
A personality, is far and away the most important factor
involving health.

He followed a group of doctors, lawyers, and workers
over a twenty-year period after their taking the MMPI—
the Minnesota Multiple Personality Inquiry—and compared death rates with the resulting ratings. In a group of
255 physicians, those scoring high in hostility were five
times as likely to develop heart problems as the balance
of the sample. Cynical thoughts, angry feelings, and
aggressive behavior were the basic behavioral elements
that made up hostile behavior, according to Williams.
People who suspect that others are unworthy, deceptive,
and selfish are considered to be cynics in Williams's
topology.

THE HUMAN SIDE OF ENTERPRISE

One of the best observers of the workplace and motivation was MIT's Douglas McGregor, who, building on Abraham Maslow's needs hierarchy, developed his Theory Y approach to motivation in the workplace. His seminal book *The Human Side of Enterprise*[3] caused the displacement of the old Theory X carrot-and-stick approach to motivation. McGregor's *X-Y* axes found immediate acceptance because they were great for plotting behavior.

Theory X

Theory X managers assume (a) the average human being has an inherent dislike for work and will avoid it if possible, and (b) the average human being prefers to be directed, wishes to avoid responsibility, lacks ambition, and above all wishes for security. One motivates people only by promise or threat, or offering or withholding the means of meeting physiological and safety and security needs.

But these needs are easily satisfied in the developed world, and especially in America. So McGregor reasoned that fulfillment of the higher-level needs is the prime motivator in the workplace. "A satisfied need is not a motivator of behavior," said McGregor. "It is a fact that is unrecognized in Theory X."

The higher-level need for belonging, after physiological and safety and security needs have been met, is a drive by the individual that takes place in society everywhere. In modern business, "belongingness" is central to the concept of "teams" and "teambuilding," which in turn is essential to long-term success in the entrepreneurial environment.

The Theory X manager perceives teams as a threat, as "ganging up," and in reaction attempts to discourage the formation of new groups and discourage the continuation of those already formed. As a result, people become resistant, antagonistic, and uncooperative. But this behavior is a consequence, not a cause, of Theory X perception.

At the next higher level, self-esteem, McGregor notes that even very slight differences in wages can precipitate trouble. Why? Not for purposes of economic survival, but because they can be interpreted as evidences of favoritism. This results in loss of self-esteem, dissatisfaction, and a resultant drop in productivity. The toxic executive does not realize how important these things are to people fighting for self-esteem, especially those who have been put down all their lives. Unless there are opportunities at work to satisfy the higher-level needs, people will feel deprived, and their negative, uncooperative behavior will reflect this deprivation.

In short, the carrot-and-stick method of Theory X works only when the lower-level physiological and safety needs are unmet.

Theory Y

In contrast to Theory X, Theory Y proponents contend that (a) the expenditure of energy in the workplace is as natural as the expenditure of energy at play, and the average human has no inherent dislike of work, which is a source of satisfaction, not dissatisfaction; (b) the threat of punishment is unnecessary, and people will self-direct and self-control in service of a known objective; (c) commitment to objectives is a function of the rewards associated with their achievement, and these rewards are a feeling of belonging, ego satisfaction in the form of self-esteem, and eventual self-actualization; (d) the average person can learn not only to accept, but to seek responsibility; (e) the capacity to use imagination, creativity, and ingenuity in the solution of organization problems is widely distributed throughout the working population; and (f) the intellectual capacities of the average worker at every level are only partially utilized in the Theory X environment.

The thrust of McGregor's Theory Y is that the goals of the organization must be integrated with the goals of the people who are working to realize those goals. In the Theory X environment, in contrast to the Theory Y environment, the goals of the organization are set independent of the fulfillment of the higher-order needs. Clearly the T.E. is a Theory X person all the way, and needs to move toward Theory Y.

Theory Z

Theory Z management deserves a brief mention. William Ouchi, who coined the term *Theory Z management*, has taken all the work on the application of Theory Y and the Japanese consensual decision-making style and rolled them into a system. His book, *Theory Z: How American Business Can Meet the Japanese Challenge,* published in 1981, goes into some detail about Japanese decision-making and problem-solving patterns. It concentrates on showing how mistrust between union, management, and government in Great Britain was largely responsible for its pitiful production effort after World War II. Ouchi finds mutual trust to be one of the most important factors in getting high, effective production rates from workers and management. However, Theory Z does not add a true third dimension to McGregor's Theory Y construct.

IS THEORY Y A COP-OUT?

No, it is not an abdication of management's obligation to channel the efforts of others in productive directions. It is not "soft" management, not a "country club" atmosphere. It is an attempt to factor in the need for achievement that lies inside every human being. While perhaps dormant in some of the working population, that need is still there.

THE LEADERSHIP AND CONFLICT GRIDS

Robert Blake and Jane Mouton published an article in my *Directors & Boards* magazine, (Summer, 1980), positing that much of progress hinges on the resolution of different drives in the corporate arena. They call their special embodiments of leadership theory, "The Leadership Grid" and "The Conflict Grid." They try to resolve the problems of sharing of power and influence in an organization. In the Blake/Mouton construct, the Y axis is labeled "Concern for People," and the X axis, "Concern for Production." Purely Y- or purely X-type people will be relatively unproductive. Blake's and Mouton's "Conflict Grid" is used to depict and thus help in the resolution of internal conflicts.

In all of this gridwork, please note that, in general, the T.E. operates along the X axis unless forced by circumstances to modify behaviors to accomplish some result in the middle ground.

Following the Blake/Mouton grids you will find my own version of a conflict grid. Invented to teach situational ethics in lectures at Georgetown University, it can be applied to any group, from historical figures to a board of directors.

Notice that, in general, the toxic executive will find himself or herself in the lower right-hand quadrant along with Hitler, Pontius Pilate, and all the heels of mankind.

Following is the editorial that accompanied the grid, which was titled "On Right and Wrong":

The line that divides right from wrong, moral from immoral and even legal from illegal, will never be drawn finely enough for any director of any modern corporation. Directors must make decisions based on their own consciousness of what is considered to be in the interest of their various constituencies.

They simplify things for themselves if they consider their sole constituency to be the stockholders. But because the right to operate in the corporate mode is a right given by the State they have a larger constituency: the public. They also have responsibilities to themselves—to fulfill themselves as human beings. Doing what is good and decent and

THE LEADERSHIP GRID®

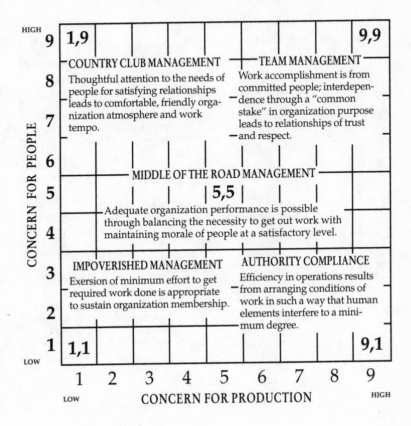

THE CONFLICT GRID®

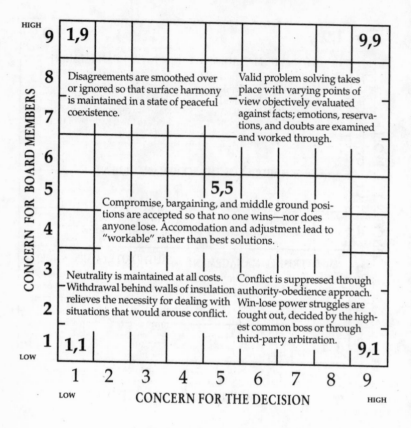

CONCERN FOR BOARD MEMBERS (vertical axis, HIGH 9 to LOW 1)

CONCERN FOR THE DECISION (horizontal axis, LOW 1 to HIGH 9)

1,9 — Disagreements are smoothed over or ignored so that surface harmony is maintained in a state of peaceful coexistence.

9,9 — Valid problem solving takes place with varying points of view objectively evaluated against facts; emotions, reservations, and doubts are examined and worked through.

5,5 — Compromise, bargaining, and middle ground positions are accepted so that no one wins—nor does anyone lose. Accomodation and adjustment lead to "workable" rather than best solutions.

1,1 — Neutrality is maintained at all costs. Withdrawal behind walls of insulation relieves the necessity for dealing with situations that would arouse conflict.

9,1 — Conflict is suppressed through authority-obedience approach. Win-lose power struggles are fought out, decided by the highest common boss or through third-party arbitration.

Source: "The Fifth Achievement," by Robert R. Blake and Jane S. Mouton. *Journal of Applied Behavioral Sciences,* 1970, 6(4), p. 418. Reproduced by permission of the authors.

SFR'S AXES OF INTEREST OF CHANGE

THE PUBLIC INTEREST

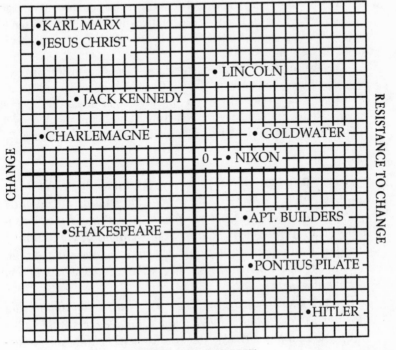

THE PRIVATE INTEREST

of benefit to each—stockholder, public, person—is vastly complicated. It cannot be resolved without conflict. A director of a major cigarette manufacturer, acting in the stockholder interest, votes in a CEO who has special skills in creating legal ways to convince children to smoke cigarettes. He does this knowing that his own children, poor little fish that they are, will, most likely, be caught up in that awful net, and some will die. Early, slowly, painfully. But why not? "If we don't sell them, someone else will!"

The answer as to why this conscience-saver is no answer, is complex, convoluted, and takes much time. Generally, the reader or listener, regardless of his or her educational, intellectual, or interest level, gets bored with this moral ambiguity. So we must invent a pictorial method to show the fatuity of the "if we don't, someone else will" syndrome.

Here is a typical ethical problem, set in the city of Washington, D.C. I tell the class: "Any of you can get a permit to build apartments in Rock Creek Park. You know that the city of Washington is desperate for park space. But, without doing anything illegal, you can get a permit, and can make a substantial profit, by building apartments in Rock Creek Park. Now, which of you would build them?"

Usually about half the hands go up. "But if you don't build them, someone else will," I add, and most of the remaining hands go up—with a few diehards (mostly women) holding out, refusing to have anything to do with building apartments in beautiful, and needed, Rock Creek Park.

Next, the group is divided into independent study groups of five or six. They are given blank Axes and asked to plot the ten most famous people of all time that come to mind. The average results of some 150 plots are shown on the chart.

It is interesting to note that Karl Marx and Jesus Christ fight for the same spot on just about everyone's chart—quite a revelation for students at a Jesuit institution. But the big game we are hunting are the apartment builders.

Pontius Pilate occupies the lower right-hand quadrant along with Hitler. But note that, after discussion, some of it quite heated, the apartment builders are forced to plot themselves into the same quarter as Pontius Pilate, who condemned Christ to death! And this was very traumatic for the apartment builders.

Another bit of trauma involved one poor kid (they're still kids even at twenty-one) who was forced to plot his own father in the Pontius Pilate quadrant because his father was the president of one of the large cigarette manufacturers.

As I recall, he cried. But directors don't cry. Except at night.

SECTION TWO

TYPES OF
TOXIC EXECUTIVES

6

THE SELF-INVOLVED
TOXIC EXECUTIVE

ON NARCISSISM

Ego can be a powerful instrument for both success and failure—mostly the latter. It is so much inside us that it is invisible, yet its powers are so great in some that it overpowers respect for the law itself.

Most narcissists have no idea that they are driven by ego until a business or a marriage fails or the prison bars close behind them. Only then (and sometimes not even then, as in the case of Washington, D.C.'s former mayor Marion Barry) do they look in a real mirror and finally can see themselves adoring their own image. "Every age develops its own peculiar forms of pathology, which express in exaggerated form its underlying character structure," wrote social critic Christopher Lasch.

The Narcissistic T.E.

Nearly every student of human behavior knows about simple narcissism and its mythic sources. In one version, Narcissus was a very handsome Greek youth who fell so much in love with his own image, reflected in a lake, that he fell in and drowned. Another version is that, unable to consummate his love, he pined away. Executives who are so involved with themselves that they spend time admiring themselves and their own personal accomplishments rather than the group accomplishment will lead short economic lives.

Narcissism doesn't show up as a sickness—like a fever that can be detected and quantified with a thermometer. Most successful people—though short of Napoleons or Hitlers or Mussolinis, with their trademark strutting, funny uniforms, and weird body and hand motions—have a little bit of narcissism in them. More and more people are becoming sensitive to the dangers of too much self-love as opposed to self-esteem, which is a quite different thing.

Narcissism is excessive self-love. The narcissist is not an egomaniac but one whose ego is in fact too weak to support an independent self, so he or she creates one.

Pathological Narcissism

This is from an interview by Richard Behar in *Newsweek*, November 4, 1991:

Pathological narcissism is on the rise says Harvard Medical School psychologist Dr. Steven Berglas. Just when certain people seem to have it all, their kingdoms come crashing down. Berglas believes they are often victims of a syndrome that a bigger bank account won't ever cure.

Berglas goes on to explain that pathological narcissists have at least three of the following four traits: arrogance, a sense of aloneness, a need for adventure, and adultery. He calls this the "Four A's Syndrome." Though each might start out as a healthy narcissist, he or she eventually implodes.

In his book *The Success Syndrome,* Berglas tells how Donald Trump said his bankers were "tossing money at him," and how Salomon Brothers' attempt to corner the treasury bond market cost Gutfreund his job and cost Salomon at least a half billion dollars in fines, penalties, and law fees, and when every other Wall Street house was having its best year in years, Salomon lost $30 million![1]

Berglas goes on to discuss Dennis Levine's "adventurous" attempts to dupe SEC investigators when they were hot on the trail of his frequent and poorly disguised illegal insider trading acts. And he has special spots for Leona Helmsley, Pete Rose, Gary Hart, Imelda Marcos, Jimmy Swaggart, Jim Bakker, Ivan Boesky, and Michael Milken. All seem to have committed self-destructive acts that followed on the heels of enormous success.

Someone with all four "A's," which Berglas calls "hitting a quad," is rare, except with the televangelists. Many people commit adultery. But Gary Hart did it, incomprehensibly and nearly publicly, at the very height of his campaign for the presidency. Arrogance increases with success and then the rules start getting broken as success becomes too much to handle.

Money loses its meaning. Levine's progression from $100,000 per year to $200,000 to $1 million to $2 million left him less and less satisfied. The pursuit became the thing, not the money. Someone on a money kick should stand back a moment, take a look, and ask, "Why do I take such little satisfaction in moving from one level up to the next?" If they don't find an answer to that question, they continue in the same pattern.

Berglas points out that if he were Levine, dragged off to jail in front of his family, he would want to commit suicide or die. But Levine has bounced back and is lecturing at business schools—on ethics, of all things—as though nothing has changed. "It happened, but it wasn't Dennis Levine that did all that," Levine says. Constant repetition will soon convince both the audience and Levine himself that some alter ego was responsible. (He's already involved himself in some suspect deals and may be headed for more troubles.)[2]

Leona Helmsley, according to Berglas, was trying to escape from being one of the "little people" who brought her down. Like the televangelists, she had a massive ego deficit. Leona is in jail for cheating the government out of some $4 million in taxes by charging millions of dollars of expense for personal items—namely the refurbishing of her and husband Harry Helmsley's chichi estate in Greenwich, Connecticut. Her housekeeper testified in court that Leona had told her that she never paid taxes, "only the little people paid taxes." Neither she nor Harry were ever sure that they deserved anything they got, never were sure that they were loved for themselves, and the only way to find out was to dispossess themselves of their possessions by the most public and asinine of behaviors, as did James Bakker and Jimmy Swaggart. But Leona has an enormous problem. How do you dispossess yourself of *billions*?

Berglas points out that Joe DiMaggio didn't have Pete Rose's problems. DiMaggio had many sources of ego satisfaction. In contrast, Rose, Levine, Milken, and the Helmsleys come across as fundamentally limited people.

How to prevent a repetition? Community service is Berglas's answer—before, not after the crimes are committed. The only antidote for narcissism is to become, early on, a part of a community group.

A Wall Street psychiatrist, Jay B. Rohrlick, once wrote, "There seems to be an inverse relationship between the amount of success narcissists achieve and the amount of praise they got from their parents," adding that the problem is not confined to young adults. He sees "men 45, 50, and 60 years old still trying to win their parents' approval."

The Self-Absorbed T.E.

One pre-Milken candidate for T.E. status is the "self-absorbed executive," according to a 1982 *Fortune* magazine article, written at a time when the "bad guys" were people like John DeLorean, the brilliant but erratic General Motors executive who was having troubles with wives and drugs and debts.[3]

Naming his company after himself was a self-absorption tip-off. DeLorean couldn't name his car after an explorer. He *had* to name it after himself. The result of his across-the-board self-absorption was personal and financial ruin. (He missed a long jail sentence by a hair's breadth.) A few years later, an unknown operator by the name of Jovanovich, attached his name to the honorable and long-distinguished name of Harcourt Brace, and moved it from N.Y.C. to Florida and in other egocentric acts such as a goofy, way over-leveraged buyout, quickly brought this fine firm to ruin.

Though barbers and bartenders have no problems with understanding such complex behaviors, it takes a great amount of skill to see inside someone else's head. But the evidence, such as it is in the case of massive narcissism as outlined in the people mentioned so far, seems to point to some massive disappointment in their lives that impacts self-esteem and leads on to inordinate fantasy in order to recapture it. To ensure its recapture, actions must be grandiose and brook no opposition, no delay. The self-involved T.E. is a menace, says Abraham Zaleznik of Harvard, an executive behaviorist of formidable insights. "Narcissists don't get anxious when they ought to. Civilization depends on people feeling anxious."

The narcissist's reaction to a bad run of luck is to walk outside, look at his name on the building, and, taking what little cash is left, head for Vegas (or its stock market equivalent). There, against known odds, narcissists expect to recoup their losses. They are usually alone in such ventures, because it's long after all the rational people who originally believed in the narcissist and his or her ideas are gone. Those followers who stay are the people who die poor and bewildered, their lives in ruins, and often in jail or disgraced. They are all those who "went along" with what they knew was wrongful behavior. (I still cannot believe that the fifteen hundred people who at last count worked for Jimmie Swaggart were all suck-ups in it for the bucks. There must have been at least a few people who finally saw him for what he is, in their lexicon, the Antichrist.)

According to Christopher Lasch, today's narcissists are the children of middle-class parents who were radically estranged from normal parental feelings and actions by the intrusive influence of child psychologists, social workers, educational specialists, and so on, all of whom knew more than Mom or Dad about bringing up kids.

Most parents in the first half of this twentieth century were conned into being afraid to punish their young, worried that they would inflict permanent damage on their issues' psyche. As a result, we are a nation of grown-up brats, who have the weird idea that there is nothing wrong with them. Even if they poop in their own pants, they don't smell it, or if they do, they think it's the other guy.

Such people really have no "self," though they are regularly described as being self-involved. The "self" that they are involved with is a narcissistic self, a self of all rewards and no punishments. This surrogate self has been created for them by thin-lipped preachers and other outsiders to the family experience, by television advertising executives, by legions of social workers, by ranks of nonloving, money-hungry, discriminating teachers, and all taught by the institutionalized professionals of the progressive school. They were taught that any punishment, no matter how richly deserved, would not be understood by the child and would inflict permanent, irreversible trauma on the child's persona, for which the parent and community would eventually pay. The self-involved T.E.s of today were thus incubated by the millions.

People with such synthetic personas can rise high in our modern society because it admires the illusion of self-confidence above the reality of performance. In an image-conscious world, we elect intellectual vacua to high office, whose rote recitation of the epic past allows them to escape involvement in an urgent present. These are the people who loved to watch *The $64,000 Question* on TV because they believed that the recall and repetition of dissassociated facts was excellence in action. (Some of them are still around, watching *Jeopardy*.)

In this unnatural world, where learned or imitative behavior is everything, there is no more room for "natural" behavior. The worst crooks in the nation—Milken of UC Berkeley–Wharton, Levine of CCNY–Baruch, Marty Siegle of Columbia–Harvard Business School—were all products of our graduate schools of business, where imitative, imagistic teaching—rather than their own experience as modified by the ages-old parenting relationship most of them never knew—governs their behavior. Most likely, the first punishment most ever received was by the State.

In the unreal world of the narcissist, meeting one's own self-set objectives is self-reinforcing, and not meeting them is destructive. I've hired a few young men whose sole intellectual qualification, as it turned out, was, "I want to be a millionaire by the time that I'm thirty." For the narcissist, and sometimes for me, that was enough if it was backed up by a top scholastic record. Most had no concrete idea how this millionaire-by-thirty goal was to be achieved. Since I was in the deals business, they believed I could show them how to do it, and along the way they'd allow me to make a profit too, which was very generous of them.

THE OVERINVOLVED T.E.

Out of narcissistic behavior one also gets the overinvolved T.E., one who must have his finger in every pie. Nondelegators, they trust no one to do a job adequately. To many people, it is insulting and enervating for their superior to check into every little job they do. It is impossible to build management muscle in people who are never allowed to make decisions.

My first editor of *Mergers & Acquisitions* magazine was one, Richard L. Gilbert, Jr., who at age thirteen became an

Eagle Scout, the youngest ever. Super-smart, he came to me after resigning as a special assistant to Commerce Secretary Luther H. Hodges.

Dick quit the job with Hodges because, according to Dick, "He kept checking up on me. I'd have everything ready for a trip, and the Secretary would say he didn't trust me and would insist on checking every single thing in my briefcase to make sure I hadn't forgotten anything. It destroyed me."

But I discovered that Secretary Hodges had good cause for his concerns. Dick was smart, but he was sloppy. He would not make that final check on a galley of type, that extra phone call to make sure that a quote was accurate. Luther Hodges should have shown his mistrust of Dick's *behavior* not of him *personally*. Dick, most likely, would have corrected his ways and would have stayed in the job.

In the modern meat grinder of business, people develop feelings of inadequacy if they feel they are being second-guessed every step of the way. Like a rubber band that stays in the drawer too long, it breaks when used. People *must* be allowed to make mistakes. Otherwise the decision-making muscle atrophies over time and develops in an unexpected way: the creation, over time, of one of the most complicated and pernicious of the toxic executives, the *non*involved T.E.

THE NONINVOLVED T.E.

At the opposite end of the T.E. spectrum from the overin-volved T.E., noninvolved T.E.s are created in reaction to the constant picky-picky of the overinvolved toxic. But many others think that it's "cool," not to get involved, or even to *appear* to be involved. They are to stay aloof. Never to emote. I've hired a few myself.

One of them, I discovered, rain or shine, crisis or no, would not begin work until he'd done the crossword puzzle in the *New York Times*. Dave ran my computer operations at *Mergers & Acquisitions* magazine. If there was a problem to solve, it waited until the puzzle was done. Further, he was out the door every evening at 5:15 in order to get to his seat at the local pub. His interests were crossword puzzles and discussing women, sports, world affairs—just about anything except the business at hand, publishing a journal about mergers and acquisitions. Dave was simply not interested in *M&A* or even computers. It was just a job. But we had a great time playing golf and tennis. Perhaps that was the reason I hired him in the first place.

The noninvolved T.E.s are the zombies of business. They are the preoccupied toxics who stay apart from the day's, week's, month's, or year's happenings, letting matters take their course. *Qué será, será!* And when things go really wrong, they turn out to be *lavabos* executives, those who wash their hands of involvement as Pontius Pilate reportedly did in not opposing the crucifixion of Christ.

The noninvolved T.E. doesn't like trouble of any kind and will spend more of his or her energies in compromise, accommodation, and peacemaking than ensuring that conflicting views are properly reviewed and discussed. Anxious to avoid involvement, these executives can create even more trouble as they dump their friends and agree with aggressors. This only exacerbates the problem.

Most noninvolved executives are also "no-goals" executives. They have no stated goals and resist goal formation: "How can I have goals when I don't know what's going to happen tomorrow?" This is bad for everyone, as research has proved that goal-directed people have much higher productivity rates than do those without goals.[4]

There are other reasons for the advent of the noninvolved toxic executive.

a. They could have been reprimanded and even disciplined for turning off their subordinates by overinvolvement in their affairs, and not letting subordinates exercise the decisionmaking muscle. As a result, they go the other way, to noninvolvement.

b. They may not have the experience or basic knowledge necessary to the job, they have made mistakes, and they have subsequently withdrawn to a self-protective, noninvolved mode.

c. They may not be natural leaders or supervisors and may have fallen into their jobs by default.

d. They may have interests that lie mainly outside of the job—church, family, sports, politics, travel, school.

e. They may never have "come over to management." The latter overidentify with the nine-to-five contingent and only get involved when they defend some stupid action of a low-ranking employee. They are antimanagement even as an integral part *of* management.

Whatever the reason for the noninvolvement, it is usually bad for the institution, as the result may be the doppelgänger effect in which other noninvolved, nondecision-making executives are added to the group in top positions and they reinforce each other. In such a group, sins of omission are not punished but sins of commission are—just the opposite of that required in a successful organization. Additionally, the noninvolved executive will not only avoid making decisions, worse, he or she will make half decisions: "Do this, but I won't tell you why." Further, the noninvolved T.E. will often be consistently inconsistent with a series of ambivalent or even conflicting statements and instructions.

Employees at all levels need the involvement of others, especially their superiors. They need understanding and encouragement in addition to supervision, guidance, and training. Without executive involvement, there is decision-making blockage as the noninvolvement virus spreads to all members of the group.

The noninvolved T.E. must get involved or leave.

THE SUPER-JEALOUS T.E.

I suppose that everyone feels a twinge of jealousy once in a while. But what of the person who is consumed by it?

I had an editor who worked for me who wrote a story about an American entrepreneur who attended a Harvard Business School seminar to learn about doing business with the Russians. As a result, the entrepreneur went over to Russia and cut a $5 billion deal to make inexpensive shoes to ship to the United States. It was a ten-year deal for fifty million pairs of shoes.

The story passed over my desk and a quick calculation showed that the shoes would cost $100 per pair, not "inexpensive," so I asked my editor for his source.

His source was an article in the *New York Times* by Isadore Barmash. I pointed out that someone had made a mistake. At $100 a pair, those were not "inexpensive" shoes, and I asked him to check the facts out with both the company and with "Ike" Barmash, an old friend of mine.

He refused. It was in the *New York Times* and that was good enough for him and should be good enough for me.

I told him I was not going to run something that was obviously wrong, and I was going to call the company and Ike and check it out. He was livid with rage, again refused to call the company to check the numbers, and insisted on running the item as coming from the *Times*. "Let them take the rap if it's wrong."

I first called the company and confirmed that it was fifty million pairs of shoes *per year*, or five hundred million pairs over the life of the contract at an average price of $10, and I then called Ike to point out the error.

Ike was grateful for my correcting the error, which he blamed on a printed release from the company. I had a nice long talk with Ike recalling the early days of *Mergers & Acquisitions*, for which he'd written a few articles. After I finished with him, I made the few necessary corrections to the manuscript and then went to talk to my editor. He refused to speak to me.

I couldn't figure it out. It was an error that was easy to make. We were simply boiling down a *Times* piece to add to a piece about opportunities in the USSR. It was no big deal. What in hell was he so mad about?

Only much later did I realize that he was *jealous!* He didn't know Ike Barmash, one of the nation's premier business writers, and didn't know his nickname was "Ike." It was as simple as that. His jealousy destroyed our relationship.

Never underestimate jealousy. The green-eyed monster can show up in many ways, both positive and negative. In publishing, I've seen jealousy make millions for people who were driven not by the profit motive, but to "beat out" their competitors. I've also seen those same people spend millions of unnecessary dollars imitating someone else who'd stolen a lead in the marketplace. Jealousy ate them up and destroyed their reason. Sometimes they couldn't quit until they went broke.

I have a research assistant, Elina Sternik, a recent émigré from what was then Leningrad. She tells me that in Russia there are two kinds of jealousy: "white jealousy," in which you are inspired to imitate and improve your own behavior, and "black jealousy," in which you are aggressively hateful to someone who is successful.

I think that jealousy can pervade an institution, where the persona of the CEO and other top officers is reflected in the behavior of the institution as a whole, as it did recently at Random House.

The largest publisher of reference books in the nation, Random House, a division of Advance Publications, which is a unit of the Newhouse Group, wanted to put out a college dictionary for which there is a huge market. The lexicographic work was easy without plagiarizing the main competitor, *Webster's New Collegiate Dictionary*, published by the Merriam-Webster company. Random House had its own base work, the marvelous *Random House Dictionary of the English Language, Second Edition, Unabridged,* which sits on the table right next to me as I write.

The word *Webster* has long since passed into the public domain, but Merriam-Webster dominates the huge college dictionary market. Random House set out to build market share for itself in the college dictionary arena.

Random House called its publication *Webster's New College Dictionary,* rather than *Collegiate,* and then did a jealous, foolish, and very costly thing: Random House copied the "trade dress" of the Merriam-Webster product, with its distinctive red and white jacket, nearly as familiar to college students and their parents as a Coca-Cola can.

Merriam-Webster sued Random House for trade dress infringement, for copying the "look" of its dictionary, and won handily and handsomely. With the judgment, punitive damages, and legal and court fees, the total bill for the infringement most likely totaled in the $5 million area. Widely publicized, it was not only a financial blow but a public relations disaster for famed Random House.

It seems to me that Random House executives were driven more by jealousy than by a conscious decision to engage in fraudulent and predatory trade practices. As the largest publisher of reference books in the world—especially dictionaries—Random House executives felt they simply *had* to have a *dominant* entry into the college dictionary market.

That kind of toxic activity seems to be on the rise. I served recently as an expert witness in a merger case involving hospital admittance bands in which, under the guise of a merger negotiation, the potential buyer (the defendant) learned everything about the process and then bought up the band company's principal supplier, effectively putting the band company out of business. This was bad enough, but the defendant didn't change the design! The band company's products were plaid and trademarked "Mac Lee." The defendant couldn't use the name, but copied the appearance, which is known as "trade dress," and is protectable. Mac Lee sued, and I not only testified as to what was standard trade practice, but in a pretrial deposition condemned the behavior of the medical doctor who perpetrated the fraud. I made a computer model of the business and computed the damages. Mac Lee won the suit and was awarded some $3.5 million and costs.

One of the increasing frauds by toxic executives in the United States is the copying of competitors' original and successful designs and ideas. The U.S. Supreme Court recently confirmed and extended the protections accorded to "trade dress," in the case of Taco Cabana, Inc., which had sued a sleazeball competitor, Two Pesos, Inc. Two Pesos had copied the distinctive external and internal decor of the highly successful Taco Cabana. Taco Cabana won the suit in a surprising 9–0 decision, upholding a damage award of $2.8 million.[5]

Jealousy destroys logic.

THE NONMENTORING T.E.

In Greek mythology, Mentor was the trusted friend of Odysseus and the tutor of Telemachus, Odysseus's son. During the Trojan War, Odysseus entrusted the care of his household to Mentor. The word *mentor* now means a trusted adviser, someone who teaches others, usually one-on-one.

Perhaps one of the most despicable creatures in our business society is the executive who will not teach subordinates for fear they will "get my job."

One of my first jobs in the Washington, D.C., area was with an air-conditioning firm out in Bethesda, Maryland, the Columbia Specialty Company. We were installing all the heating, ventilating, and air-conditioning (HVAC) equipment on the new extension of the F Wing of the Shoreham Hotel.

It was January 1940. It was cold. The owner, Bernie Bralove, was pushing us to get the job done in time for the Cherry Blossom Festival.

I had worked on enough big HVAC jobs to suspect that the system, as designed, with that exposure, would not work as expected. It was an either-or system: warm air in winter and cool air in summer. The occupant could not control the temperature of the air, only the *amount* of warm or cold air coming from a common source and shared by all the suites in F Wing. I predicted that the system, as designed, would be impossible to "balance"—that is, some rooms would be too hot or too cold, winter or summer.

I had been admitted to membership in the American Society of Heating and Ventilating Engineers, which published the *A.S.H.V.E. Handbook,* and I worked out what I thought was a better system of damper control so that the system could be balanced. I then asked my graduate engineer boss to teach me how to calculate the actual air flows for both winter and summer conditions so I could properly size the dampers.

The engineer refused my request. I pressed him. He still refused. Finally he said, "If I teach you that, they'll soon not need me." Here was a thirty-five-year old experienced graduate engineer afraid of a twenty-two-year-old student. He was a toxic executive of the first water. The system was installed the way he designed it.

I liked the job. But I like learning, too. And I hate doing a bad job. With his answer I started looking and I wound up at a Bethlehem Steel shipyard in Baltimore designing heating, ventilating, and air-conditioning systems for large ships, in particular, the U.S.S. *Alcor,* a troop transport being readied for World War II.

Unfortunately, the same thing happened there. My boss was sending out a ship with a main blower rated at ten times less than I calculated was necessary. I asked him to take me through the calculations he'd made. He refused, giving me the same answer as had the earlier Mr. Asshole Engineer. But this time I wasn't concerned with Bernie Bralove's hotel guests and a few frozen tushes; I was concerned with a naval vessel unable to do its job. I took my calculations upstairs. My boss was fired, the proper-sized blowers were installed, and I was promoted.

In all of the companies I have owned and operated, I tried to instill in everybody the important function of mentoring. It is an integral part of every executive's job to "bring the juniors along." Only a truly toxic executive would refuse to teach and train.

I have been on the corporate board of the Culinary Institute of America for some years, and served on the Education Committee. One of the most important educational processes at the institute is what they call the "extern" program, in which student chefs spend time off-campus at some famous or leading restaurant. Each candidate restaurant and its mentoring program is carefully checked out before it is allowed to participate in the program. We want our students to be *taught*. We want them to *learn*.

Every executive—in business, government, education, the armed services—has automatic mentor responsibilities. They are simply part of his or her job. It's the way that great institutions are built. The idea of *nonmentoring* to preserve one's job gives me the shudders. A nonmentoring executive is a toxic executive.

It's now fifty-two years later. I called the Shoreham—now the Omni Shoreham—and talked to the chief engineer, who's been there forty-four years. Sure enough, the system could never be balanced, and everything was ripped out a few years after it was installed and individual room units were substituted in F Wing. Did I feel good? Yeah, sort of. But I still must ask myself, was there something about me and my approach to him that forced that engineer to act in that toxic fashion? I am forced to answer that there could well have been.

THE TOXIC TALKERS

This category of self-involved toxics has a number of different subcategories, but in the main, this kind of T.E. talks to the exclusion of others. That is, no void in a conversation must ever be allowed to go unfilled lest others fill it first. The quiet person, perhaps the only thinker in the group, is squeezed out of the conversation or discussion.

Toxic talkers believe passionately that they talk considerably less than others, and when shown a tally or asked to listen to a tape, they refuse to look or listen.

Generally, the toxic talker will substitute talk for action. It is amazing to me is how long the toxic talker can be kept on the payroll without being fired. It can take years for a corporate planner, spouting off about "strategic alliances," "diversification," and "vertical integration," to be exposed as a phony who's never even read the literature—a typical characteristic of the toxic talker.

But there are other types of toxic talkers that inhabit and inhibit organizations of all types.

The Meetings Talker

Just before attending a Young Presidents Organization seminar at Harvard Business School, I got the following notice in a mailing to registrants:

CLASSROOM DISCUSSION

In a survey of those who attended previous seminars, the one aspect most often complained about was the too-often disorderly nature of the discussions.

Some YPOers tended to monopolize the discussion, others consistently talked off the point, still others constantly interrupted. Obviously most of this is a result of interest and enthusiasm, but with only approximately 20 class hours during the week, every minute counts, and when discussion gets out of hand, valuable time is lost.

A few suggestions to make the classroom discussions as useful as possible:

1. If you have not read the case, don't talk about it—at least not in the beginning.

2. Keep to the point being discussed.

3. Try not to talk when someone else is talking.

4. Don't monopolize the discussion.

It surprised me at the time that the Harvard Business School faculty would need to give this kind of high school advice to the presidents of some of America's largest and most dynamic corporations. But there did indeed seem to be more talkers than listeners. At the seminar, a few of the more aggressive participants, in spite of the warning, talked much too much. But their most annoying habit was interrupting.

This was a shame. We were there to learn and if the rules had been followed, in a more controlled environment, we could have learned from both the Harvard Business School staff and from our fellow seminar participants. After all, more than 50 percent of us got to our positions on our own—we hadn't inherited our businesses, we'd built them. Many of us had case-related experiences that we could have shared with our fellow members and the faculty. Not only did the toxics recite off-the-case, self-promoting non sequiturs, they interrupted, especially during one-on-one discussions with faculty.

But some of the warnings seemed to have been taken to heart. I served as a director on several YPOers' boards. It was remarkable to me how the preseminar rules were observed for board meetings. I was on one board for ten years, and the only interruptions I remember were my own!

Communications guru Muriel Solomon author of *Working with Difficult People,* has a special category of "difficult people," those who interrupt at meetings. Your only relief is to interrupt the interrupters or to ignore them. One way is to summarize the interrupters' remarks—their egos will be served. In your office, discourage interrupters of your work by remaining standing during their visit.[6] But remember, *always* be nice!

There are other types of toxic talkers.

The Rumormongering T.E.

The T.E.'s inner fears and anxieties are sometimes expressed in his or her giving life to rumors. "A rumor is a kind of hypothesis, a speculation that helps people make sense of a chaotic reality or gives them a small sense of control in a threatening world," says Temple University's Dr. Ralph Rosnow, a psychologist.[7]

A domestic manufacturer of coats repeats a rumor that a woman, trying on a coat in a department store, put her hand in the pocket and was bitten by a snake. The coat had been made in Taiwan, "where a viper laid eggs in the pocket." The woman died. The manufacturer's anxieties about foreign competition made him repeat the rumor— perhaps with some embellishments. If believed by fellow employees, it can hurt rather than help the manufacturer. Why? Rather than listening to or repeating rumors, the staff should be trying to discover how to meet foreign competition by concentrating on style and service and reducing costs. All the American automobile industry did for years was complain about Japanese cars and never concentrated on developing quality, beauty, serviceability, safety, and economy of operation. And they did little to reduce the costs of production by making the necessary capital investment rather than spend their cash on nonautomotive diversification.

The Phonaholic T.E.

This T.E. spends most of his or her life on the telephone. He or she can have a four-hour conversation, and in the meantime the rest of the world can go hang.

This T.E. takes calls during conferences and meetings.

Phonaholics simply cannot pass up a telephone call, even from people they don't know. They don't understand how you can.

This is a sickness just like alcoholism. The telephone is used, as alcohol is used, either as a substitute for reality or to blank it out.

With some phonaholics, it's to avoid the reality of face-to-face meetings.

In others, it's to show how important they are. This is emphasized in one version of the New York Treatment in which you are asked to leave the phonaholic's office because the subject is "confidential," as are most conversations with bookies.

I've had a number of personal experiences with phonaholics.

The advertising agency that handled the ad placements for my M&A seminars was the Washington, D.C., firm of Abramson & Himmelfarb. Dave Abramson arranged for me to meet his brother-in-law, Marshall Cogan, formerly of Carter Berlind & Weil, Cogan Gerland Weil and Levitt, and even later CBWL-Hayden Stone. I wanted information on the coming shakeout in the investment banking business. His firm was a subscriber to my *Mergers & Acquisitions* magazine. It was involved in some coming deals within investment banking.

Abramson set up the meeting. I confirmed it by talking to Cogan, who set the time at 3:15 P.M., well after the then 2:30 P.M. market closing.

I was there on time. But before I could even begin the interview, Cogan took a phone call. That phone call took fifteen minutes. There was no apology when he hung up. No sooner did I go back into my interview mode when he took another call. Still no apology. I had flown to New York City for this particular meeting and after the fourth phone call, I was steaming. I told him I was unhappy with him and asked when he would quit taking calls. He persuaded me to stay, and I began the interview for the fifth time. But even before I got an answer to the first of my questions, again with no apology, he took another call, his fifth. It was already 4:30 P.M.

For years I carried a small pair of folding scissors in my pocket. I use them, for example, to clip newspapers or trim nails. They are very sharp. So I took out my trusty scissors, carefully unfolded them, and then reached out and cut his phone line about ten inches below the handset which he had up to his ear.

Cogan's reaction was incredible. He held the phone out in front of him, with that silly little piece of wire dangling from it, and looked at it. He then put the obviously dead phone back to his ear and said, "Al, you can't believe what happened. This crazy guy Reed, you know from *M&A* magazine, just cut my phone line. Al, can you hear me? Al?"

It wasn't the greatest thing I ever did, but it was a proud moment for me to walk out the door with that jerk sitting there with the phone in his hand and a stupefied look on his face like he'd just had a lobotomy.

Come to think of it, that's what it was, a "phonabotomy." All phonaholics should get one.

The Phonaholic Salesman

A year after I founded my quarterly, *Mergers & Acquisitions*, I launched a companion, *Mergers & Acquisitions Monthly*, to launch my M&A *Roster*, a report on financial details of M&A deals, the most popular department in the magazine. (The *Roster* is still going strong today, twenty-eight years later, is on-line and is used by thousands annually.)

The quarterly, which was hardbound, did not take advertising, but the monthly, which was stapled, could, and we hired an experienced ad salesman to sell advertising space. Unfortunately, it turned out he was a phonaholic and never left the office.

After one unproductive week, I listened to his side of a few conversations. After one nonproductive phone call, he had a megachat—from 10:30 A.M. to 12:30 P.M.—in which he and a friend discussed, one after another, a long list of restaurants where they might or might not go for dinner that evening. Next, he had a conversation with his tailor, another with another personal friend, and, with lunch in between, he managed only two business calls that whole day.

The next day I put him out on the street with call-report forms to fill out—detailing, for example, whom he'd seen and at what time. He quit after two days. He was, and still is, a phonaholic and has had maybe twenty jobs in the meantime.

THE NONLISTENING T.E.

Michael Schrage, a columnist for the *Los Angeles Times*, wrote a great piece that appeared in the *Washington Post*.[8]

Schrage listed example after example of why America's top executives, either out of pique, ego, or ignorance, have stopped listening to suppliers and customers. They are instead relying on their in-house skills and "marketing departments." This is a cop-out.

The nonlistener T.E.s are only interested in what *they* have to say or do. They are entranced with the sound of their own voices, their own ideas, their own products. At home, that kind of a T.E., you will discover, has no interest in anyone else's children, only his or her own, whose dopey drawings adorn his or her office walls. They are "behavior blind." The worst of them will interview you with the TV on, which they watch with one eye. Others will have a radio playing. Asked to turn it down, they'll comply, but a minute later they'll automatically turn it back up.

In meetings, the nonlistener will inject a non sequitur, something entirely irrelevant to the subject at hand. If the nonlistener is in a position of authority, this can wreck the meetings process.

Schrage cited, as a positive example of someone who listens, Edwin L. Artzt, Procter & Gamble's CEO, who brought in suppliers to brainstorm a severe problem with Pampers design that they had been unable to solve internally. They explained the problem, and then *listened* to them. Bingo! One of the suppliers had an idea to use the rubber-band windings they use to make golf balls to get a better fit. It solved the problem.

James C. Morgan, CEO of Applied Materials, makes chip production machines, which he regularly sells to Japanese companies in competition with Japanese machines. Morgan tells how he personally and regularly visits his Japanese customers and *listens* to them. Only by listening, says Morgan, can one discover firsthand what customers really want. Then he gives it to them.

On the basis of such examples, journalist Schrage went on to point out that suppliers and customers are really partners in a business's enterprise. And partners should have a voice in the business's affairs. Schrage believes that by learning to listen, American CEOs can regain some of the competitive edge their companies have lost to competitors abroad.

Nonlistening T.E.s are so involved with what is *theirs*, whether it is products or people, that they never see a sunset. Every conversation will be turned to something about them: *their* children, *their* house, *their* illnesses. Notice that they rarely look directly at you. To do so would mean that they are listening to you, and listening means that they have lost control. Like a fickle date at a dance, their eyes are roving along with their brain as they seek to escape from the reality of you and yours, to the fantasy of them and theirs.

That's why so much market research is conducted as a search for validation of decisions already made, not as a search for usable information. If there's no match between the *desired* answer and the *actual* answer, there's a negative report. The customers' needs may never be discovered. Businesses should instead ask "What is it you need?" or "What can we do to help you?"

One form of the nonlistening T.E. is the "no-bad-news" toxic. Subordinates are never eager to give this guy or gal bad news—too much chance of being fired. Effective managers are eager for information not only as to what *has* gone wrong, but what *might* go wrong. They are thus two steps ahead of the game instead of two behind. It's easy to get information when things are going well, when there's lots of good news. But when things turn bad, watch out—the information flow dries up.[9]

Nonlistening executives are toxic executives no matter at what level they serve. (There is a kind of sickness called "attention-deficit disorder" that affects not only children but adults as well. Read about it in the *Wall Street Journal*, Jan. 11, 1993).

THE NONCOMMUNICATING T.E.

Many a T.E. is a noncommunicator, an information sink rather than a source. He or she keeps everything to himself or herself in a proprietary way. "The quiet man is oft' endowed, with gifts stole' from the gifted loud." If you just sit there and say nothing, you will be seen as "cool," and in control of yourself and thus your environment. But just as often, that controlled quietude is desuetude, a desert of dead ideas and massive ignorance of the here and now. It may be years before anyone in a power position discovers that under that quiet shell is a dead body and a dead brain. Such executives are easy to identify because they never make mistakes. How come? Because they never commit themselves. Never take a stand. Never make any decisions.

THE SUPER-SECRETIVE T.E.

I worked for Vladimir I. Yourkevitch, the designer of the fabulous *Normandie*, perhaps the greatest passenger ship to ever plow the oceans. (At least it went faster with less horsepower than any other ship of its size ever built before or since, due to "Yourky's" special underbodies.) I loved working for him, except for one thing.

Brilliant as he was, Yourky was also super-secretive. If I went into his office, the first thing he did was start turning over all the papers on his desk. After the third time, I reached over and turned them all back up and told him, very gently, that this was America, not Russia, and it was considered rude to do that with papers. I finally convinced him that I had no interest in anything he was doing except my current job, which was designing a very fast garbage disposal ship to follow the fleet so the Japanese subs couldn't follow a garbage trail.

But Yourky couldn't get over that bad habit. While he stopped it with me, he couldn't stop with the other people who worked there and he lost them, one after another. It was a shame. Such a marvelous man. He did not realize how important it is to be trusted.

THE NAYSAYER T.E.

One kind of toxic executive that drives everyone nuts is the naysayer. No matter what is proposed, the answer is nearly always no. Generally they are found in mature companies that have one or two basic products or services that yield a steady stream of revenues. The naysayer T.E. probably got his job because his predecessor mortgaged that steady stream of revenues to take one or two fliers in some new and unrelated area—perhaps a "whyncha," q.v., that bombed.

I've noted that there are various kinds of naysayer executives. Here are some that I have encountered.

• Profession-specific naysayers. They turn down ideas from accountants but not from engineers.

• Gender-specific naysayers. They invariably turn down ideas from women but not from men.

• Hierarchy-specific naysayers. Will ignore or turn down ideas from subordinates but not from superiors.

- Race-specific naysayers. Will turn down ideas from Blacks, Jews, Asians, East Indians, etc.
- Religion-specific naysayers. Will turn down ideas from Protestants but not from Catholics.
- Age-specific naysayers. Will turn down ideas from older people.

There are really no defenses against a career naysaying executive. The best thing to do is leave. Let someone without any ideas have the job, someone who *likes* rote work and paper shuffling and wants to leave every evening to catch the 5:08.

THE TOXIC ENTREPRENEUR

A toxic entrepreneur is one who is "a rich owner with a poor company." I have known many of them. The toxic entrepreneur sees a business and its employees only as a source of cash, never as an organic whole. While the business is starved for cash, he or she will *force* it to pay him or her excessive amounts of it. In moderation this can be good, because, like the stimulus of heavy debt, a cash-starved company may be far more efficient than one that is cash-surfeited.

But that can be carried too far, and often is, as short-term goals replace the long-term, the best people leave, and the draubs take over. The career toxic entrepreneur sucks the last drops of cash out of the business, lets it go in the tank, and without a quiver of remorse walks off with enough cash to do it all over again.

THE AGGLOMERATING T.E.

A *con*glomerate is a group of companies under a common operating head with a common theme—say, high-tech production of electronic equipments. On the other hand, an *ag*glomerate is a jumbled-up heap of companies composed of disparate elements that have no operating or market commonality or congruence.

The agglomerator buys companies (a) because they *can* be bought and (b) for the sake of owning them. He or she will buy anything if the price seems right. With no operating, marketing, or even financial unifying elements, the *ag*glomerate cannot last, while the *con*glomerate can, has, and will. Unfortunately, Wall Street and the investing public cannot tell the difference between the two. The toxic executive *ag*glomerator will hold on to these disparate elements even as they are failing.[10] In the long run, and sometimes in the short run, they must all die. In the process, many lives and quite a few fortunes are ruined.

THE PERKAHOLIC T.E.

Perhaps the worst of all the self-involved T.E.s are what I call the "perkaholics." Those are people who are far more interested in the perquisites of the office than the welfare of the stockholders or the discharge of their responsibilities.

In the corporate world, takeover king Carl Icahn's most telling point in persuading investors to support his corporate raids was his statement that "most executives are far more interested in perks than profits." He also implied that most were not too swift in making decisions and that they were happy recruiting less-swift people to support them. They are sitting ducks for takeover raids, claimed Icahn.

But even rubber-stamp directors can get fed up with perkaholics, as they did with toxic executive William J. Gilliam, the free-spending chairman and CEO of Rexene Corporation and a perkaholic of vast proportions. He was forced out by some of his own hand-picked directors, a rarity in corporate America. How come? Because Gilliam, as CEO of Rexene, spent some $400,000 as a sponsor of the Ryder Cup tournament held at the Ocean Course on South Carolina's chichi Kiawah Island barely three weeks before filing for bankruptcy. "Beyond the company's actual cost of sponsoring the international match, the highly publicized expenditure made potential investors leery of the company's stocks and bonds. Gilliam has personally extracted at least $23.2 million in profits from his investment in Rexene and is leaving with what one person called 'a tin handshake,'"[11] reported the *New York Times*.

In the public sector, the most famous pursuit of modern perks was John Sununu's. He was President Bush's former chief of staff. He was forced to resign in 1991 for excessive perking, he of the palindromic surname and philatelic obsession was not the first governor of New Hampshire to serve as chief of staff and to be fired for perking. Sherman Adams was also a former governor of New Hampshire, also chief of staff, to President Eisenhower, and also forced to resign his office—in his case for taking gifts, namely a vicuña coat.

I remember it vividly because I was, at that time, up for membership at Burning Tree Golf Club, where the Washington power elite, including President Eisenhower, played golf. While waiting to tee off with my sponsors, I made a very mild joke asking the pro, old friend Gene Larkin, if he sold vicuña club covers. There was an embarrassed silence. President Eisenhower was only ten feet away and I just hadn't noticed. I'm quite sure that he did not hear me, and if he had, I'm not so sure it would have bothered him. I shot a seventy-five, but my sponsors suggested that I wait for a while to be formally proposed. (It's now nearly forty years later. I'm still waiting.)

At the time, the Eisenhower campaign had featured some of the peccadillos of the Truman administration, and it was two months to reelection. Adams did not have a significant policy-making role as did Sununu, but guarded the gates to Ike as Sununu did for Bush. Adams was known as the "Abominable No Man," and like Sununu was heartily disliked for his arrogance. It was easy for Ike to drop Adams. Not so easy for Bush to drop Sununu.

They say that Will Rogers never met John Sununu. In

common with many toxic executives, according to William J. Bennet, Reagan's former Secretary of Education, and Bush's Drug Enforcement Czar, Sununu would berate someone in front of four or five other people. At the end, according to Bennet, Sununu had no friends.

Sununu never seemed to realize where his authority began and ended, nor that the legislative branch of our national government is coequal in power to the executive branch. But then, few chiefs of staff seem to have known it. Donald Regan, chief of staff under Ronald Reagan, had been an arrogant T.E. And according to Tom Wicker of the *New York Times*, so was H. R. Haldeman under Nixon.[12]

But Sununu was by far the worst. He never quit making an ass of himself. Even after he was in serious trouble from excessive perking, he verbally assaulted a *Washington Post* reporter at an otherwise happy White House affair, the signing of the 1991 Civil Rights Act. He called her a liar for saying that he was responsible for writing into a Bush speech a call for lower credit card interest rates. Sununu compounded the problem by publicly blaming Bush for that bad idea.[13] No matter, he certainly did not follow the suggestions of Louis Brownlow, head of a 1937 presidential commission that was supposed to modernize the executive office of the president, that the modern chief of staff should have "a passion for anonymity."[14]

In addition to being a perkaholic, Sununu broke a bunch of rules summarized by the *New York Times:*

1) Don't make enemies you don't need to make.

2) Don't start believing you're indispensable.

3) Don't confuse what is good for you with what is good for the President.

4) Don't forget that you are not the elected official.

5) Don't start blaming the boss if you get into trouble.

6) Don't unilaterally announce you are going to run things. Let the President make the announcement.

7) Someone must pay the price when the polls plummet, and the high-profiler usually is the target.[15]

In addition to violating all of these rules, Sununu developed a "bunker mentality" after being caught flying government planes to Boston to see his dentist. Rather than lying low, he flew even higher and oftener, and soon a pattern of abuse of government planes for personal use—at tens of thousands of dollars per trip—emerged.

But he still couldn't quit. He was now a confirmed perkaholic, an addict. At the height of the press's feeding frenzy, he *still* took a government car and chauffeur to New York City to attend a stamp auction. What a perk jerk.

Perhaps the worst thing he did was blame the Jews for his troubles. This came from at least four different sources, and William Safire, one of those columnists who early on had taken aim at Sununu's pursuit of perks, accused him of descending "into a gutter of bigotry." (As governor of New Hampshire, he had been the only governor out of fifty that refused to condemn a U.N. resolution equating Zionism with racism.)[16]

Sununu reportedly has a very high IQ. But for years there has been controversy as to whether people are tested for the right things. Obviously his IQ test was off, as Sununu did a lot of really dumb things. (He got the chief of staff job because, as governor of New Hampshire, after Bush's bad showing in Iowa, he delivered the state to Bush in the Republican primary, perhaps saving the Bush candidacy.)

I can imagine how difficult it must be to discuss anything important with someone like Sununu. He was opposed to limitations on the use of the chemicals that have caused the ozone holes in the atmosphere. Now that the holes have appeared over Bush's summer place in Kennebunkport, Maine, and without an ignorant Sununu to hold him back, Bush is all for accelerating the chemicals' replacement.

Let us hope that we never hear from the perkaholic T.E. Sununu again.

(Unfortunately, we did. He had to pay an additional $4,242 to the government for plane perks. And *Spy* magazine's publisher, Gerald Taylor, in an Exclusive Spy Prank, posing as an executive headhunter from New York, tape-recorded a thirteen-minute conversation with Sununu discussing a job that would pay in the high six figures. Sununu came back that he'd like to talk about $3.5 million per year and that he "didn't mind traveling." He never caught on. IQ 180?)[17]

Is it only a coincidence that Sununu's successor, Samuel K. Skinner, while Secretary of Transportation was also a notorious perk hunter? He flew government planes twice as frequently as any other cabinet member. He took 150 flights on FAA and Coast Guard jets at more than a million dollars' cost to taxpayers, fifty of them to his hometown of Chicago and many of them tied to playing golf. In an apparent violation of FAA rules he used his position to upgrade his flying skills from prop to jet. He also took $40,000 worth of training and logged more than 250 hours flying a twin-engine Cessna that the FAA rents for $1,111 per hour.[18] But that's not all. In 1991 he accepted nearly $11,000 in gifts and paid for two others worth $6,000 "to eliminate any questions that might arise based upon his new, broader duties."[19]

John Sununu and his successor perkaholic Skinner are mentioned in this section because of their recent prominence. But perkaholics abound in business as well as in politics. Business records, however, are not nearly as available as are government records forced to the surface by Freedom of Information Act filings. There is no such equivalent act in business. In fact, the April 1992 issue of *Directors Monthly* reports that even stockholders have been barred from getting such information, although some of the larger pension funds have been trying to change that.

The rules should be changed. Digital Equipment Corporation, in late March 1992, reported that, while the company was losing some $617 million in the fiscal year ending June 1991 and laid off 6,950 employees, just in one division some $30 million was misspent on limousines service and at luxury resorts, on "dinner cruises," and the like. Such "blatant misuse of company assets" must stop, said James A. Wallace, a Digital finance manager.[20] But it will not stop until the stockholders have a right to see the books of America's public corporations.

A few years ago CBS did a show in prime time on the Super Bowl in which they photographed hundreds of executive jets in New Orleans. The interview team, headed by Mike Wallace, tried to interview a few of the executives and their guests at the elaborate wingdings they put on at stockholder expense, but got nowhere. There is now substantial stockholder resentment building in the United States against T.E. perkaholics, especially CEOs. Some changes are bound to be made in the future.

One real full-time chief executive perkaholic in the public sector is also a religious nut. He's the governor of Alabama, Guy Hunt, who hunts perks like a coon hound hunts raccoons, howling after his prey.

Hunt is a member of a church called the "Primitive Baptists." He's also a preacher in that church. He has primitive ethics as well, and he's been using state-owned airplanes to fly all over, preaching and passing the collection plate, *and* pocketing the proceeds!

He tried desperately to derail a possible grand jury inquiry after a state ethics board found he may have committed a series of felonies by illegally using state resources for personal gain.[21] A Republican and former Amway salesman, Hunt made eighteen trips on state planes for preaching assignments for which he was paid. But it doesn't stop there. At state government expense he retained four top lawyers to file a lawsuit arguing that the governor, the state's chief executive, should not be subject to the state's ethical guidelines. (How's *that* for primitive?)

Fortunately, he lost, and while the grand jury was looking at an indictment, Hunt went off on another of his preaching trips—this time by car.[22]

An Associated Press report also detailed that three of his state-paid bodyguards pruned trees, wormed cattle, and performed chores at his farm. Hunt finally gave back about $10,000 he got from the collection plates and promised not to use the planes anymore. But it was only the drumfire of publicity that made him come clean. (Hunt was recently indicted on thirteen felony charges for diverting $200,000 of the state's inauguration funds to his own pocket, according to a *New York Times* story on December 29, 1992.)

Writing in the July 8, 1991, issue of *Newsweek*, Scott Shuger, in a piece entitled "Stopping the Next Sununu," suggests that Sununu would be embarrassed if the public were to be regularly informed of his peccadillos—that he was "betting you wouldn't find out." And the way things are now, the public learns only by luck.

Shuger thinks we need a voter-friendly law that will require every public servant to report regularly on trips, gifts, and other perks. If senators are allowed to mail good news postage-free to their constituencies, by law they must be made to include the bad news as well, such as who's giving them money or gifts. The same should apply to government contracting firms like Northrup, one of the biggest corporate liars in America. They take full-page ads in the *Washington Post* hyping their nonworking aircraft, with crappola about how their B-2 bomber will protect us from the Martians. Just as cigarette ads warn that they are bad for you, Northrop should be forced to include a big warning label that the plane advertised had completed only six hours of testing rather than the three hundred to four hundred required by the contract, and further, that they've recently paid a succession of fines at the seven-figure level not only for defrauding the U.S. government, but for firing the guy who blew the whistle on them.[23]

I would like to extend Shuger's kind of notification to the broad corporate sector as well. Let's have corporate annual reports with first-page disclosures of all of the bad things the company has done, like convictions for stealing from government, for EPA and FDA violations, for all kinds of civil and criminal convictions for their transgressions against the public. These should be printed right up front with the good news and/or excuses, in big type rather than in the tiny type in the footnotes where by design it is nearly impossible to find and very difficult to read. Stockholders should also be made aware, in easily understood language and numbers, of exact figures for executive pay and bonuses.

Shuger points out that if his proposed law were in effect for Congress, some major S&L scandals might have been detected earlier, some S&Ls might not have gone under, and the taxpayers would have saved a large part of the $500 billion it's estimated it will take to bail the S&Ls out.[24]

THE BAD-MOUTHING, JOB-HOPPING T.E.

One of the people to watch out for in business is the bad-mouther. He or she is the one who applies for a job after working for many years—say, for a competitor—and then says mean things about the company and the people. Never hire them. Why? Because they'll bad-mouth you if they leave you!

Further, out there are many job-shopper/hopper T.E.s who will offer their present company's secrets in return for a job. Again, be careful; if they leave you, (and they probably will), they'll take your secrets with them.

There are many proto-executives who fake an academic and a work background. After twenty years at one pharmaceutical company, in preparation for an overseas assignment, a background check was run on an executive. Dismaying! The institution he claimed gave him a Ph.D. did not even exist! "His certificate was a phoney,"[25] reported New York City's McAward Associates, which runs background checks on executives along with Bishop's Services and the huge Kroll Company that has offices all over the world. But there's hope for those phonys. The Centennial Press unit of Cliff Notes—the firm that helped students fake it through *Beowulf*—now offers twenty-five "Bluffer's Guides" in such fields as management, computers, marketing, and golf.[26]

I myself have hired people produced by an executive recruiter or "body snatcher," also called a "headhunter." One in particular comes to mind. Not only had our new CEO no engineering degree as he'd claimed, he'd never attended Carnegie Tech at all. He had never worked in half the places he claimed on his résumé and never held the positions at the level defined. We had paid the headhunter firm a substantial fee to find him and took it for granted that the firm had checked his background. It hadn't. During his time with us, believe it or not, he charged a whole house to us! I mean he bought a house in his own name and signed the purchase agreement as an officer of the company to guarantee the payments! I was chairman, and the principal stockholder, and I knew nothing about it until I got suspicious and got a Bishop's report which confirmed we had made a bad hire.

In another case, in selling one of my inventions, a two-chamber air-mattress that preserved body heat, the buyer told me with great pride that he never paid any taxes. I asked him how he did it. Amazingly, he told me he kept two sets of books. I asked him which set he would use to record the sales of my invention to compute the royalty. He had no answer. End of deal. I also have had executives applying for jobs who bragged that they stole parts and materials from the dumb companies they worked for who had no inventory controls.

Another kind of bad-mouthing T.E. is one who blames everything that goes wrong on a former employee—one who may have worked for the T.E. for years. Now he or she is gone and can't defend himself or herself. But the T.E. can play the blame game for years.

Other T.E. bad-mouthers deride the competition, suppliers, customers, superiors, peers, and subordinates. Their toxicity can infect an entire organization.

THE NONSHARING T.E.

Some of the most execrable toxic executives are those who don't share. Here are six types with whom I have had personal experiences.

1. *Mr. Fishhooks.* We had a business group that met to discuss marketing and afterward we'd go to dinner. One wealthy young bachelor executive never paid for his dinner. We called him "Mr. Fishhooks," because his wallet was figuratively covered with them so that he couldn't get it out to pay a restaurant check when it was his turn.

After a full year of this, one evening eight of us hungries met at the Carriage House in Georgetown. We ordered everything on the menu, including drinks, wine, a huge dinner, dessert, brandy—the works. Fishhooks was in seventh heaven until we all walked out and left him with the check. He paid a bill of some $400 and we got rid of the fishhooks. Permanently.

2. *The Disappearing Executive.* I had complaints that one of my department heads went to lunch with subordinates and invariably went to the john when the check came. I stopped that in a hurry. They should have complained directly to him—possibly with a joke or by hinting, and not complained to me, as it hurt my relationship with the *desaparecido.* Don't complain about things like this to your spouse, to your fellow workers, or to the boss. Do something about it. Tell him or her how much you resent it. If you don't, you deserve to get stuck.

3. *The Sponger.* Another toxic is the executive who attends home parties of fellow executives with his or her spouse (and sometimes the whole family) year after year, and never invites anyone back. That's wrong. Again, don't complain about it, tell him or her or at least make some

strong hints. My advice for the sponging executive: If you can't reciprocate, I suggest that you stay home.

4. *The Muncher.* We had one woman executive who used to come into the office in the morning with a bag of dough-nuts and then sit in meetings with the bag up to her mouth as she stuffed one doughnut after another into it like a horse eating oats. In two years she never offered a single doughnut to her fellow executives or even to her subordi-nates. A real weirdo, that one.

5. *The Gobbler.* Many employees cook and bake and buy and bring—cookies, cakes, sweet rolls, and more into the office to share with the others. But not Esther. Esther would gobble up everything and anything that was put out or stored in the refrigerator. She'd complain when the coffee ran out, but would never make any. In two years of nosh-ing she never brought in even so much as a cookie. As a kinder, gentler executive, I know *now* that someone should have told her how much her behavior annoyed her fellow workers. There was not the usual going-away party when she left, only *after.*

6. *The Shirker.* In spite of a sign in the kitchen, in those three years Esther also never washed out her coffee cup, waiting for the once-a-week maid to wash it. And neither did Ed after he saw Esther get away with it. Unfortunately, no one ever faced them with the office's collective resent-ments at their shirking. Again, I wonder if there was some-thing wrong with *us* that induced them to act in such an antisocial manner. Today, I would be sure that the very first time Esther left her coffee cup unwashed, she would be reminded to correct her behavior.

THE **TOXIC** DISORGANIZER

One thing is nearly certain with toxic decisionmakers: Everything they do leads to eventual disorganization.

ON BONDING

The toxic executive lacks the ability to bond with subordinates. Bonding is important if an executive's wishes are to be carried out. I said *wishes*, not *orders*. Most people don't like to be *ordered* to do things. Even the armed forces are discovering that participative decisionmaking, rather than autocratic order giving, works out better.

Of course, in the end, someone must have the final say. The soldier has no alternative but to obey. Neither does any subordinate who has become economically dependent on a particular job. But the executive who brings any relationship involving an instruction to the point of compliance for strictly economic rewards will most likely never bond with his or her subordinates for the institutional good.

It is difficult for bonding to take place if the T.E. has no respect for the individual and his or her special talents. The typical T.E. will force people into jobs they are unsuited for or will try to get them to do things they don't want to do. When performance evaluation time comes around, the T.E. visits despair on those subordinates that have been slotted into unsuitable jobs because the executive was sensitive only to his or her own needs and insensitive to those of the subordinate.

The typical T.E. never considers that a person does best in a job he or she *wants* to do. Further, what a person wants to do will change with age, education, experience, market conditions, technology, family circumstances, and the economics of the reward process. The quiet desperation in which many people live out their lives is generally caused by a failure to match talents to job requirements.

In my experience, the most frequent misallocation of job responsibilities by the T.E. is giving executive responsibilities to people who have never "come over to management." The T.E. assumes, wrongly, that everyone wants to be a manager. That everyone wants to have people to order about. That everyone wants profit and loss responsibility. T.E.s wrongly transfer their own personal ideals, drives, ambitions, values, and work ethic onto subordinates. For many years I would start an interview with a potential hire with, "If you could have any job in the world, what would it be?" Often the answer was a job description completely different from the one at hand. Taking this as a challenge, I would then try to sell the prospect on changing his or her perspective to fit our institutional, and my personal, needs. That was not right. It was toxic behavior on my part. No way could the necessary bonding take place with such diverse notions of what was needed in that job.

Perhaps the most common cause of bonding is shared stress.

In the armed forces during World War I and for some units in World War II, the higher-ups feared that bonding between blacks and whites would not take place. They knew nonbonding could mean death, for soldiers in battle must depend on one another, so they kept the races apart. What they didn't know then, and what they learned in Vietnam, was this: As soon as the bullets started flying, bonding between black and white could, would, and did take place. And fast!

Recently, in Desert Storm, another myth was destroyed: that the addition of women to fighting groups, even in support roles, would interfere with the male bonding thought necessary to successful military operations. But according to West Point graduate Carol Barkalow, who commanded an air-defense platoon in Germany and a truck company at Fort Lee, Virginia, men and women did bond in the Gulf. There they had a common and merciless enemy in Saddam Hussein. (Barkalow is one of the authors of *In the Men's House*, a book about her life in the military.)

I cannot imagine any executive in business being an effective decision maker without bonding with those who must carry out his or her decisions. And this bonding is not only vertically downward to subordinates, but upward to superiors, and sometimes horizontally toward peers. Competitors are perfect for the role of enemies, and even without them, there is the economy itself to contend with. The good executive must make common cause with his or her subordinates and convince them that the enemy is everywhere and that just staying in business is a challenge!

Once basic bonding has taken place, the nontoxic, or caring, executive will use that base to build a successful organization through participative decisionmaking.

But bonding can also cause problems. There are two dimensions to bonding: internal and external.

The *internal* dimension is inclusive bonding: mutuality of objectives, reciprocal self-enhancement, reciprocal task help, mutual support (including emotional support), and caring about and for each other.

The *external* dimension is exclusive bonding. Bonded groups, once formed, are highly cohesive and may evolve into cliques, rejecting newcomers who should be made members. Generally, a toxic executive will be a member or a leader of an excluding group, concentrating on the external at the expense of the internal.

THE BUSYBODY T.E.

Another type of disorganizing T.E. is the executive who is perceived to be overconcerned with the life-styles of his or her employees. In attempting to bond with or establish a relationship with a subordinate, many an executive believes it is necessary to control, at least in part, the employee's life outside the plant or office. If carried to excess, this makes a toxic out of an otherwise nurturing executive. The driving forces are both economic and moral.

Topping the list of the economic forces are ballooning health costs—currently compounding at 15 percent per year. Smokers', drinkers', and noshers' medical costs and lost time from work are much higher than the average. Smoking mothers have low-birth-weight children whose medical problems often add to a company's health costs. Thus, many companies will not hire inveterate smokers, regardless of whether they smoke in the office. Further, it costs money to smoke—the cost of cigarettes has increased much faster than the Consumer Price Index and smokers need more money to live on—perhaps more than they are worth. The disgust that nonsmokers have for smokers is often verbalized: "How could you do this to yourself? What a jerk!" This inhibits communication by encouraging the formation of nonsmoking and smoking cliques that avoid each other, and the situation is exacerbated by isolating them. Finally, the quit rate for smokers subject to a nonsmoking environment is very high and training costs are not recovered.

In addition to smokers, there's a similar area—high-cholesterol noshers, who show it by their weight. They are usually not hired in the first place because of obvious neurotic problems. Further, after being trained, they often die of heart attacks. If they travel, they may be forced to buy two seats.

People who drink to excess off the job often can't perform the morning after. They may also drink on the job.

Many T.E.s (such as Mormons) do not smoke or drink for religious reasons. They can make life miserable for those who do—especially those poor souls who are hooked on nicotine. Unskilled attempts at behavior modification will often fix bad habits in the target's mind and the target will continue smoking, drinking, or noshing out of stubbornness, listening to an inner voice that says, "Leave me alone."

Letting superiors know that you can't stand the smell of tobacco smoke and you don't want secondhand smoke in your lungs, hair, and clothes is not only your right, but your duty. Because otherwise, you're going to bitch about it and only make things worse.

But busybody T.E.s, especially reformed smokers, with their holier-than-thou attitude, often make things worse. Behavior modification is usually accomplished by skilled insights into the causes of the behavior. Moralizing about it won't help. Trying to shame a smoker out of his or her habit won't work either. Changing behavior is a skill that is taught at an academic level. Untrained counselors should butt out of the behavior modification process.

One busybody T.E. even forbade his executives to ride motorcycles, even though the late Malcolm Forbes, one of the nation's really smart executives, rode all over the world on them.

Busybody bosses are an old tradition in the United States. That old busybody boss Henry Ford had his "Sociological Department" employees enter the homes of employees to be sure they were not cohabiting with anyone but their wives and to look for booze. It was deeply resented.

One of the factors that led to the dissolution of the USSR was the state's insistence on getting involved in the private lives of its citizens. According to my research assistant, a Russian émigré, one of the favorite methods of disciplining a child in the Soviet school system was teachers and administrators threat to call not the child's parents, but his or her parents' *bosses!* And they actually did it, too.

THE T.E. AND LIFE-STYLE DISCRIMINATION

The *Economist* says that there is growing "a decadent puritanism in America: an odd combination of ducking responsibility and telling everyone else what to do." Life-style discrimination is wrong. The sole criterion should be on-the-job performance. And someone with a ring in her nose should not be fired for it. (It wasn't even a ring, it was a diamond. But Hilton Hotels fired Sandra Morgan anyway.)[1] While there are solid *economic* reasons for not hiring off-the-job smokers, drinkers, and noshers—they can run your health insurance right out the door—a person's life-style is his or her own business absent behavior that threatens the economic viability of the company.

But *caring* is another thing. If you really care about your employees, you'll do your best to help them improve their health through nonsmoking programs, healthy eating programs, exercise programs, and *skilled* counseling of all kinds. The operative word here is *skilled*. Behavior modification is a science. There are people who spend their whole lives in the profession. The amateur efforts of self-appointed didacts will only set bad habits deeper and build a resentful, uncooperative work force.

Unfortunately, the tobacco lobby, with the help of substantial campaign donations and the American Civil Liberties Union, has succeeded in getting "Smokers' Bill of Rights" legislation passed in twenty-one states. The measure forbids employers to "harass or discriminate against an employee" who smokes after work hours. In some states the legislation prohibits local governments from enacting tougher smoking restrictions than those ordered by the state. This will eventually mean litigation under the state's constitution.[2]

THE WESTINGHOUSE EXPERIMENT

When, after World War II, Westinghouse Electric got in a little trouble and needed some consulting help, it hired one of the then most effective management consulting firms in the world, Cresap, McCormick & Paget, to make Westinghouse over in the modern image.

And the consulting firm, led by Mark Winfield Cresap, did a marvelous job—at first. Cresap himself did such a good job that the Westinghouse board of directors persuaded him to leave his firm and made him, first, assistant to the president; next, an executive V.P.; next, president and COO; and finally, in 1959, CEO.

This brings us to one of my favorite stories.

A famous marine artist, Don, and a wealthy real estate developer, Dan, were longtime friends and next-door neighbors. They bought a horse, Exploder, at an auction for $50,000. They hired a trainer and raced him and, true to his name, he exploded down the track and won, again and again. For the next eight years Exploder made them millions before being retired to stud.

One day the two lifelong friends went to visit Exploder, when Dan had an idea. "Don, old Exploder has been good to us. I think you should paint his picture." Don allowed as how he was a marine painter, painted only boats, and refused. Dan was furious and said that if Don wouldn't paint a picture of Exploder, their friendship was at an end.

Don finally gave in: "Okay, Dan. I'll paint his picture. But that horse is gonna look like a boat!"

And that's the way it was at Westinghouse. It was turned into a huge experimental campus for testing various ideas in management consulting, and Westinghouse went straight downhill. Why?

With Cresap in charge, the only constant was change. Nothing was ever allowed to settle down. Change is what management consultants are into. They constantly change the way things are done. Thus, there is often misallocation of scarce resources: money, space, machinery, and man- and womanpower. Talk about putting monkeys in charge of the banana plantation! Imagine giving carte blanche to a consultant to run one of the largest and most important companies in America. It is my bounden duty to warn the reader that such executives are toxic executives! *Never* give a consultant line responsibilities.

At Purex Corporation, the Federal Trade Commission lawyer who started the successful antitrust action against Procter & Gamble to force its divestiture of Purex's main competitor, Clorox, was made CEO out of gratitude. But what a dumb choice! William R. Tincher decided to "prepare [Purex] for the future by diversifying out of the grocery store." He went on a crazy buying spree.[3]

From manufacturing, bottling, and marketing laundry bleach, he put Purex into a series of totally unrelated product lines such as remanufacturing jet engines. He also decided that Purex was going to grow broccoli 365 days a year and soon had forty thousand acres under cultivation. Purex bought Cessna Aircraft dealerships, a helicopter manufacturer, Ferry-Morse seeds, a swimming-pool supplies distributor, and made fifty more dopey deals. At the time, Dean Harold Williams of UCLA's Graduate School of Business Administration, a former chairman of the Securities and Exchange Commission, said the program, which Tincher described as acquisitions in "safe niches," "was a poorly conceived acquisition program."

When Purex got in real trouble with many of its acquisitions, it hired me to plan a divestiture program. I began the project and started looking for reasons I could use to resell its acquistions at a good price. But in trying to develop a history of some of the acquisitions, to answer questions I knew would be asked by potential buyers, I made the mistake of asking Tincher for quantitative data: "How did you price the acquisition? What reasons did you have to buy this company?" Tincher took it as personal criticism, since he was the smoking gun. As an attorney he knew that the "business judgment rule" protected him from stockholder suits for making mistakes, *provided* that his decisions were backed up by solid studies. Unfortunately, he seemed to have made none—at least his staff couldn't come up with them—and if the record showed how macabre his entries were, with no fit with present operations, he could be in trouble with the stockholders. He was so defensive that he never came up with anything that I could use to downsize the company at reasonable cost and the project was abandoned. If there was ever a toxic executive, it was the egomaniacal Tincher.

What he wanted was advice from someone self-effacing, someone compliant, someone worshipful. I wasn't hired for that.

As the result of the research for this book and my current research and writing on the new edition of my book *The Art of M&A: A Merger, Acquisition, Buyout Guide,* I now know how precious is an executive's success/failure acquisition record. What most executives want is only pass/fail. What they don't want is quantification: How much did that dopey acquisition cost? How much money did you actually lose? What reasons did you have for making that deal?

General Grant, a soldier, made a lousy president. Eisenhower never did anything much except stay out of trouble, which is the military way in peacetime. Cresap, a consultant, put Westinghouse on such a toboggan slide that the directors eventually couldn't wait to replace him. Westinghouse has never really recovered from the Cresap regime, and neither did Purex under a nonmerchandiser lawyer who so decimated the earnings picture that it was eventually gobbled up by Greyhound and is now part of Dial Corporation under my old friend John Teets.

Cresap, Tincher, and General Grant were what I call toxic disorganizers. Eisenhower followed in the Grant pattern and was so irresolute that he let Joe McCarthy and McCarthyism run rampant in the United States and never lifted a preventive finger, never took a stand. Soldiers know how to run armies, not countries. Consultants know how to give advice, not how to run day-to-day operations. Lawyers know how to win court battles, not how to manufacture, distribute, and market even one product line, much less several hundred. Ignace Jan Paderewski was a marvelous pianist and composer and after World War I and in 1919 was named Poland's first prime minister, but never brought Poland into the twentieth century. Knowing how to form a diminished ninth chord doesn't help much in running an emerging country, and he did a poor job. Jim Rand, founder of Remington Rand, told me that when he made General Douglas MacArthur Chairman of Remington Rand, mainly for cosmetic purposes, he expected at least some comprehension of the job and was surprised at how little the general brought to the job.

THE REED RESEARCH EXPERIENCE

Companies get into trouble by trying to fix things that aren't broke. It happened to my own company, Reed Research.

In 1959, after fifteen years of steady growth and profits, as a member of the Young Presidents Organization, I attended a week-long program at Harvard Business School. It was great. Warren Avis, who founded Avis Rent-A-Car, was one of my roommates. He and I wound up as heads of opposing teams in a vicarious acquisition negotiation.

During the week, we were exposed to many case studies and I learned that it was highly unusual to have more than five or six people reporting to one executive, especially a CEO.

I had about twenty reporting to me because each research contract was a task, generally one that I had conceived and sold either to the government or to a firm in the private sector. It appeared that, by Harvard Business School standards, my Reed Research was critically *under*-managed.

All of the shop and lab heads, four of them, also reported to me, as did all of the research task leaders, of whom there were fifteen or sixteen, each of whom had a written plan and a budget. This gave us one of the lowest overhead rates in the whole country for a research laboratory. With some sixty professionals, good budget controls, and Price Waterhouse as auditors, we'd had fifteen years of steady growth and fifteen years of modest profits.

But I came back from the seminar loaded with ideas and started to reorganize the flow of information and responsibility with the help of Kearny & Company, a management consulting group from Chicago. We moved some people around and, with new hires, finally got to the point where only six people were reporting to me. Relieved of much of my daily routine, I was now free to dream up and sell new programs. Reed Research was ready to take off.

But it didn't work out that way. Projects got behind and budgets were overrun as the new people "protected" me from problems that they couldn't solve. So they went unsolved! The new people also cost money, as they were, in the main, not billable to the projects and our overhead went up alarmingly. Change orders, which are especially complicated in research tasks and require both technical and accounting knowledge, got behind. Billings, cash flow and bank balances fell off sharply and we were soon back in the banks.

And the very simple, flat organizational chart that looked like a Frank Lloyd Wright home and that had worked so well in building the company, now looked like a Babylonian ziggurat.

It turned out that we were now *over*managed, something that Harvard Business School forgot to teach. It took me a full year to discover what was happening and to correct it. While we did not lose money, we made a lot less, lost some good people, and, more important, lost a few longtime clients.

Was I a toxic executive? You're damn right I was. I was a disorganizing toxic executive and nearly destroyed my carefully built company. As an experimenter in a research laboratory I had been very successful. But when I carried those experimental skills into the day-to-day management area, just like Cresap at Westinghouse and Tincher at Purex I reaped the whirlwind.

T.E. DISORGANIZERS AND MERGER MISMANAGERS

Probably in no other area is the disorganizing function so apparent, so frequent, and so unexpected as in the merger and acquisition area, and I'm talking about *friendly* deals. Like kids with toys in kindergarten, possession is everything. "That's mine," the acquirer says, as the latest acquisition toy is hugged to the corporate chest.

The three most frequent lies: "The laundry is on the truck," "The check is in the mail," and "Easily assembled," must be expanded to four. Add "You will continue to run the company after the deal."

After twenty-seven years in the M&A business, and as publisher of *Mergers & Acquisitions* for seventeen of those years, after reporting on some forty thousand mergers in my *Roster*, I can tell you, "Ownership means managership!" I've seen solemn agreements with owner-sellers and seller-managers broken not in years or mouths, but in *weeks* following a deal.

I was so concerned with this factor that when I put A&T Ski into Fuqua Industries, in 1974, I made J. B. Fuqua promise me that he would let Hank Simons, who'd founded A&T Ski and built it up, continue to run it. But even as the deal was closing, one of Fuqua's brand-new Harvard MBAs met with me and showed me a reorganization plan for A&T. I was horrified. I called J.B. and he was called off.

But other people have not been so lucky. Here's the pattern of merger manageritis:

    1) The deal is finally cut, usually after a long and difficult negotiation.

    2) The buyer or its representative insists on change to show who's boss.

    3) Standard operating procedures (SOPs) are introduced from headquarters so they "know what is going on," but really for control purposes.

    4) Often the SOPs, derived from other profit centers, are unsuitable for the new business.

5) Headquarters costs are loaded into the acquired company's G&A at from 3 to 5 percent of sales.

6) Headquarters takes over legal, accounting, advertising, consulting, financing, and sometimes sales and distribution—especially export—and the operation is billed at excessive rates for these services.

7) Often the headquarters people are unfamiliar with the business and don't take time to learn it.

8) Brownnosers, toadies, sycophants, and suck-ups to the acquirer are promoted and top people leave as a result.

9) They are replaced by uninformed people from headquarters.

10) The people who built the company are fired. ·

The result is a failed acquisition.

UNFRIENDLY TAKEOVERS AND THE CLOCK SYNDROME

There are types of toxic disorganizers other than the consultant type and the merger mismanager.

For instance, change for the sake of change is endemic in the *unfriendly* takeover area. Because it's not a friendly deal, many buyers are unfamiliar with operations in the businesses they suddenly own. In such a deal, the real structure, conduct, and performance of the unit and its subsidiaries might not be known until the new owner arrives on site to discover what makes it tick.

One method to discover how the unit works is to take it apart, like a kid with a clock. And just as kids lose clock parts, companies lose people. Kids break clock parts, reorganizers break people. The clock doesn't work afterward because it's put back together wrong. Neither does the company work, for much the same reason.

Finally, a whole new group is brought in, just like buying a new clock. In the meantime, several years have been lost, along with pots of money. The new clock might cost twice the old and will never run as well, if at all.

For both friendly and unfriendly deals, ownership is managership. Except in the most enlightened of companies, sooner or later ownership power will be invoked and the restructuring will start.

Like the chap searching for a lost coin under the streetlight because the light is better there, the major T.E. disorganizer trademark is his or her insistence on installing management procedures and methodologies that he or she understands. The acquired company is made over into something familiar, no matter how inappropriate.

In a worst-case scenario, the new owner will fire the people who built the original, successful organization, out of jealousy. My name was removed from the masthead of *Mergers & Acquisitions*, contrary to agreement, because the new manager did not want to give credit to me for its founding. That seems to be endemic in the M&A area. I founded LogEtronics, hired people, and got so many orders I couldn't finance them, so at the end of the first year I sold it. LogE took off and soon the new owner, Richard M. Johnson, who didn't know an electron from an elephant and who'd evidently never had a success in business before, announced himself to his Harvard Business School classmates, Class of '29, as the "founder." I never imagined that anyone would need kudos so badly that they would do something so crass.

In *The Prince*, Machiavelli said that a conqueror of a city should either kill off or exile all the former leaders and then build loyalty by promoting second-tier people to ruling offices.

One of the reasons for the horrendous problems of the Texas banking system in the nineties is the hundreds of bank mergers that took place in the sixties, seventies, and early eighties. There, the top managers were fired and second-raters, fake Texans usually from New Jersey, were moved in who didn't know banking but knew how to bow and scrape and do a passable "you-all."

They were dead meat for the experienced borrower, and the Texas banks are still not out of the woods as a result.

THE "WHYNCHA" SYNDROME AND THE T.E.

Airplanes are fun. I love them. I always meet interesting people, some of whom have become lifelong friends. But I've also met toxic disorganizers of the worst kind, the kind I call the "whyncha" types because that's what "why don't you" sounds like when said frequently and quickly. *"Whyncha* get in the bowling business? Good money in bowling."

Worse than attending a Young Presidents Organization–sponsored seminar and merging with a company represented there is meeting someone with knowledge and persuasive abilities on a plane. Plane friends can be dangerous. The space is too cramped to check credentials, even if you had enough nerve to ask. Yet the physical closeness, the food, and wine are all conducive to the striking of an alliance, even though you cannot see into your potential partner's eyes, something essential to proper deal-doing.

One of the really bad things about chance meetings of any kind is their impact on planning. A CEO will spend up to 10 percent of annual revenues on planning, taking great care that the programs "fit" the company. But that same CEO takes one little plane trip and all of that planning goes out the window. Why? He brings home a "whyncha."

On the plane, the CEO hears of fantastic doings. Too busy to read, he hears about high-definition television, about raising shrimp, eels, fish, and even *lobsters* on farms, about the unsatisfied learning drive of one *billion* Chinese, about million-dollar plants full of brand-new machinery that can be bought for a hundred grand. Wow! Opportunity, here I come!

Our CEO has told his seat-mate that he has a successful business and is looking for more worlds to conquer. His new friend says, *"Whyncha* get into the fish-farming business? It's wide open and run by a bunch of ignorant farmers who don't know how to market. In fact, I know one for sale." The CEO is entranced. He comes home and completely distracts the whole organization by trying to push everybody in completely new directions, into areas in which they have no skills and no interest.

This happened to one company of which I was a director, a family-owned and -operated company with a large free cash flow. I mentioned to our CEO that I was looking for someone to buy up a transmission rebuilding plant that was for sale in Alabama. There were huge contracts to be had with General Motors dealers under their new drive-train warranty programs for their new fuel-saving "lockup" transmissions.

Before anyone on the board knew it, the CEO had jumped in the company King-Air, flown to Alabama, made a deal to buy the failed operation, and cut a deal with a bunch of people with big bellies, Italian suits, pointy shoes, and leased Lincolns to run it. He also committed us for many millions of dollars to finance the operation. This business, its technology, its marketing were quite foreign to us. We dropped $10 million before we knew what hit us. But worse, the whole company was distracted from its core business, some of which was lost to overseas companies.

Afterward, we ran it through my "Fit Chart," a multivariate analytic construct which identifies operating and financial synergies, and it scored only 250 points out of a possible thousand—a 25 percent efficient acquisition and a sure loser. But the CEO liked warm weather and southern women. He controlled the company and we could do very little about it—especially since he did not tell us what he was about. I also must admit that he was so enthusiastic about the prospects and so grateful to me for bringing the deal to his attention that he even sold *me* on the potential—but he'd already bought it!

There are thousands of good solid acquisition opportunities out there. They must be properly evaluated for "fit." The word "properly" means some kind of formal evaluative process. A plane ride and a few random "whynchas" is not the way to solid growth—not the way to make money as they disrupt the planning process.

THE TOXIC NONFINISHER

One of the worst of the disorganizers is what I call the toxic nonfinisher. They're the ones who form up task groups, have big hairy meetings where they outline a complicated project, and then make assignments for follow-up to people who (a) have no real interest or stake in the project, (b) do not have the requisite skills, and (c) are busy with things of higher priority.

Nonfinisher T.E.s make project schedules but then don't follow up. It's as though the job is finished when the Gantt Chart, which plots sub-sector completions against time, is first drawn up.

Some businesses, at the urging of academicians like Theodore Levitt of Harvard Business School, make the creative person responsible for carrying out his or her idea to a higher level, as he outlined in his *Harvard Business Review* piece, "Creativity Is Not Enough."[4] However, this is not a good idea, as it may turn a good idea into an *idée fixe* on the part of the ideator. The efforts of a *group* of people of complementary talents—one with creative abilities, the next with analytical, the next with organizational, and the last with managerial skills—is frustrated by the Levitt thesis. Making the ideator responsible for all those other skills in order to get a hearing for his or her idea is simply another way to torpedo the innovative process.

But the egomaniacal T.E. will fall into the trap that Levitt has set. He or she will try to do all those things—innovate, analyze, organize, and execute a project—and that is usually impossible and the project is left unfinished.

Failing to assemble and maintain groups of people with complementary talents is the primary reason not only that projects never get finished, but also that many never even get started![5]

Career criticophiliacs, the toxics who live off the discomfiture of others, are happiest when they have some poor trembling ideator in their sights. Bereft themselves of ideas, they dislike people who have them and make a career of killing off the creative act along with the creator, and many bought into Levitt's thesis.

Toxic executives don't like to see themselves in the subservient but important role of making something work, though this follow-through is often far more important than the idea itself! In a proper environment, the ideator and completor would be considered a team and would be equally rewarded. But in today's strange society, it's the idea-killer who is rewarded, not the ideator.

Watch out for the nonfinisher executive. He's toxic!

One of the prime problems in America today is that MBA graduates of the Levitt persuasion, exposed to a continuum of simplistic and super-reductionist instruction supported by massive quilldriving in a captive *Harvard Business Review*, are running much of American business, and are killing it! Perhaps one of the most celebrated *Harvard Business Review* pieces of all time was Levitt's "Marketing Myopia," which urged their hundreds of thousands of readers to look beyond their day-to-day experiences and discover what business they were *really* in. This brought about numerous business tragedies of great scope. For instance, oil companies convinced themselves that they were not in the "petroleum business," they were in the "energy" business, or the "extractive" industry. This led them to substantial investments in coal and/or copper, which are extracted, processed, priced, and marketed completely differently from petroleum. It was a disaster for them and for the thousands of companies which followed Levitt's advice as I followed their fates in issue after issue of my *M&A* magazine.

THE COMPLICATOR T.E.

One of the worst of the disorganizing T.E.s in the decision-making area is the undue complicator. He or she has never heard of KISS—keep it simple, stupid.

Because I founded the magazine *Export Today* and the

low dollar is currently driving up our exports, I have had two recent visits from people in the export-import business. Both have set up wildly involved corporations and partnerships involving such disparate elements as American nationals, overseas and American investors, foreign corporations, and tax haven countries. Both sets of visitors have used every possible device, every kind of corporation and partnership (both limited and regular) that interlock, and codeal in such a complicated way that I am amazed that anything gets done at all. Some of the arrangements are tax-driven. But the benefits are minuscule compared to the ongoing administrative costs of solving problems created by the complicated structures.

I call this "high school organization." Why? Because in high school they learned that 51 percent was 1 percent more than 50 percent and that in a corporation you always wanted that 51 percent so you would have "control." But there are many legal ways to control a company other than through the percentage of equity. There are, for instance, voting trusts and agreements and nonvoting stock. And remember that the law is evolving so that minority shareholders seem to have more rights than the majority and that an overly complicated structure creates suspicions of hanky-panky and is an open invitation to minority stockholder suits.

THE NITPICKER T.E.

One of the primary disorganizers is the nitpicker. Generally nitpickers are underworked, or they wouldn't find the time to nitpick. They get more satisfaction out of spotting a misplaced comma than a misplaced employee. They insist on seeing every letter before it goes out and then make petty changes in form rather than function. They are far more concerned with process than product, things rather than people, and ideas not at all.

Also known as the "who, what, why, where, whenners,"

they drive people nuts with their acerbic questioning. In the research and development area, with which I am most familiar, they will never take an "I don't know" for an answer. In research you really can't answer who, what, why, where, and when questions in as quantitative a manner as you can in, say, publishing or hard-goods manufacturing.

The nitpicker T.E.'s job as he or she perceives it is to lower risk by making sure that all the *i*'s are dotted and all the *t*'s are crossed. That's important. But it puts them in the position where they can extend their inquiry into areas where they have no knowledge or skills. I had a partner when I founded *Mergers & Acquisitions* magazine in 1965. He was a Harvard Business School graduate and insisted on doing a "market survey" before launching the magazine. I agreed. He then talked to twenty-one lawyers, accountants, and businessmen. All of them said it was a dumb idea—they could get all the information they needed from Commerce Clearing House and similar services, from the *Wall Street Journal,* and from a dozen more publications. But while my partner was talking to all those people, I talked to Austin Kiplinger, one of America's most successful publishers. He said it was a dynamite idea and confirmed my notion that to pull everything about mergers and acquisitions into one publication was a great idea. My nitpicking partner pulled out. I launched *M&A* myself, it was an instant success, has made money for years, and is now beginning its twenty-eighth year of publication.

I have always heard that Samuel Goldwyn, the famous and very successful movie producer and one of the founders of Metro-Goldwyn-Mayer, had said that the most important component of success in business is *enthusiasm.* Nitpickers can kill off this great quality of the human spirit. What my partner tried to take away, my enthusiasm, was displaced by Austin Kiplinger's approbation. I will always be grateful for it. (I discovered later that my prospective partner had not tried to discover why people *would* buy the magazine, but why they would *not!*)

On a personal basis, the career nitpicker will concentrate on trivia. He or she will point out a spot on your tie, a misplaced chair in your office, an eraserless pencil, your clothes, your car—anything and everything.

The nitpicker executive is very clothes-conscious. He or she has a dress code and will not hire outside of it. At client Baltimore Gas & Electric, I ran a long-range planning meeting on a hot, hot day in mid-July. I wore a comfortable cool and crisp Brooks Brothers three-piece seersucker suit. I sat at a table with a dozen others who were all dressed like undertakers. At the end of the meeting I was taken aside by the executive who had retained me and was warned never, ever again to wear that suit to a BG&E meeting, or no more contracts. He spoke the truth. I never had a chance to wear it again to Baltimore, for there were, in fact, no more contracts. Incredible! *Their* loss!

THE OVERORGANIZED T.E.

Many a T.E. has devoted his life to organization charts. He or she is positive that most business decisions are made in a certain way and that unless the decision path is laid out for individuals and groups, bad decisions will be made.

Few people realize that decisionmaking in most companies is an informal process that takes place by osmosis; ideas and actions slowly permeate the membrane of the corporate psyche or culture. Institutional memory—decisionmaking dictated by past performance—plus organizational diagrams for dictating required flows of information, responsibilities, and authorities have a very short effective life in which change is or should be endemic. Not even the newest in matrix organization theory and practice can depict the way that decisions—especially those made under stress—are actually made in any organization. While there are a thousand books on how decisions *should* be made, there are very few on how they *are* made, and diagramming a decision path in a modern corporation is a near-impossible task, though many attempt it.

In my experience, any company is a collection of potential strategic business units (SBUs) that are created every time something happens that falls out of line with what has happened in the past or has been formally predicted to happen. Unexpected things are always happening in business and no organization theorist has yet come up with a solution that works for all companies all the time.

For instance, a manufacturer of farm machinery, bidding on a contract to supply seven bean-pickers to a major canner, suddenly learns that a competitor has put in a low bid at the very last minute and has put a proprietary twist to it. What to do? There is really no time to call a full-scale meeting of executives. The CEO is in Europe. You need the work or the overhead will go up. Inventory will lie unused. Something must be done.

In an overorganized environment, believe me, nothing *will* be done and the order will be lost. But if people can be trained and permitted to think and act as members of all those little SBUs that are created each day by problems just like this, and if they are given the authority to meet and create solutions to urgent problems at middle-management levels without having to follow some pyramidal organization chart created by some overorganizing zealot, the firm will soon rise above its competition. Decisions will be made and things *will* get done. The company will get the order!

While it's nice to have a formal organization chart, far more important are the *informal* processes that take place. Learn what they are. Discover what they should be. Watch out for the overorganized T.E.

THE DOPPELGÄNGER EFFECT, UNIFORMITIS, AND T.E.S

For some years I was on the board of directors of the largest affinity-group travel company in the world. Called

Intrav, the St. Louis–based company was built by a genius, Barney Ebsworth, who knew that people of the same cultural, educational, and employment backgrounds much prefer to travel together.

Barney built a highly profitable business taking such affinity groups on trips all over the world—medical doctors from the same geographical area or specialty, lawyers from the same local bar association or legal specialty, alumni groups, golf club members, and so on. Barney insisted that I join several of the groups to learn more about the affinity-group travel business, the better to discharge my director's responsibilities. He also insisted that I take my family along.

Often a single group was not large enough to fill an entire plane and I noticed that when two different groups—say, members of the Harvard Alumnae Association and the Erie County Medical Association—made the same trip together, they very seldom mingled.

The doppelgänger effect in business works the same way. (The word *Doppel* in German, means "double," a spirit-double in German folklore as distinguished from a ghost.)

Executives like to hire people who look alike, dress alike, talk alike, and act alike, people who have the same backgrounds, are of the same political persuasion, and make decisions the same way they do.

Thus affinity groups are constantly being formed in operating companies. Some executives, and almost all T.E.s, find them much easier to administer, as communication is simplified.

Further, while affinity groups and doppelgängers work well on the assembly line where one is dealing with "things," they work out less well in middle management, where one is dealing primarily with "people" who are not "affinitied" in any way. And it certainly cannot work at the CEO level where one is dealing primarily with "ideas," which should know no affinity.

One of the prime reasons for doing away with the

"track" system in primary and secondary schools was this: Those in the more advanced tracks never learned how to deal with those of lesser learning ability—something most successful executives must learn early in life.

These same problems cross over into business decision-making where cultural differences play a role; they can cause real problems for those coming out of the track system. Diversity is a near-necessity in business today, while lockstep decisionmaking by clones at any level can bring down a whole company.

Canceling out the doppelgänger effect in business has been the subject of many books and articles, in particular those of Warren Bennis. Bennis, in his 1989 book *Why Leaders Can't Lead*, notes:

> One of the most striking things about the Iran-Contra hearings was how much all the alleged conspirators resembled one another in manner, posture, and speech. All seemed cast from the same mold— clean-cut, trim, conventional, full of humorless purposefulness, and empty of any moral sensibilities. In these ways they resembled their commander-in-chief, as if they were all doppelgängers, ghostly doubles.

Bennis goes on to explain that these "doubles" screw up the administrative process. Drawing on his six years as the president of the University of Cincinnati, he writes:

> The desire for a congenial and closely knit management group is . . . understandable. The sheer size of [modern] organizations makes it impossible for the top people to verify their own information, analyze their own problems, and decide with whom they should spend their time. They [must] rely on their assistants to double for them . . . those assistants should be of kindred minds and compatible natures . . . but since they control access to their boss, choosing the . . . people and the material their boss will see, they control the boss. . . . [In the Reagan White House] operating on the assumption that Reagan wanted them to aid the Contras, North . . . and company broke a number of laws, lied, even deliberately shredded evidence, and, by their own lights "protected" him by not telling him what they were doing.

[Meanwhile] Reagan, who campaigned against big government, had the biggest staff in the history of the White House and, with the exception of Nixon's, the most inept.

The one thing a president—whether of the United States, a corporation, or a university—needs above all is truth, all of it, all the time. And that is the one thing a president is least likely to get from his or her assistants if they are cut from the same cloth.[10]

Ronald Reagan, as the chief executive of the greatest nation on earth, had his ideological doppelgänger assistants in place. Just because they shared his ideology did not mean that he wanted them to share his power or his decision-making responsibility. But they took it anyway. (Doppelgänger ideologues tend to exercise much more authority than they have been given, since they feel protected by their ideological affinities.)

The toxics in this case were North and Poindexter. North was a lying little sycophant who ideologued his way into the Oval Office on more than one occasion.

Reagan had plenty of experience dealing with people with secret agendas and plans when he was in the movie business—one of the reasons he was elected and served for some years as the head of the Screen Actors Guild, a trade union. There he came up against some of the most exploitive people in the world and traded them out of benefits. How come he was fooled, as he claims he was, by North?

It simply *had* to be the uniform, which amplifies the doppelgänger effect. A very simple, but honest man, Reagan had played parts in at least ten films where he wore a uniform. And they were *always* heroes. For Reagan, North just *had* to be a hero!

Further, "uniformitis," as I call it, becomes endemic in a society that has chaos at home. For instance, kids will latch on to anything that is, like a uniform, the same from one day to the next. That's why the first thing a boy answers, when asked what he wants to be when he grows up, is "a policeman," "a fireman," or "a soldier." Later he opts for the sports uniforms. A little girl would answer "a nurse" or "a stewardess" when asked the same question.

It was for those same reasons that Lyndon B. Johnson, coming from the variability of the political world where few are honest or believed, placed his trust in the military. He actually *believed* the men in uniform when they gave him numbers of how they were decimating the Viet Cong. Would they lie to their commander in chief? Of course not. And when they drew all of those silly expanding circles of control on the blackboard, telling him how they would win the war in a few months given the troops, he believed that too. The uniform inspired trust.

How very wrong he was. And how very wrong we remain when we continue to trust and revere our military establishment as a result of the Desert Storm victory in which we had a four-to-one numerical advantage over the Iraqis, an army of religious and political zealots commanded by another nut with a mustache. We must ask ourselves the question: If it were not for the oil, which made us all covert doppelgängers, would we have fought Desert Storm? If it were oil-poor Kenya being occupied, whose leaders are only slightly less despotic than those of Kuwait, would we have organized the whole world to come to *their* rescue? Hell, no. It was the oil.

THE UNPRINTABLE T.E.

One of the most disorganizing of the toxic executives is the one who swears, not in anger, but as a matter of course. This is not the educated cusser who can come up with an occasional oath or a profanity at an appropriate time. I'm talking about the executive who can't complete a sentence without an expletive, usually something scatological.

Swearing offends many people and is a sign, some say, of an inability to express one's ideas or emotions in a mature way. I've known people to quit their jobs because they were very uncomfortable in such an atmosphere. Ross Perot even cited it as a reason to be released from his service commitment to the Navy. I myself have been guilty at times. At the University of Colorado where I was lecturing, after listening to Norman Mailer, a skilled cusser, I tried to imitate him. It didn't work. I only embarrassed myself. One has to *know* how to swear. And "recurring incidents, like the use of foul language that eventually amounts to sexual harassment of female employees, are the most likely to damage morale."[11]

The offended person simply must tell the offender that it is bothersome. The offender may not be aware of the effect that a constant use of expletives can have on a relationship. In executive ranks, proof that continuous execration has not become an integral part of their communicative process is found in their ability to turn it off and on. If you are offended by it, sing out. But don't moralize about "taking God's name in vain," and don't try to use psychobabble on him or her as to *why* the invective stream. Simply tell him or her how uncomfortable it makes you feel.

THE UNPRINCIPLED PROMISING T.E.

In the hundreds of interviews I conducted in preparation for this book, one of the most frequent complaints I heard was of executives who failed to meet their promises. Feel-good promises are easily made by the T.E., but uneasily met. Excuses range from "I never said that" to the execrable, "I might have said that, but that's not what I *meant*."

Many businessmen use high-level politicians as their role models. To them, a promise is easily given. The public writes it off as "campaign rhetoric," forgives them, and votes them back into office. Ronald Reagan's oft-repeated and solemn pledge to balance the budget in his first three years in office and create a surplus in his fourth was probably the single most wildly improbable and inaccurate unmet presidential campaign promise in history until Mr. Bush came along with his "read my lips, no new taxes" and his promise to create thirty million new jobs during eight years in office. During the first two years in office, the Bush administration produced the smallest annual growth rate since that of President Herbert C. Hoover. And Bush's '92 campaign to convince the public that "recovery is everywhere" sounded just like Hoover's "prosperity is just around the corner." In public life, and now in our corporate life, it seems that the Pollyanna Complex, taken from the turn-of-the century American novelist Eleanor Porter's child heroine, has replaced the Cassandra Complex.[12]

At my Reed Research, I once hired an executive vice president. Financially trained, he was to relieve me of my administrative load. But just as he got into the job, he came down with the flu. It was winter and he had one flu bout after another. He was absolutely useless. In desperation I sent him to my doctor, who suggested that he go to Florida and lie in the sun and "bake out for two or three weeks." We said we'd pay for the trip for him and his wife if he promised to stay in the sun and get well. He came back three weeks later. He wasn't tanned. He still had the sniffles.

"Did it rain all the time?" I asked.

"No."

"Well, how come you're so white?"

It turned out he'd stayed home, a half hour's drive from the office, with all the blinds down for three weeks so we would think he was gone. We paid him off and I refused to give him a recommendation for his next job. Curiosity led me to go back over the calls I had placed to his former superiors who had given him a good recommendation. I had asked questions only as to his analytical and administrative capabilities, not his behaviors. I had not asked the key question: "Does he honor his commitments?"

He was a toxic executive of the first water.

8

THE FISCALLY ABUSIVE T.E.

While we have already met some fiscally abusive T.E.s in the form of perkaholics, we have isolated a few more who use their company or institution as a personal fiefdom, wasting company assets in their drive to carry out personal vendettas and jealousies, and to deal with their own personal demons.

THE TOXIC LITIGIST

One of the most difficult to identify, the most difficult to control, and the most difficult to classify of the T.E.s is the toxic litigist executive. His or her main mission in life is to contest every competitor, every supplier, every customer, and every employee, either in a court of law or before an arbitration tribunal. The medical profession even has a name for this kind of person. A "litigious paranoid" is a person suffering a psychosis (usually paranoia) who is "habitually engaged in lawsuits which he pursues with fervor, treating even minor issues as major causes celebres."[1] "America's favorite sport after baseball is suing other people," said a character on the *Wings* sitcom. I agree.

Unlike the abrasion junkie (see chapter 1), who gets a *short-term* charge out of daily conflict, the toxic litigist gets a *long-term* charge out of keeping a law case going for years and will waste the company's money on lawsuits that there is little or no hope of winning. The accompanying rhetoric, such as "upholding the honor of the company," is usually crappola because the litigating company is often proved to be wrong, perhaps after ten years of expense. The toxic litigist executive should be identified early, disciplined, and forced to settle, quit, or be fired. The forcing function is the growing use of the "English Rule," in which the loser pays the court and legal costs of the winner.

Identifying Characteristics of T.E. Litigists

Here are some of the identifying characteristics of toxic litigists.

1) The *variety* of lawsuits. They will insist on litigating *everything*.
2) The *number* of lawsuits. They will have a dozen or a score going at once.
3) The *duration* of lawsuits. To prove themselves right, they will keep a case alive for eight to ten years, even to the point of bankrupting their own company.
4) The *cause* of lawsuits. Often the litigating executive was the cause of the trouble in the first place.
5) The *frivolity* of lawsuits. In some courts that have adopted the English Rule, legal costs of the winner are paid by the loser.
6) The *vagueness* of lawsuits. In cahoots with the lawyers who are living off them, it's nearly impossible to get a reading from the toxic litigist as to:
   a) The *total* of sunk costs to maintain the action to date
   b) The *present value* of the loss if the case is lost, including the effect on ongoing business, rated against the present value of the gain if the case is won
   c) The *present value* of the future recovery, which may be negative after deducting the costs of the lawsuit even without factoring in executive and staff time lost from the business

d) The *continuing cost* of maintaining the action, including the internal costs of executive and staff plus overhead

f) The *cash costs* of immediate settlement

g) The *probability* of settlement

h) The *relationship* of the law firm maintaining the action to the internal legal staff, board members, the CEO, COO, or other top executives

7) The *effect* of the lawsuit on the morale of the entire organization. This is especially keen in the SLAPP (strategic lawsuit against public participation) suit usually filed against homeowners who protest the actions of real estate developers. The SLAPP suit compels them to recant in the face of overwhelming legal costs to defend themselves. (In New York State the Coalition Against Malicious Lawsuits has successfully lobbied legislators for passage of anti-SLAPP legislation.)[2]

Early detection and prevention of toxic litigists and their actions is nearly impossible, since they are often highly effective executives in every other department. They just like to play lawyer using company funds.

Some of the same qualities that make an aggressive salesman and company-builder are the same qualities that will keep an executive in court on a piddling little case for years. But his or her addiction to litigation may soon destroy his or her executive effectiveness as attention is diverted from the job to the litigation.

The Toxic Litigant Board Member

Board members who get income from litigation are dangerous to have around. They're of several kinds: the in-house lawyer/litigator whose job may depend on his keeping an action going; the outside litigating counsel whose income flow will be impacted by a settlement; and the board member whose law firm is retained to litigate. All should be closely monitored as they are often the hench-men of a compulsive litigating CEO or COO. Together they will oppose settlement.

Where there are a number of suits, or one very large one, a committee should be formed of non-involved directors to monitor the litigation and report to the board. Many boards schedule meetings where the first item on the agenda is a review of pending litigation. Why? Because the corporate secretary is often either an inside or outside attorney, has a stake in the outcome, and wants the board to know how hard he or she is working in order to support his or her salary and/or billings.

I was on one board where one case alone took eight years of litigation and we had to listen to the details every meeting as we lost appeal after appeal. Often, the board never got to some of the really important items on the agenda as the dopey lawyers went on and on and the CEO whose ego was involved kept the suit alive year after dreary year.

Directors are often unfamiliar with the effect that an ongoing suit can have on company morale and on cus-tomer relations—especially when the company is in the wrong and the employees know it. Determining this would be the job of the litigation review committee.

Inside directors who are also involved in ongoing suits present a problem. Often they are not as interested as they should be in settling, which might mean that they were responsible in some way for the problem. They should not serve on the litigation review committee.

There's some current literature that backs me up. Rather than the common impression that the federal courts are jammed with overeager lawyers fighting tort claims against major corporations, professors Marc Galanter and Joel Rogers of the University of Wisconsin argue that the blame has been misplaced. The boom in civil corporate liti-gation—complaints brought by businesses against each other—has been virtually ignored in loading up our courts, as they take far more time than do criminal cases.

Contract cases between corporations in federal court grew from 518 in 1971 to 6,277 in 1986, an increase of 1,112 percent. The litigation included disputes with suppliers, distributors, creditors, competitors, customers, and government. Involved were misleading advertising, civil racketeering, bankruptcy law, and intellectual property rights.

Senior Litigants

One of the prime identifiers of the toxic litigist is age. The more advanced the age, the more frequent and the more aggressive the litigation. With advancing age, the stakes for the litigant are constantly diminishing and many a lawsuit is settled after the death of one or more of the primary supporters of the actions.

Litigation as Strategy

Businesses have come to think of litigation as a management strategy. "If you couldn't negotiate, you can sue," says Carl Liggio, general counsel for the accounting firm of Ernst & Young. Liggio commented to the effect that our commercial society is much more open today. "The old-boy network, where you washed your dirty linen in private, is long gone," says Liggio.

But Galenter says that product specialization, heightened competition, and the increased complexity of business transactions is causing the boom in litigation. Judges also are to blame in allowing frivolous actions into court. (Remember, we are talking here only about federal courts, not state and local courts, where the number of cases runs into the millions.)

I am not alone in believing that we have a major problem here. Vice President Dan Quayle said as much in a rather raucous dispute with the president of the American Bar Association in Atlanta at the group's annual meeting in the summer of 1991, asking the audience whether "America needs 70 percent of the world's lawyers . . . and 18 million new lawsuits a year." Quayle called it a "$300 billion-a-year self-inflicted competitive disadvantage" in the world economy. ABA president, John Joseph Curtin, Jr. replied with a smarmy "Who will protect the poor, the injured, the victims of negligence, the victims of racial discrimination and . . . violence?" Curtin was much criticized within the ABA ranks for his overprotective response. Played up in the press, it was the first time that many people learned that lawyers were *protecting* the poor, the injured, the victims of negligence, racial discrimination, and violence, rather than *exploiting* them!

Quayle continued the attack in September. With his mail running fifty to one in his favor, he expanded his attack: \"It matters that . . . foreign companies often have product liability insurance costs that are 50, 80, even 90 percent lower than their counterparts in the United States. It matters that liability concerns have caused dramatically higher prices for some everyday items—from stepladders to medicines—that some beneficial products may never reach the market at all!"'

If the CEO is opposed to settlement of long-running litigations, the board should take away his or her authority to maintain long-term legal actions and should actively pursue settlement on its own. If this is foiled by the CEO, he or she should be fired.

Dispute Resolution

Business Week recently did a cover story on corporate litigation. It reported:

Motorola Inc.'s 100 in-house lawyers must seek all possible alternatives to landing in court: arbitration, mediation, even private judges who settle disputes for a fee. After all this, Motorola lawyers who still want to go to trial must fill out a form estimating legal costs, likely damages, and chances of victory. "The form is so onerous that they gladly work out an alternative settlement rather than screw around with that form," says Motorola General Counsel Richard H. Weise, and "Our energies should not be spent on recreational litigation," says PG&E's general counsel.[4]

Many firms are firming up their resistance to litigative solutions to disputes. There are a growing number of firms that specialize in settlements of ongoing lawsuits. Generally classified in the area of dispute resolution, or alternate dispute resolution (ADR), such firms cut short the time and costs of pretrial discovery and run "mini-trials" that are similar to court proceedings, but without recourse to the expensive and time-consuming pretrial discovery and at-trial hallowed rules of evidence that so delay, extend, and complicate formal juridical processes.

ADR is one of the fastest-growing fields of professional consulting. Lawyers and their firms have traditionally argued that ADR is not cheaper, and if forced to arbitrate will wilfully increase their charges to discourage the process. Since such people as judges, court clerks, and bailiffs are displaced, they too generally oppose any out-of-court processes. However, former chief justice of the Supreme Court Warren E. Burger, an old friend of mine, expressed his personal belief to me that the next century would see many formal court processes replaced by administrative procedures of one kind or another.

One example of the new attitude is Procter & Gamble's recent settlement of its seven-year "diaper war" with Kimberly-Clark over competing disposable diaper technology. A federal district court in Charleston, South Carolina, in 1989 had held that a Procter lawyer had committed "inequitable conduct" before the U.S. Patent Office by deceiving a patent examiner with a false affidavit. Kimberly had sued Procter in an antitrust action for attempting to control the market and wanted reimbursement for $20 million in law fees. This is heavy stuff. There were bitter feelings on both sides. The settlement is a tribute to the management of both companies.

(A caveat *against* arbitration: One effect of the U.S. Supreme Court's June 1987 finding upholding a stockbroker's right to enforce the mandatory arbitration clauses in many customer account contracts is that it has ignited a national debate over how Wall Street handles investor disputes. The Government Accounting Office recently reviewed the arbitration processes that are used in settlements and, in a 114-page report abstracted by the House Subcommittee on Telecommunications and Finance of the Committee on Energy and Commerce, found that investors "cannot be assured of getting a fair hearing unless improvements are made in the way that arbitrators are recruited and trained for their task.")[5]

No matter what lip service is paid to the alternate dispute resolution process, never, never, never use your regular law firm in an arbitration. Get a firm or service that does nothing but dispute settlement.

Finally, there's too much opportunity out there to make real money without diluting executive time and diverting corporate resources to excessive litigation. My advice to companies across America that are involved in a long series of lawsuits (and that's most of them) is to get rid of the litigating executive and hire a good ADR firm to take a close look at every lawsuit your company has, with one object: settlement.

THE EXECUTIVE COMPENSATION PROBLEM

The rule of thumb that executives should be paid no more than ten times the lowest paid employee in a company is long gone. Today, fiscally abusive CEOs can use a multiplier in the thousands in paying themselves, even while a) they are firing tens of thousands, b) the company is losing money, and c) when the stock is falling. How come?

The directors of a typical American corporation, who are supposed to represent the stockholders, are like a train of little cars hooked to the CEO locomotive, running on a management-laid track that twists and turns around stockholders' interests to generate excessive executive compensation, including that of the board members themselves. The typical corporate board is a bunch of overpaid rubber-stampers who by law are supposed to represent the stockholders but in fact represent only management and themselves. Mostly CEOs themselves, with a smattering of lawyers who keep the company in constant lawsuits, they are currently shoveling the stockholders' assets into one another's pockets at increasing rates. Mutual back scratching by exchange of outside directors on compensation committees is standard practice.[6]

Right here in the Washington area, under the very noses of the legislative and regulatory bodies, the average base pay for the top executives at sixty area companies in 1991 was $697,899, up from $664,378 in 1990. Add in long-term compensation, and the number rises to a current $1,147,212 compared with $1,107,039 the year before, a 3.6 percent increase. Meanwhile, total profits at those sixty companies dropped by nearly one-third. The top local executive, Jeffrey J. Steiner of Fairchild Industries, got a whopping $19.3 million, most of it based on his sale of one of the Fairchild divisions at a top price.[7]

According to *Business Week,* executive salaries nationally rose a full 7 percent in 1991, and 11.8 percent the year before, in the middle of a severe recession. A survey by Standard & Poor's Compustat Services, Inc., using a sample of 363 leading companies, reported that executive compensation was up a surprising 26 percent[8] in 1991, while profits were off some 15 percent.

One of the principal local pay malpractitioners is US Air. After a loss of $454 million in 1990, the worst year in its history, it *raised* retiring CEO Edwin I. Colodny's salary to $726,900 from $624,726!

UAL Corporation, parent of United Airlines, had a poor year in 1990. But UAL chairman Stephen M. Wolf had a grand year. While UAL earnings dropped by more than two-thirds, Wolf received more than $18 million in total compensation, of which $17 million came from a single source—cashing in the stock options that UAL had given him in previous years.[9]

And even that bastion of corporate rectitude, Marriott Corp. in the person my friend Bill (J. Willard) Marriott, Jr., CEO, was taken to task by the *Washington Post* for bumping his 1991 compensation by 76.3 percent to $1.278 million, while earnings shriveled to a meager $82 million and the stock price dropped by more than 50 percent. (He had taken a 28 percent cut in pay in 1990.) In addition, he was given an option on another 125,000 shares of Marriott stock at the much-reduced price.[10]

General Dynamics, headquartered right next door in Falls Church, Virginia, cut a deal with its twenty-five top executives like this: Get the stock up $10, hold it there for ten days, and we'll pay you a bonus equal to your salary. Each subsequent $10 bump will be at double your salary. It was passed by the board in February 1991 with the stock selling at only $25.56 because of a loss of $578 million in 1990. With announcement of the plan, the stock took off and in May, after the plan was approved by the shareholders, it hit the magic number of $35.56 and some $20 million was paid out. (However, they didn't pay it out right then. The plan called for half the bonus to be paid in 1994 and the other half at age 65. In the meantime, General Dynamics would pay interest on the bonus money at 14 percent, ten percentage points above the going CD rate.) Management then targeted the next $10 jump. This was no problem at all. In September, with $500 million of excess cash and securities in the till and with the shrinkage in defense spending reducing the need for capital investment, management announced that they were going to return their "excess cash" directly to shareholders. With the announcement, the stock price jumped the targeted $10 and $40 million was paid out to those same executives who pumped up the stock. Also, out went ten thousand workers.[11] Later, General Dynamics sold off its information technology unit to EDS for $184 million. Then it sold off its profitable

Cessna division to Textron for $600 million. Altogether, this gave it a total of some $1.2 billion in excess cash and securities for the promised special dividend. However, General Dynamics did not make the promised dividend. Instead, it made an offer of up to $75 per share to buy up to thirteen million General Dynamics shares—that's $975 million.[12]

This might have been the inspiration for Mark Russell's bit of doggerel:[13]

> The country's in recession but I'm cheerful and I'm chipper,
> As I slash employee wages like a fiscal Jack the Ripper,
> And I take away their pension plan and never mind their hollers,
> And pay myself a bonus of a coupl'a million dollars.

To many, the General Dynamics bonus plan appeared to be at the cost of long-term benefits. The United Shareholders Association wrote letters to the company protesting the plan. The Washington-based Investor Responsibility Research Center also filed its objections.

About this same time, General Dynamics went to trial on charges of defrauding the U.S. Government of $160 million.[14] The outcome of which has not been determined at this writing. Run for years by retired Navy and Air Force officers, they not only rip off the stockholders but the government as well. I've had personal experience with this.

My Reed Research staff were experts in measurements of physical phenomena—cold, heat, radiation, underwater sound, light, x-rays, cosmic rays, etc. We had built all kinds of measurement and telemetering equipment for hundreds of jobs—monitoring the first launches at Cape Canaveral, the detection of atomic bomb explosions in the USSR, and measuring the force of the hydrogen bombs at Eniwetok. We'd had basic groundbreaking contracts with the National Academy of Sciences as well.

I personally sold the Office of Naval Research (ONR) a project to review all the present methods of sensing and recording the entire electromagnetic and inertial spectra. We wrote a long and complicated proprietary proposal and waited for the contract. But during the evaluation period, General Dynamics hired away our Pete Marenholtz—who'd assisted me in writing the proposal—capturing him by nearly doubling his salary.

Apparently the people at General Dynamics took our bid, made a few minor changes, cut the price, submitted it, and got the job. I insisted on seeing the General Dynamics proposal so I could compare it with mine. The Navy refused. I was told if I persisted, Reed Research would be barred from future Office of Naval Research contracts, possibly from all Navy Department contracts. That's the way General Dynamics has historically done business.

Meanwhile, at ITT Corporation, CEO Rand V. Araskog was vigorously defending his 1990 salary as shareholders repeatedly questioned whether his performance justified his compensation of $11.4 million. This had doubled while profits were up only 4 percent. Araskog said he didn't set his own compensation, the board did. Who appointed the board? Araskog. Some, but not enough stockholders knew that Araskog had pumped up ITT's profits, General Dynamics–style, by selling off long-held assets, like its 30 percent stake in Alcatel N.V. to its partner, Alcatel Aisthom. This produced a reported one-time after-tax gain of $186 million (which eventually turned out to be much more), which Araskog cited in support of his salary and bonus bump. Such sales of assets, at inflation-adjusted prices, provide shadow earnings. That doesn't take much executive talent. But ITT stockholders are powerless—as stockholders are in most American corporations—to rein in fiscally abusive T.E.s like Araskog, who is cashing in on the perspicacity of ITT's former CEOs like Sosthenes Behn, who, with his brother, Hernand, bought the overseas operations of AT&T in the early twenties and thus created ITT.

Managers at ITT are rewarded if the average return on equity is boosted to 15 percent by 1994, compared to the base of 11 percent, and by getting the stock above $71 per share and holding it there for ten days. By selling off long-held assets they can draw down the bonus.[15] And with all the cash from the asset sales, management can go into a stock buy-back program that will certainly bump the stock price enough to earn them the bonus.[16]

In 1991 Araskog drew down a hefty $9 million, lower than 1990, but with added incentives that could be worth another $7 million for improvements in ITT's return on equity, cashable depending on whether the company falls short of, or exceeds, its goals.[17] This is still mega-tapping the corporate coffers for multimillions far out of proportion to performance, as earnings were off 14.7 percent.[18]

Executive compensation abuse is widespread. The leaders of public pension funds grilled Andrew C. Sigler of Champion International Corp. at a meeting of the Council of Institutional Investors, whose members control $400 *billion* of funds, and found his answers wanting. Sigler currently pays himself in the $2.4 million area. Over the seventeen years that Sigler has been running Champion, the firm's return was lower than that from a no-risk investment such as Treasury bills![19] Earlier, California's two principal state pension funds had announced they would vote their shares against management to protest Sigler's compensation level, and Champion's attorneys threatened to sue compensation guru Graef S. Crystal for repeatedly listing Sigler as one of the nation's most overpaid executives.[20]

And in Wall Street it's even worse. Drexel, just before announcing bankruptcy, paid out $208 million in cash bonuses. Before closing up shop, the fifty top people got an average of $3.5 million each. Leon Black got $10 million, but claimed he was "robbed" and got it increased to $20 million: $16 million in cash and $4 million in Drexel stock.[21] Morgan Stanley's three top executives got $8 million each in 1991, which included stock options worth some $2.7 million to each of the three. And PaineWebber paid its chief $7.2 million.

At Goldman Sachs, the last major house still in partnership form, its two co-chiefs, Robert Rubin, now President Clinton's chief economic advisor, and Stephen Friedman made $15 million apiece. (In that particular partnership they only draw out $2 million in cash and the balance is left in to finance the partnership's activities. Interest is paid on the money.)[22]

And Bear Stearns has been forced to revise its bonus pool formula after its top executives, Alan Greenberg and James Cayne, drew down $15.8 million and $14.7 million respectively for 1992—tripling their 1991 compensation. (It must be noted that the Wall Street houses make most of their money by trading for their own account—which is really trading against their own customers. In-house trading brought in some $20 billion of profits in 1992 as compared to only $10 billion in brokerage commissions and $5 billion in underwriting fees.)

Complicating the whole problem of executive pay is the problem of figuring out what it is. According to David McLaughlin, a consultant who sits on several boards, "There are companies that will go out of their way, within the letter of what is permissible, to obfuscate compensation data."[23] Deciphering all these elements requires leafing through at least a dozen pages of dense text and proxy statements for several years. "Normal practice is to obscure total compensation by scattering elements of it among footnotes, tables and paragraphs of dense legal language," says E. Webb Bassick, compensation specialist with Hewitt Associates.[24] Professor Graef Crystal of the University of California at Berkeley, an executive pay consultant who used to defend CEO pay, "got religion," and is now opposed to the out-of-scale salaries paid to U.S. corporate managers. His book *In Search of Excess*[25] made the best-seller list. But Crystal himself has trouble figuring out how much a CEO is paid because of contrived obfuscation on the part of the in-house legal staff that writes up or at least approves the final draft of the Annual Report.

According to a piece in the *Wall Street Journal*, the system of compensation for executives at Merrill Lynch & Co., now a public company, was changed twice in three years, each time making it more complex and difficult to decipher. It takes a supercomputer to calculate how much

Chairman William A. Schreyer (a) actually received in restricted shares, (b) when they vested, (c) which of these were "performance" shares, and (d) what long-term cash payments were made. The determination of what he really had been paid required detailed searches through five years of proxy statements. Even Merrill Lynch, in assisting the *Wall Street Journal* in analyzing proxy data for the *Journal*'s article, made several mistakes, as did Sears Roebuck in a parallel report.

The Council of Institutional Investors, a non-profit group that represents some seventy of the nation's largest pension funds, recently held a proxy-reading contest at its two-day meeting in April 1992. The names of the companies and officers were disguised. The "experts" came up with huge variations in their answers from those of Crystal for the compensation of three CEOs: Martin S. Davis of Paramount, from $2 million to $4.2 million; Robert Stempel of General Motors, from $1.1 million to $4.0 million; and Robert C. Golzueta of Coca-Cola, from $4.7 million to $66 million.[26]

The major corporations are trashing the stock option route to performance incentives as well. It costs the company zero cash to inspire the executive to extra effort. If he doesn't perform, his options are worthless. It costs the stockholders dilution if the stock price rises. But lately they've changed the rules. If the stock price falls off, they simply cancel the old option and give the executive new ones. This stinks. It's an incentive to *poor* performance, to drive the price down to lower and lower levels so that the cash-out when the price does turn around will be bigger and bigger. Just before his June 1992 appearance before the Senate Finance Subcommittee, Crystal cited American Micro Devices as a typical abuser of stock option incentives. American Micro over five years, as its stock price declined from $20 to $4, repriced their CEO's options so that, when the stock did turn around, the CEO cashed out in the millions.[27] U.S. Surgical granted options now worth about $120 million to its CEO, Leon C. Hirsch, diluting its stockholders' interests to some great extent. "AT&T, Equimark, Merrill Lynch, Paramount, Philip Morris and Westinghouse have joined the rush, each dishing out 300,000 shares or more to their chieftains,"[28] according to an article in *Business Week*. The Westinghouse deal is extraordinary. CEO Paul E. Lego, in the face of a loss of $1.1 billion, lost his annual bonus, reducing his cash compensation for the year by about $1 million. But he got two grants of options to buy seven hundred thousand shares of Westinghouse; one grant is currently worth $1.25 million.[29]

The investing public is getting more and more upset with the arrogance of corporate boards and the CEOs who appoint them. The Business Roundtable, a group of two hundred CEOs of the country's two hundred largest companies, spelled out its recommendations in its first position paper ever on executive compensation coincident with the SEC's preliminary report on corrective action to rein in the "complicated, self-serving, compensation plans that inadequately disclosed long-term compensation. The corporate proxy statement reporting the pay of its top five executives all too often became an exercise in obfuscation."[30] In essence, the Roundtable told stockholders to complain to the board if they believe the compensation to be excessive.[31] Hah!

Tying CEO pay to performance as the SEC is proposing has many problems. The fiscally abusive CEO can screw the stockholders in various ways. For instance:

1) Tying salary and bonuses to earnings. This can soon break a company. There are too many ways for the fiscally abusive CEO to bump the bottom line, short-term, by cutting down, for instance, research and development, advertising, or insurance, and even changing accounting practices. He or she then cashes out at stockholder expense.

2) Tying salary and bonuses to return on assets. Here again, changing accounting practices or dropping research and development and other outlays that ensure

the long-time effectiveness of the company can bump CEO compensation at the expense of stockholder value. Further, a retiring CEO's severance and retirement pay are often linked to late-term earnings, which exacerbates the situation.

3) Tying CEO pay to the stock's market price. This is probably the worst ploy of all, as there are many ways to get the stock price up, as did General Dynamics in selling off profitable operations and promising a special dividend. Further, stock buy-backs can temporarily bump stock prices. For instance, Ralston Purina in 1986 agreed to award management nearly half a million shares if the stock closed above 100 for ten straight days. What did Ralston executives do? They used borrowed funds and much of the company's free cash to buy back nearly one-third of Ralston's outstanding shares. The stock price doubled, management was paid off, and the stock price soon dropped back to a split-adjusted 91.[32]

JAPAN BASHING AND AMERICAN CEO SALARY INFLATION

In the last days of 1991, President Bush left on a Japan-bashing trip to reverse our negative $41 billion trade imbalance with that country, crying unfair competition. In support, he took along a twenty-member group of American manufacturing CEOs. Based on the past ten years, the companies they represent were below average.[33] (Included was a nonmanufacturer, the notorious T.E., James Robinson III, then CEO of American Express, currently under fire for his alleged role in Amex's role in promulgating a massive smear campaign against Banker Edmond Safra, as recounted in the best-seller *Vendetta*.)[34]

These CEOs' average salary was $2 million per year.

Bush shot himself and the country in the foot. The CEOs went along to discuss problems with Japanese CEOs, whose companies are far more successful, but who are paid at one-sixth the rate of the Americans![35]

Furthermore, the Japanese execs cut their salaries in bad times and for bad performance. American CEOs' pay is not geared to performance. With a fall-off in sales and profits, some even raise their salaries, claiming that they must work harder—or they didn't lose as much money as their competitors. Moreover, Japanese executives' take-home pay is considerably less than the Americans', as up to 60 percent of their salary goes to Tokyo, and only 33 percent of Americans' goes to Washington.

The Japanese complain that American industry has become uncompetitive because of overpayment of its executive corps and because of those executives' short-term view of the economy. The Japanese say that American executives mistakenly place immediate profitability and personal compensation above their company's long-term welfare. Closing plants and laying off tens of thousands of workers, while keeping executive salaries at the old levels, or even increasing them, is incomprehensible to the Japanese.

This point was made sharply and clearly by the Japanese in May 1991 during the Structural Impediments Initiative talks as a forerunner to these more recent talks. The Japanese openly wondered why executive pay is not matched to performance and suggested that some substantial part of the cost differential between U.S.-made and Japanese-made autos is impounded in excessive executive pay and collateral benefits. The American executives' reply was that Japanese execs receive huge perks like chauffeured limousines and golf course memberships. But a golf course membership is a one-time charge and is often a capital asset that can be sold. As for chauffeured limousines, American execs have them too, along with fleets of corporate jets, unknown in Japan. And even if expense accounts are high in Japan—remember, a bottle of scotch is $50 there—no way could these piddling perks ever make up for the 600 percent differential in pay.

Bush also brought along Chairman Lee Iacocca of Chrysler, which had lost nearly a billion dollars the year before. But Iococca was doing great at a salary of $4.5 million per year. Two years earlier he pulled down $24 million. Recently, he was unhappy that two of his excess homes were not selling in a depressed real estate market, so he had Chrysler buy them.[36] James Robinson III, CEO of American Express at $5.9 million, according to Graef Crystal, was one of the most overpaid executives in the United States. He deserved $2.6 million at most.

No CEO is worth 100 times what his secretary is paid, says Boston Consulting Group's Koichi Hori. On average, American CEOs earn 160 times their average worker's salary, says Graef Crystal, while the Japanese ratio is sixteen times. "Bush couldn't have chosen a less appropriate bunch of business executives because they represent collectively what is wrong with U.S. society today," said Yoshi Tsurumi, a Japanese professor of international business at Baruch College in New York. "All these executives help themselves to hefty bonuses and fire their employees."[37]

GM's CEO, Robert Stempel, who received $2.18 million in compensation last year while the company had a net loss of $4.5 billion (after absorbing $8 billion of losses in automobiles), was closing down twenty-one plants and laying off seventy-four thousand people in 1992. A *Wall Street Journal* article quoted management guru Peter Drucker, "In Japan, somebody like Mr. Stempel would have announced his resignation by now."

But all the fiscally abusive T.E.s pale before Time Warner, Inc.'s late chairman and CEO Steven J. Ross, with his megamillions compensation package, his company helicopter trips to his summer house, and reports of a "golden coffin" arrangement should he die prematurely.[38]

On September 25, 1991, owners of Time Warner's stock joined with current and former company employees at the annual meeting to vent their anger at the big pay packages of top executives and the axing of more than six hundred employees in the magazine division.

"We are shocked that your compensation this past year is two times the entire compensation of the 605 employees who are being eliminated," Key Martin, chairperson of the Newspaper Guild at Time Warner told Ross. Longtime shareholder activist John Gilbert, who attended the meeting in a clown costume, reminded Ross that Ben and Jerry's Ice Cream, an extremely successful company, has a policy of limiting top executives' salaries to seven times that of the lowest-paid worker. (Herman Miller, Inc., modern furniture manufacturer, is also modern in its approach to executive pay. "The CEO's cash compensation including salary and bonus is limited to 20 times the average paycheck ($28,000) earned by the company's hands.")[39]

Ross countered with the argument that out of the Time Warner deal he'd gotten close to $200 million, and that the $74.9 million he received in compensation was deducted before the deal closed. He said he paid for the helicopter trips. (If you believe that he fully reimbursed the company for their full cost—including depreciation, hangar costs, maintenance, pilot standby, etc.—you probably believe that babies come from cabbages.)

Time Warner lost nearly $100 million in 1991, but Ross still drew an annual salary in the $3 million to $4 million range.

There was also the sticky question of interference by *Fortune* editors with Graef Crystal's analysis of executive compensation at Time Warner, which owns *Fortune*. *Forbes* had computed Steve Ross's compensation package at $78.1 million, *Business Week* at $78.2, and Crystal at a significantly lower $39.1 million. But still *Fortune* editors gave Crystal a hard time about the Ross calculation and also that for cochief executive of Time Warner, which Crystal had figured at $7.1 million. Crystal said that none of the other 199 companies out of the 200 in the survey had questioned his methods and there was no reason for him to give Time Warner that special privilege. But *Fortune* lives off of advertising revenues and the pressures from Crystal's CEO targets were impacting revenues, so after four years of doing the survey, he notified *Fortune* editors that he was through because of their interference.[40] This encouraged *Financial World*, which had similar problems with advertisers, also to drop his column. *Financial World*'s majority owner is Carl H. Lindner, Chairman of Penn Central Corporation, who Crystal lists as another overpaid-by-twice executive. Overpay seems to run in the family. Lindner's former daughter-in-law is the daughter of Champion International's Andrew C. Sigler, another overpaid CEO according to Crystal.[41]

Vice President Dan Quayle, after taking on the head of the American Bar Association about America's excessive corporate lawyering, targetted the problem of excessive executive pay with his White House Competitiveness Council, saying, "Some of these exorbitant salaries paid to corporate executives [are] unrelated to productivity."

Meanwhile, U.S. executive pay hit new highs in 1991 despite the recession, slimmer profits, and widespread layoffs. *Forbes* said 407 of the chief executives of the country's 800 largest publicly held companies earned $1 million or more in total compensation last year, up from 386 in 1990.[42]

Bush certainly did not pick the best firms to be represented on his hat-in-hand trip to Japan. While many were in the deep doo-doo on recent profits, on a ten-year basis the thirteen companies represented have returned to the stockholders less than the 13.8 percent of the average annual return of the companies included in the Standard and Poor's 500 Index.

The Severance Pay Bash

Pan Am went bankrupt, and its new CEO, Thomas Plaskett, demanded his agreed-upon $1.5 million in severance pay. This was the "golden hello" he negotiated after taking the creditors committee to heaven with a program to "save" Pan Am. (Should be "golden halo!") Creditors screamed about the $1.5 million, but he finally collected $1 million for piloting the airline into the tank only a few months after he took over.

Troubled companies are having more and more problems with "golden handshakes," which pay two or three years' salaries if a company is sold or taken over. Originally designed by Marty Siegel of Kidder Peabody as one of a half-dozen "shark repellants" to *prevent* takeovers, it was soon turned, by exploitive, fiscally abusive executives, into just the opposite. They would sell out the company just to cash the parachute if it was big enough. So they made the parachutes bigger and bigger. Many such deals were voted in by rubber-stamp, CEO-appointed directors, who were not above voting themselves long strings of benefits at the same time.[43]

Perhaps the worst practice was that of very sick savings and loans without the cash to pay off depositors except with government money: They voted their officers huge terminal payments. Charles Zwick was finally ousted in January 1991 as the $500,000 per year chairman of the money-losing and failing Southeast Banking Corp., after agreeing to take severance pay of $1.25 million in thirty monthly payments of $41,667 each. The payments were halted because Southeast didn't have the money. Any normal person, responsible for such an enormous failure, would crawl away and hide. But not Zwick. He's suing.

In a really weird-deal, Nicholas J. Nicholas, departing co-chief executive of Time Warner, Inc., will receive $15.8 million in severance pay, plus $2.9 million in salary and bonus for 1991. He will be permitted to keep his stock options, which already have a built-in gain of $8.5 million. The unusual deal keeps Nicholas on the payroll, in a position that "will not require a material portion of his time," at $250,000 per year, plus full company benefits, plus an office, a secretary, and a $6 million life insurance policy! Graef Crystal said of the deal, "They ought to be lining up in the corridors of Time Warner hoping to be fired."[44]

And R. H. Macy's creditors are screaming to the bankruptcy court that the termination pay for CEO Edward Finkelstein, who was responsible for the Macy mess in the first place, is too rich—a four-year consulting contract worth $3 million, a pension worth about $300,000 per year, and part of the proceeds of the sale of his Macy-purchased town house worth somewhere from $3 million to $5 million and loaded with antiques that may belong to Macy's.[45] "Unofficially, I've heard they spent a lot of bucks on that," said Kevin Collins, a financial advisor to Macy's bondholders.

But one retiring CEO, Hamish Maxwell of Philip Morris, got a $24 million going-away package which included the value of his stock options.[46] (Reportedly a heavy smoker, Philip Morris we hear, Maxwell may never get to reap the benefits of his retirement before the Grim Reaper gets him.)

And megabank First Chicago will pay its former chairman, sixty-one-year-old Barry F. Sullivan, who took early retirement, more as a consultant than it paid him as chairman—from about $770,000 to $780,000 plus his annual pension of $136,000. In addition he gets office space, a car, secretarial help, and if he goes to work someplace else he still gets the $780,000![47]

THE TOXIC "SPENDOR"

There are some toxic executives who get a "rush" out of spending money—generally "OPM"—other people's money. I call them "Toxic Spendors." I've hired a few of them myself. The Toxic Spendor won't bargain with suppliers: They think it's demeaning. They will never dispute a bill, whether for supplies or in a restaurant. They have the idea that people who add up a restaurant bill before paying are cheapskates.

One such young executive who worked for me was on a continuous ego trip. A highly productive employee in other ways, he loved to spend money as long as it was not his own. He ordered a thousand sheets of stationery and envelopes to match for $850. The salesman bought him lunch and told him that was only eight and a half cents a letter. He did the same thing the following year, buying at a remarkably reduced price of only $250 per thousand, or two and a half cents each! It was so cheap he bought a ten-year supply! He *loved* to spend money. He also flunked math.

He rented fifteen hundred square feet of fancy office space at $30 per square foot, but never measured it. It was only a thousand square feet and really cost us $45 per foot. That was twice the going market price.

Trying to build decision-making muscle in executives can be costly if that executive is what I call a compulsive and thus a toxic, "spendor" or a "BTO," Big-Time Operator.

Further, many executives do not follow the "prudent man rule"—that is, to treat company money not as their own (because many are personally profligate), but as a "prudent man" would. This has been the basis for a hundred court decisions, but has recently been modified to assume that a prudent man will have acquired the knowledge needed to make a prudent decision.

In big companies, toxic spendors spend money on "show" items. They buy bigger and bigger jets. They buy, rent, or build buildings they don't need. They buy machinery with a lot of flashing lights that looks important, but brings nothing down to the bottom line. They hire secretaries they don't need. Why? Because successful executives are "supposed" to have secretaries to answer their phones, even though the executive is gone more than half the time and the secretary has little or nothing to do. The Toxic Spendor likes big offices, usually with gold-toned cork on the walls, and big expensive desks with large ego-chairs to sit in. On the bookshelf are the 100 Great Books, still wrapped in the plastic they were delivered in years before.

On the walls are arriviste paintings. In the garage is a seldom-driven Rolls-Royce—it was the *spending* that was important, not the driving!

Give me someone who gets a rush out of *saving* money, not *spending* it. Give me people who take pride in being "conservators" not "spendors."

THE NEPOTIC T.E.

One of the fiscally abusive toxic executive types is the executive who loads up the payroll with family, close relatives, mistresses, and other bodies that do not contribute to the bottom line. The U.S. government and local and state governments are especially sensitive to nepotism; you can be fired for hiring a relative because it's against the law. But American business has never subscribed to that notion. Like Saddam Hussein, who would be long dead if he were not surrounded by blood relatives, toxic executives feel they can trust family over nonfamily.

At Bethlehem Steel's Key Highway shipyard, I had to work with the beer-bellied nephew of my good friend the head of the sheet metal shop. On the ships, I designed the ductwork, the Navy approved it, the shops fabricated it, and Beer-Belly tried to install it. But he couldn't read blueprints, would guess at it, and when he was wrong would try to cover up by blaming it on someone else. He should not have been hired in the first place and should have been fired long since.

I believe that he resented my friendship with his uncle, since I could run every machine in the shop and Big-Belly didn't even know their names. After a particularly egregious and costly error, we nearly came to blows. Big-Belly rushed at me. I gave him a "hip" from my basketball days, and his beer belly carried him over the rail and into the drink. He was disciplined but not fired, as nepotism was a way of life at Bethlehem, from the CEO on down. But he was off the job, thank God.

Nepotism is bad. People get jobs that in the normal course would and should go to others. Those others resent it. Miscreants like Big-Belly also *keep* their jobs after making horrible mistakes, which is another cause for general disaffection.

There are also ethical questions involved. Would you discourage an applicant for a job you had reserved for a relative without telling the applicant? In the nepotic company, the word gets around that hard work will get you nowhere. *Who* you know is more important than *what* you know. This not only discourages applicants for jobs, but accelerates turnover.[48]

In the matter of CEO succession, choosing family members can lead to disaster. Take Wang Laboratories, Inc., founded by Shanghai-born and Harvard-educated An Wang in 1951 to build word processors and minicomputers. It grew to $3 billion in annual sales in 1988—too fast to properly service its equipment, according to one of my studies. An Wang got sick and passed the word that his son, Frederick A. Wang was to take over. Dr. Wang died, his son did take over but he'd never learned how to reduce staff and disaster followed. Wang Laboratories is not expected to survive.[49]

THE HIRE-FIRE T.E.

Many executives have trouble with the hire-fire syndrome. In this one area they suddenly become delegators. They dislike the tedium of the exhaustive analysis and intensive interviewing necessary to finding the right person for a job. They practice decision avoidance by dumping the decision on someone else—the personnel department, for instance, or their superiors or even their subordinates or peers. Then, if it doesn't work out they have someone to blame! Furthermore, they avoid the most distasteful part of the job of being an executive; the firing of a bad hire or, worse, a layoff for economic reasons. They thus avoid the "You hired him, you fire him" dictum.

At Otten, Liskey & Rhodes, Naval Architects, of Washington, D.C., Ernest Liskey had hired me away from Bethlehem Steel in Baltimore. Two months later Jim Rhodes called me in and told me that I was being terminated. I couldn't believe it. I was the only one with shipyard experience at the firm. I loved the job. Why? I couldn't get an answer.

I was personally decimated by the decision. What had I done wrong? Economically it was a disaster, as my house in the Annapolis area was still not sold. Neither Otten nor Liskey nor Rhodes gave me a reason for my termination.

In desperation I called my friends at the Maritime Commission. They told me the contract I was working on had been moved from OLR to another firm. I called that firm and was welcomed with open arms and made assistant coordinator of design. Jim Rhodes simply could not face up to telling me that his company had lost the contract. But I forgave him.

Two years later, I was made an associate of OLR. I brought in some major contracts. I worked hard and late and went to the hospital for three weeks with an ulcer. When I came back someone was sitting at my desk. Without any notice, I had been *dis*associated. But the company still had the contracts I'd brought in. But not for long.

Within a few weeks I had those contracts transferred to my new firm, Reed Research, Inc. I hired John Otten away, and Otten, Liskey & Rhodes soon folded. All this grief because they couldn't face reality.

THE EMPIRE BUILDERS

Some of the most difficult T.E.s to identify before employment are the empire builders. They are the ones who like to hire people—more and more and more of them. They are the most frequently encountered of the fiscally abusive types, and are the most fiscally dangerous.

I violated two or three of the unwritten rules of corporate conduct when I hired one of my sailing buddies, "Cap" Alberts.

Cap came aboard at Reed Research to head all the non-scientific, nontechnical activity. Cap was a find. Purchasing, the mail room, print shop, switchboard, stockroom, tool room, office supply room, and guard and janitorial services were finally under control. Cap and one person administered about fifteen people in those various services.

But Cap had some problems as an executive. He decided that he needed more help and before we knew it, his administrative staff was up to six people, and the services staff up to about twenty. This was not matched by sales growth, and since many of those services were in nonbillable overhead, our costs began to climb. We told Cap that he had to cut down. That he had to let some people go.

Cap had hired them. Cap would fire them. But a week later, they were still on the payroll. What to do? My best friend, my neighbor, my sailing buddy!

Cap just couldn't stand to see his little army defeated. He left the job rather than let them go. We stayed friends for many more years. But we never talked about it. It was much too painful.

Under Cap nothing ever ran more smoothly, if expensively. But, like many tyro managers, Cap had problems in "coming over to management." Unfortunately, he identified with the people he had hired and would have to dismiss rather than with the company.

Andrew Grove, CEO of famed Intel Corporation, has a Knight-Ridder column called "On the Job." In one column he suggests that, in hiring personal friends, you owe it to both to take some extra measures. Tell your boss of the relationship and have him or her do the interview. Use peers as well.[50] I would add to Grove's advice that the background check should be extra thorough.

Time after time, on consulting jobs at companies in trouble, we have run into inflated ratios of overhead people to shop people. At one client, a division of Foster Wheeler Corporation, during one downturn in the economy the ratio of overhead bodies to billable bodies went from one-to-four (50/200) to two-to-four (40/80). With such a disproportionate number, the overhead went out of sight, which locked the company out of potential contracts. When we interviewed the department heads, they were adamant that they could not operate with a lesser number of people. Yet we knew that many had very little to do all day except listen to the silence from the shop floor. Like Cap, each had built his little empire and just couldn't stand to see it fall.

In my experience, just about every company that got into trouble in the late 1980s played the blame game. It was "excessive government regulation," "the unions," "unfair foreign competition," and so on. Few would look at the excessive growth of support staff in relation to billable bodies. There are many places where expense can build up that simply cannot be carried by a company's direct labor in a downturn in the economy. That's why I like to use the term "factory burden" rather than "factory overhead," because it is a *burden* the direct labor employees must shoulder. You must ask the hard question, how much more money will this extra expense bring in? The toxic executive will defend such costs because those extra bodies build up his or her ego, in addition to defending a salary level that is derived from the number of people he or she supervises.

A recent special issue of *Business Week* suggested that the ABC system, or "activity-based costing," which allocates *all* costs in an operation directly to units of production, be installed everywhere possible. The ABC system ties every dollar of expense to its ultimate yield and quickly reveals the empire builders.

9

THE VALUELESS T.E.

The valueless T.E. runs the gamut of intolerant behaviors—from crude, rude, inappropriate, organization-destroying hatreds to disruptive favoritism, cheating, and lying. But his or her principal failing is lack of respect for his or her fellows in the workplace. Valueless T.E.s hate and mistrust their fellow workers, their bosses, their company. And they're into intolerance, especially of minorities, as a career.

I have been elected to membership in quite a few clubs, some good, some bad, and have been a guest in hundreds more, mostly bad. I am, therefore, talking from the inside looking out. I know many people who are members of some of the "best" clubs, which usually means the ones that are hardest to get into, and which usually have the worst food. I currently belong to three clubs: the New York Yacht Club, the Racquet Club of Philadelphia, and Washington, D.C's International Club. None of these clubs discriminate against anyone; otherwise I would not belong. But I have belonged to clubs that did discriminate: the Washington Golf & Country Club, and Pelham Country Club, where I was a member Honoris Causa. Most of the members of all of these clubs are businessmen. Business is not allowed to be discussed in the public rooms of the New York Yacht Club, nor at the "best" clubs, nor should it be. But much of the conversation at many clubs is about business or about hate. Not dislike, but pure, undisguised hate.

THE COUNTRY CLUB EFFECT

Someone who has never joined a country club, or a major social club would only be speculating as to the behavior of its members. I dislike generalizing about such an important subject. In chapter 3 I discussed bonding and the natural, if inefficient, formation of exclusionary groups derived out of a *meritocracy*; however, you must also realize that there are exclusionary groups which have developed out of a blooded, landholding, or business-based *aristocracy*. For instance, 50 percent of the members of some of the "best" clubs in New York City have never had a job! The envy that builds in them then emerges in the most venomous of forms. One such very wealthy member of one of the "best" clubs told me, when Bobby Kennedy decided to run for senator in New York State, that he was trying to think of a way to get Bobby killed. He stated that if he saw Kennedy crossing a street, he'd step on the gas. It was at lunch and he was cold sober.

For many others, money, and money alone, has bought them a membership in the clubs. And the manner in which they or their ancestors have made that money is really distasteful to them. Their disgust with themselves because they have never accomplished anything recognizably useful, beautiful, or moral starts them on the hate trail against those who have. They hate their parents, their former teachers, their kids, their wife or wives. Since the workplace is no longer a forum for expression of such a continuum of hate, the country club or city club has now become the place where one can join with others of the same ilk, express one's hatred and find kindred souls who also hate their parents, former teachers, kids, and wife or wives and are ready to hate anything.

The "country club culture" is one built on a mutuality of interest in intolerance and dislike and even hatred rather than in love and equanimity. It is place to give voice to one's prejudices under the guise of recreation. Only those clubs that cater to career people-haters seem to be successful.

Collis and Claudia Stocking and WGCC

Two of my very good friends were Dr. Collis Stocking and his wife, Claudia, an educator. Collis, a distinguished economist, was on President Eisenhower's Council of Economic Advisers. They lived three doors from the Washington Golf & Country Club (WGCC). I asked why they had never joined. They said they had been turned down for membership. I was shocked. I immediately talked to the club president, Jimmy Murphy, a lawyer, and we got out the file.

Why were they turned down? Two reasons, according to letters in the file. One, Collis had written a book many years before, during the Great Depression when there was no welfare and people were starving. The book was called *Company Script as a Form of Wage Payment.* Two, he drove to work with David Lilienthal, head of the Tennessee Valley Authority and, according to the file, "most likely a communist." That was all. I immediately proposed the Stockings for membership and warned everybody on the board that if they didn't make it I would resign with a letter to the *Washington Post* that would make WGCC the laughing-stock of the city. They rushed the membership through with a special meeting.

SYLVESTER "BENNY" BENNETT

There were some really slimeball members at WGCC, one of the oldest but certainly not one of the "best" clubs in the Washington area. It was only a few blocks from my home and I was a member for many years. Like all the other country clubs in Washington, it was strictly WASP with a few token Catholics. No Jews. No Blacks. The Jews had Woodmont and Indian Springs country clubs (which also had a few upscale black members like columnist Carl Rowan), and the Blacks had "their" public courses.

At WGCC there was one long-time black waiter called Benny (Sylvester Bennett). He was my family's favorite. Every time I came back from a duck or goose hunt, Benny would pluck and clean the game for me and wind up with some extra dollars and a fat goose or a brace of ducks. Benny was always smiling. My kids loved Benny and so did I. We often talked about what he was going to do when he retired. It was the prospect of retirement that kept Benny going.

As in any well-brought-up family, north or south, the word "nigger" was never used by any of us. But I remember one member at WGCC who used the word habitually. And he used the word at the club table with Benny within earshot. I objected, but this awful person called Benny over and said, "Benny, you know that there's two kinds of 'niggers,' good ones and bad ones and you're one of the good niggers, right?" Benny, coming up for retirement soon, just smiled and said, "Yes, sir, I know what you mean." But I saw the hurt. I never spoke to that member again.

(Sadly, Benny was only a few months from retirement after forty years of near-slavery at WGCC when he died. On the job. No retirement.)

One particularly hateful member at WGCC ran an orthopedic shoe store where many people, including many black people, with foot problems went to get specially made shoes.

Martin Luther King had been assassinated the week before. The TV in the WGCC men's grill was on. On the screen was the grieving Coretta King and her two little boys. I was watching along with several other members when the member came by and said in a very loud voice, "Haven't they buried that black bastard yet?" I was the only person that objected. Also in the room, only a few feet away, was Joel Broyhill, our local congressman. He said and did nothing. But I did. I let that member and everyone know how bad I thought they were. I should have resigned right then and there. But I did not.

Another WGCC member, a doctor, was running for public office. I was sitting with him and several others a few days after Bobby Kennedy was assassinated. In a loud voice, he made the remark, "Now this will put a stop to the rumors about Bobby and Coretta King." I expressed my disgust and got up and left the club table, my lunch unfinished, while the other members guffawed.

About this same time, the WGCC women's tennis team canceled a match with the Indian Springs Country Club's women's tennis team because Carl Rowan's wife was on the tennis team. Carl Rowan, the black columnist and TV personality, was a friend and a fellow board member of the Peace Corps operation, "Books U.S.A.," chaired by Edward R. Murrow as head of the United States Information Service (USIA) who had appointed both of us.

Now I had a real problem. Do I stay a member, try to fight such discrimination from the inside, or do I resign? I chickened out and resigned, with an open letter to club members that I wanted to publish in the *Washington Post*. My wife said she had to live in the community and would not let me mail the letter. But I did resign.

I was surprised to discover much the same kind of thing going on at Pelham Country Club (PCC), in Westchester County, in the late eighties. Ironically, many of the PCC members are second generation Irish and Italians, who, for many years, were excluded from membership in any Westchester County country club. At PCC I was surprised to discover that, while racial slurs were quite frequent, the word "nigger" seemed to be used more frequently by the newer members—especially by the Irish. They were never used by members of the "founding families," and it was disappointing that the FFs tolerated this kind of language. After several arguments with members at the club table over the use of words that expressed racial prejudice, I finally resigned, but not before my new golf clubs, bag and all, with my name sewn into the leather, mysteriously disappeared, and my name, just as mysteriously, was the only name left out of the PCC membership book.

In 1990, the Professional Golfers Association (PGA) championship was to be held at Shoal Creek Country Club near Birmingham, Alabama. The club had no black members. The club president, Hall Thompson, was widely quoted in the press as saying that a member bringing a black guest to the club was "something that's just not done in Birmingham, Alabama." Six corporations immediately withdrew their advertising from ABC and ESPN telecasts. Nabisco canceled plans for its hospitality tent, and the PGA itself announced that it would no longer hold any meets at courses with membership practices that excluded anyone based on race, religion, or sex. Shoal Creek soon had its first black member as did many other country clubs across the country. Meanwhile, some nine major clubs refused to change their membership practices and lost the PGA, the Ladies Professional Golfers Association (LGPA), Women's Amateur, U.S. Women's Open, and other contests. At the same time, many clubs issued rules that have been standard at the "better" clubs like the NYYC, for many years: no briefcases, no business discussions—the club is a "social" club. The NYYC had always had that rule as a standard of simple good manners. But many of the newer clubs were simply protecting themselves against lawsuits because the clubs weren't "social" clubs at all, but provably existed for the sole purpose of expediting business deals. Excluding minorities from such business activities was in restraint of trade and therefore illegal even in the face of the "freedom of association argument."

Board Member Usage of Ethnic Slurs

I have served on quite a few corporate boards of directors. After my election to one particular board, that of a family corporation, I discovered that the word "nigger" was used by the chairman quite frequently, and infrequently by a few other members. I liked the company, felt I could make a contribution, and the pay was attractive (especially my gin rummy winnings on long flights on the company plane).

Before my arrival on the board, where I served for some eight years, board meetings had been rather informal leaving them without a proper record. As the founder of *Directors & Boards* magazine, I brought some order into the meeting process. But I was turned off by the language, which ran the gamut of racial prejudice. They had operations in Alabama and some board meetings were held there. I tried to convince the two most frequent users of racial epithets that it was not only rude, but could be dangerous. But it didn't help.

I finally solved the problem this way. I announced that if any racial epithets of any kind were used during a meeting, I would leave for the next thirty minutes. If they didn't like it, they had my resignation. (Remember, these were good, honest, church-going people that I really liked, except for their racial prejudices.)

Surprisingly, it worked. I never had to leave the meeting. Perhaps they were all waiting for someone to tell them it was wrong. Terribly wrong.

THE SUPER-ARROGANT T.E.

Ross Perot, a super-arrogant executive, on joining the board of GM after selling them his Electronic Data Systems company, wrote Roger Smith, another super-arrogant executive, a letter, excerpted as follows:

Dear Roger,

. . . . in our relationship I will support you when I believe you are right. I will tell you candidly when I think you are wrong. If you continue your present autocratic style, I will be your adversary on critical issues. I will argue with you privately. If necessary I will argue with you publicly before the board and the shareholders. . . .

You need to understand that your style intimidates people. Losing your temper hurts GM. Your tendency to try to run over anyone who disagrees with you hurts your effectiveness within GM.

You need to be aware that people are afraid of you. This stifles candid, upward communication in GM.

You need to know that GM-ers at all levels use terms like "ruthless" and "bully" in describing you. There is a widespread feeling throughout GM that you don't care about people. . . .

The foundations for a future relationship are honesty, openness and candor—or simply put, mutual trust and respect. From this point forward, actions count—words don't. We must focus all of our energies on helping GM win. . . .

Sincerely,
Ross[1]

Anyone with half a brain must know that a bust-up between the two had to follow such a letter.

Gerald Rafshoon, in telling why he dropped out of the Perot-for-President campaign well before Perot's withdrawal, wrote of Perot, *His problem was arrogance . . . The tone of the entire speech [before the NAACP] not just the 'you people' line, dripped with condescension. Perot seemed incapable of putting himself in the shoes of people different from himself. And in a country as wildly diverse as this one—so diverse that no person and no group can truly be 'typical'—a president must be able to see himself and the world through the eyes of others.*[2]

The most common and the most despised of T.E.s are the arrogant executives who think *their* ideas are better than anyone else's. They ride roughshod over others and their opinions. It is obvious that Roger Smith of GM was this way and equally obvious that Perot was too. With both it was "My Way or the Highway." Perot took the highway out of GM but with $800 million of GM's cash that bought him off and sped him on his way. And a series of well-publicized defections from his presidential campaign staff, such as Rafshoon's, brought on at least in part by Perot's arrogant ways, certainly contributed to his decision to withdraw—if only temporarily—as a presidential contender.

And arrogance is not an exclusive male trait. Dawn Steel of Columbia Pictures was notorious in Hollywood for her callousness toward subordinates. "Steel's habit of excoriating secretaries with sexist expletives kept the exit doors at Columbia swinging."[3]

And there's egomaniac Robert Malott, CEO of FMC, who said, "Leadership is demonstrated when the ability to inflict pain is confirmed." Bad Boss Malott could take a lesson from Good Boss Max De Pree, CEO of Herman Miller: "Leaders don't inflict pain; they bear pain."[4]

Not only are the Arrogant T.E.'s ideas better, so are his clothes, his car, his house, his neighborhood, and in the office or factory, his methods. And the Arrogant Executive especially hates people with ideas.

One of the most arrogant public officials of all time was J. Edgar Hoover, longtime head of the Federal Bureau of Investigation, who built files on everybody he was even slightly suspicious of, which included anyone with ideas. "He hated ideas, distrusted them, feared their contagion," wrote columnist James J. Kilpatrick.[5] Hoover even built files on William F. Buckley, Jr. from the age of sixteen on. Why Buckley, a surface scholar, who over the years has emerged as America's Number One Bore? But Hoover evidently found him interesting. Hoover even kept files on Buckley's son Christopher from age ten on after his first visit to FBI headquarters with his Dad.

There is little doubt that the military services of the United States are run by arrogant T.E.s.

I sold a contract to the Navy to be administered by the Johnsville Naval Air Station just outside of Philadelphia. It was a rush job to build monitoring equipment for some of the first missile launches at Cape Canaveral, Florida. We were due for a conference with the contracting officer at noon. We arrived on time. The Marine guard signed us in, but then put us on hold as he stood by the door waiting to hold it open for the Admiral who commanded the base to come through, which he did at 12:45. I was furious. The guard had refused to use the telephone to call the contracting officer and wouldn't let us use it. When Admiral Poot swept through, I expressed my annoyance and asked him to call the contracting officer and tell him that we had been held up for forty-five minutes. He refused. There was no apology. He couldn't have cared less. All he cared about was that for those ten seconds out of forty-five minutes, the door should be held open for him and everything else could go hang!

No wonder the Navy is held in such disfavor today. No wonder that naval officers, especially naval aviators like Admiral Poot get their kicks in such strange ways as in the Tailhook incident. If the nation wants to save money, fire those perk-seeking admirals, the door-openers, or both!

Daryl F. Gates and Robert Vernon of the L.A.P.D.

Super-Arrogants maneuver themselves into positions of power where they can gain and retain control of resources: money, people, machinery, systems. Thus, they can marshall substantial forces to prove themselves right when the rest of the world considers them wrong.

Such a Super-Arrogant toxic was longtime Police Chief Daryl F. Gates of the Los Angeles Police Department (L.A.P.D.), who resigned under fire after the 1992 Los Angeles riots. His exit line, after hearing that the highly respected Amnesty International had rated the L.A.P.D. one of the most repressive regimes in the world, was to call them "A bunch of knuckle-headed liberals."

Gates was protected from being fired by a rigid civil service structure originally enacted to prevent politicization of the office. In the words of the post-King-beating report of the Christopher Commission formed to look at the problems in the L.A.P.D., it left the city with a police chief "subject to no serious oversight in a position that carries a virtual lifetime guarantee of tenure."[6] He abused his power position by failing to cure abuse of minorities both in the police forces and in the L.A. community. Only after the videotaped savage beating of Rodney G. King, witnessed or participated in by thirteen of "L.A.'s Rottenest," where Gates was very slow in taking even the minimum of disciplinary action, did the City Council pass ten measures that would limit the power of future police chiefs and change the way they are hired and fired. The Christopher Commission called for those changes after confirming widespread bias against racial minorities and women not only in the L.A.P.D. itself, but in its relationship with the L.A. community.[7]

According to the testimony of senior officers, during his long tenure Gates had done nothing about intradepartmental biases, and was unusually lenient in disciplining his men for bias and brutality in their dealings with minorities in carrying out their duties.

Gates's arrogance was apparent when he stripped from command one of his top officers who testified to this effect.[8] Finally, it wasn't the Gates-hating blacks and Hispanics who brought the action to control the police forces and the police chief, it was the businessmen of the L.A. community who had had enough of his arrogance. They lobbied successfully for passage of corrective legislation to regain control of the police chief's function.

In the Rodney King affair, a runaway jury found for the L.A.P.D. in its nearly total exoneration of the thirteen officers charged, in spite of the hard evidence of the video tape of King's vicious treatment. Anyone with a brain knew that there would be riots if the cops got off. And they did get off. (With the exception of the lead malefactor, club-swinging Laurence M. Powell, the principal King assailant, with the jury deadlocked eight to four for acquittal. But he may be retried.)

Sixty people died and nearly a billion dollars of property was destroyed in the ensuing riots. Superior Court Judge Stanley M. Weisberg had told attorneys for both sides that, once informed that the jury had arrived at a verdict, he would wait two hours before expecting both sides in court. This was designed to give L.A.P.D. police commanders an early warning of possible trouble if the cops got off.

But that warning accommodation of the court was ignored by Gates and company. If the L.A.P.D. had been on the job they could have shut down the riot at its start. But no. After the verdict, even after the riots started, Gates left his post to go off speechifying and raising money to defeat the ballot initiative to fulfill the recommendations of the Christopher Commission for the community to regain control of the office of police chief. (Warren Christopher, the Chairman, is now Secretary of State in the Clinton Cabinet.)

After the King beating, when asked to resign by longtime. L.A. Mayor Tom Bradley, himself a former police lieutenant, Gates refused and added, by his own account, "Who the hell do you think you are?"[9]

Mayor Tom Bradley is black. Gates has a low opinion of blacks. In 1982 the *Los Angeles Times* quoted him as saying that more blacks than whites die from police choke-holds because their "veins and arteries do not open as fast as they do in normal people," and he also said that Hispanics were naturally lazy. Gates says he was misquoted.[10]

The police officials were not students of history. In the Boston Police Strike of 1919, the National Guard was not called until well after the riots started, after stores were looted, people had been assaulted, and women raped. In Boston, the incompetence of a super-arrogant police commissioner and vacillation by Governor Calvin Coolidge, paralleled the situation in L.A. In both cases the Guard was called in late.[11]

Still not clear are the reasons the L.A. police forces were called off after the riots started and not sent back until things were completely out of control, until buildings by the hundreds were burning, until people were dying. The helicopters were broadcasting live coverage of criminal activity. So, where were the L.A.P.D.'s vaunted SWAT teams? In storage? Or were they out with Gates raising money to combat the initiative?

The L.A.P.D. forces, before the riots, were often called "brutes with badges." After their delayed and hesitant response to the city's worst riot in history, they have now been additionally, and most likely unfairly, labeled as cowards and incompetents. If the L.A.P.D. failed in its duties, it was their toxic leaders' fault, not the police themselves who, in the course of duty, have sacrificed many of their brave members but who pick up the anti-black, anti Hispanic, anti-woman attitude of senior officers like Gates. It was the stubborn resentments and the resulting incompetence of L.A.P.D. officials not the police on the line that allowed the riot to get out of hand.

The Cassandra effect, where predictions of disaster are not believed, had taken over there in lala land itself.

As Gates was out drumming up money and support to defeat the Christopher Commission's recommendations, and the town was burning, one of the Gates-goofies even suggested that Gates run for president! What a great country is the U.S. of A., that this enthusiast wasn't carted off to the nearest looneybin.

Later, after his retirement and replacement by a black police chief, Willie L. Williams, Gates looked like J. Edgar Hoover in short pants when it was discovered that his forty-five-man Organized Crime Investigative Division (OCID) unit that was supposed to be infiltrating drug gangs, spent much of its time and money spying on local officials, politicians, and celebrities—people that Gates was suspicious of. He built files on Barbra Streisand, Robert Redford, CBS's Connie Chung, and even fatso-turned-slimmo, Tommy Lasorda. But his special target was long-time-foe, Mayor Tom Bradley.[12]

The tragedy of America is that people like Gates cannot be utilized to the advantage of all of us. I can't imagine his taking money. But I can imagine his being captured by simplisms that are easy outs for busy people. I suspect that he is a far better man than he himself or the pubic knows. But at some time in his life, probably in secondary school, he missed a basic course in "values," most likely because it was not taught.

Into that values gap step people like Gates's deputy, Robert Vernon, a religious nut who contributes to continuing problems in the L.A. community. Vernon headed for a Florida vacation while the Rodney King beatings' trial jury was still out. On his arrival in Florida he heard the riot news and offered to return. He was told he was not needed. It was probably for the better. The nature of the man is such that he could not possibly have helped. Here's why.

A number of years ago Vernon made six audiotapes for the conservative evangelical Grace Community Church in Sun Valley where he is an elder. He advised people to hit their kids with "boat oars" and said he'd done it many times. Why? Because children are "born sinners!" Vernon said that he has administered this kind of treatment to children right up to age seventeen.

Vernon made a tape called "The True Masculine Role." He says that women should be submissive to their husbands. "We spend a lot of time talking to your husbands... about learning submissiveness, about really fulfilling God's intended role so you will want to be submissive to them. The Bible teaches that." Also, "Police officers are ministers of God."

Given a Daryl Gates as police chief, it is not difficult to believe that this kind of trash is generated by his deputy, not difficult to believe that this nutcake is thenumber two man on the L.A. police force. But again, with Gates as his *Führer*, he was an avid *Anhänger*. There are many, many people with brains and education out there in L.A. How come they let these arrogant T.E.s, whose nonidentification with, and subsequent hate for their fellow human beings is quite evident, are given authority over *people!*

Further, people like Vernon and Gates are expensive for the community to have around. Vernon cost the city a $3.3 million judgment when Black Panther Party member Michael Zinzun proved that Vernon used a Los Angeles police computer to obtain and spread false and personally damaging information about him. Zinzun was also awarded $10,000 assessed against Vernon *person-*

ally.[13] In this case arrogance was compounded with stupidity. All of this was before the disastrous riots. But arrogance is not confined to people in uniform, they're all around.

I always wondered if it was more than a coincidence that "National Secretaries Day" is on the same date as "Earth Day." Is it because most executives treat their secretaries like dirt? In Washington, D.C., the Hard Rock Cafe issued an invitation to drop a typewriter on a lifesize cutout labeled "BOSS." The Hard Rock was swamped with applicants. They chose ten who dropped twenty-five-pound Selectrics about 12 feet from the mezzanine onto the cutout. Keerash![14]

I was on the board for some years of a company in Tulsa, Oklahoma. It was run by people I really liked and respected. But the founder and CEO was given to quixotic impulses.

It was a hot day in Tulsa. One of many. The machine shop was air-conditioned. There was a large door leading to the loading dock. There, they shipped out huge x-ray welded parts for the jet engines of America's commercial and military planes. The door was kept closed except for those brief moments when the parts were moved out onto the loading ramp. One very hot day our CEO found the door open and shut off the air conditioning to "discipline" the workers. They walked out.

This was an arrogant action. One guy left the door open and one hundred paid the penalty. But it was the stockholders who lost. The lost production cost us at least $100,000 in lost profits and considerably more in customer dissatisfaction. It was not the chairman's job to discipline shop people. He also allowed the salesmen to go on the shop floor and "hustle up" the workers to get *their* customers' orders out. This is a classic business no-no. It is *very* disruptive. He was a great guy, not at all arrogant in his family life, but, in business, he was given to precipitate actions that cost him and his fellow stockholders real money.

Jack Willis

During World War II, at Bethlehem Steel's Key Highway yard, we were converting a large, four hundred-passenger luxury cruise liner to a troop carrier, the U.S.S. *Alcor*, designed to carry several thousand. I was in charge of the installation of a new ventilating system which entailed flame-cutting holes through the decks. It was a critical operation. Pilot holes had to be drilled to make sure you were not cutting through strength members. There had already been serious mistakes made costing the shipyard a lot of money to correct and delaying a hurry-up job. I was put in charge of the cutting to ensure there would be no more glitches.

There were three shifts. I had been at the ship since about 6:30 A.M. checking on the work of the previous night's shift, and it was now 11:30 P.M. I was waiting to instruct the night shift on where and how to make the cuts since there were some new hires. I was marking blueprints with a red greasepen when I nodded off. The next thing I knew I had a foot in my ribs.

It was Jack Willis, head of the shipyard, with three guests, two of them women. Even though it was wartime, they were all in formal attire. I never got a chance to explain and was immediately ordered off the ship.

That night the cutting crew, absent my on-site instructions, cut through two structural members. Repairs cost thousands. Delivery was seriously delayed. The Navy was furious. I was rehired the next day but started looking for a new job. Within a few months I became the assistant coordinator of design for a Maritime Commission program.

I next saw Jack Willis a year later at a Propeller Club dinner–dance in Philadelphia. At the request of the Maritime Commission's regional director I was escorting his very attractive secretary to the dinner. Her physician husband had the duty and could not make the dinner but would be there later for the dance. After dinner, Jack Willis came up to me and asked to be introduced to the young lady. I did so. He then called me aside and offered me $50 to "disappear." I told him it would cost him a hundred. He gave it to me, two $50 bills. I "disappeared" just as her husband appeared.

Jack Willis was not only an arrogant bastard, he was a toxic executive of substantial proportions, a showoff, a fool, and a philanderer. I *loved* getting even with him and made sure all the old gang at Bethlehem's Key Highway yard in Baltimore knew what happened at the Propeller Club affair. (You see, there's a little toxicity in all of us!)

General Curtis E. LeMay

I first knew of General Curtis E. LeMay when he was the head of Wright Field in Dayton, Ohio, which was a research and development station for which my Reed Research was building missile flight simulators. LeMay used to run race cars around the tarmac. Later he became the head of the Strategic Air Command, flying around the country with a red telephone hooked directly into the White House.

I was scheduled to speak at an annual meeting of the American Association for the Advancement of Science. I was going over my notes in a corner of the reception area when a bird colonel, with a lot of looped braid on his shoulder and a little tiny mustache, came up and asked if I was Stanley Foster Reed. He said he was the aide to General Curtis E. LeMay, and would I mind giving up my early place on the program to the General so he could get back to protecting the nation.

"How do you know that he'll be here?" I asked. The bird colonel with the little tiny mustache said that the General was already there and was standing only a few feet away. I was really surprised. "Why didn't he come over and ask me himself?" The General heard me, looked over, but didn't move. No way would His Arrogance come over. And no way would I give him my place on the program.

(LeMay was as lacking in good sense as he was in manners, as proved by his running for Vice President of the United States with George C. Wallace on the American Independent Party ticket in 1968. They got 9,906,473 votes. That dopey duo siphoned off enough southern Democratic votes to elect Richard Nixon and [ugh!] Spiro Agnew. As a result, they took the popular vote from Hubert Humphrey and Ed Muskie, 31,785,480 to 31,275,166,[15] and the subsequent electoral vote.)

HOW ARROGANCE BLEW A DEAL

I flew to St. Louis one day with J. Willard (Bill) Marriott, Jr. to discuss Marriott's possible purchase of "Intrav," a highly successful affinity travel group of which I had been a longtime board member.

The meeting was to take place at the new St. Louis Marriott, which Bill had not visited since its opening a year earlier. We walked up to the desk. Bill said, "I'm Bill Marriott, do you have the suite reserved for me?" The clerk allowed as how she was the Queen of Sheba, and wanted to know if I was Napoleon. I pointed to Bill's portrait directly behind her and asked her to compare. Bill enjoyed all of this hugely, especially her horrified, hands-over-mouth expression on recognition.

Bill was most gracious, assured her it happened quite frequently, and we went off to the suite to meet with Barney Ebsworth, the young genius who had built Intrav into a thriving business.

The meeting was a disaster. I had known Barney Ebsworth for maybe five years. He was a wonderful guy. But with Marriott, he went through a complete personality change. He turned out to be an arrogant egomaniac. He told Bill about all of the expensive paintings he was buying, about the dumb things the competition was doing, about what a smart guy he was. It went on and on. We never did get to talk about the deal. By mid-afternoon when we headed back to the airport, Bill was furious.

He compared Barney's ego to Nixon's. "Can you imagine Barney's bringing me out there and forcing me to listen to four hours of self-serving statements? Can you imagine anyone being egotistical enough to want to record every single word spoken in the Oval Office?" Barney never even thanked Marriott for taking the time from his billion-dollar enterprise to meet with him. (Bill Marriott and his dad were arch-conservatives and super-supporters of Nixon. His obvious displeasure with the arrogance of both Ebsworth and Nixon was evident by the depth of his reaction.)

Under those circumstances, Barney's performance was the act of an arrogant executive and all arrogant executives are toxic executives.

Recently (mid-January 1993) Paul Kazarian who had turned around Sunbeam-Oster, was fired by the board because he called his people "scum" and treated them like dirt. They threatened to resign and Kazarian, who "dumped" on everybody, himself was dumped. He was a true T.E. (See the *Wall Street Journal*, January 14, 1993, for details of this sad story.)

THE SUPER-STUBBORN T.E.

One of the most common and most disruptive of toxic executive types is the super-stubborn exec. (Many of these, in my experience and based on interviews, have been women.) Once they take a position or evince a point of view, they will not change no matter how much evidence is brought to the contrary. "That's the way we've been doing it for ten years and that's the way we'll continue to do it."

Good executives have strong opinions and hold to them until persuaded by the weight of argument on the other side that they *could* be wrong. It is resiliency versus rigidity. The latter simply does not pay off in business. A good executive is a resilient executive, but not a *compliant* executive, one who changes his or her opinion based on the last person he or she talked to.

THE SERIAL SADIST T.E.

One of the worst of the Value-less T.E.s is the Serial Sadist. (The temptation to attribute this characteristic exclusively to the male executive is strong, but many serial sadists are women.) Serial sadists must transfer their self-hatred to another. That hatred is projected onto a series of people quite different from themselves, people they would probably like to be. Like targets in a shooting gallery, the T.E. attempts to destroy them one after another.

I employed a scientist, an extremely competent M.I.T. graduate electrical engineer. We were building a large analog computer to simulate heat flow in the skin of a large missile. His work was above reproach. Everything he did was engineeringly correct. He knew electrical engineering as Oliver Wendell Holmes knew law. And he knew that I knew it. However, he had problems keeping people. At a symposium at Woods Hole Oceanographic Institute (WHOI) I met a young oceanographer who had worked with my prize engineer on WHOI's research vessel, the famous four-masted sailing ship, *Atlantic.* He could not believe that I would employ such a cruel person, for my prize engineer had made life miserable for this young man. Every day was another day of criticism. Every day some reason would be found to invalidate the young scientist's work. At Woods Hole they were evidently not sensitive to this kind of thing. At Reed Research we evidently were, for upon my return I discovered that my engineer's attempts at this kind of arrogant behavior (of which I had not been aware) had been detected by our personnel director who discovered his toxicity in an exit interview with someone who had quit because of the way he was treated. When faced with the seriousness of his behavior there was a remarkable change in my engineer. He told me he was totally unaware of the toxic nature of his actions—especially at WHOI. He resolved to change and he did so.

The Serial Sadist T.E. is someone who is completely intolerant of any person who suffers any of the myriad of illnesses, physiological and psychological, that are visited on people. Serial Sadist T.E.s seek out those already in pain—especially psychological pain—and delight in inflicting even more pain and embarrassment on a succession of carefully selected targets, usually people in an inferior position who are "locked into" their job by economic necessity and can't fight back.

Every person in the world suffers from *some* kind of physiological or psychological problem. Some unfortunates suffer from many, so targets are easy to find. The Serial Sadist T.E. has no sympathy for any of them.

In particular, the Serial Sadist male T.E. will beat up on those women employees who suffer from premenstrual-syndrome (PMS), when, just before the start of their menstrual period, they have cramps, bloating, fatigue, and general malaise, and, as a result, can become irritable and hostile for a few days out of the month.

As more women attain high-stress executive positions, all executives are becoming more aware of PMS, which in some small percentage of working women can be so severe that they must stay home. But for the Serial Sadist T.E., it's a chance to vent his *or her* pent-up Theory X suspicions that most such people are malingerers who are trying to get out of work.

What about PMS-prone women executives? How many of them turn into T.E.s? Let's face it. They're out there, and for a few days a month can make life miserable for those around them. In a worst-case scenario they become Serial Sadists themselves! It is each such executive's responsibility to learn which medications work best for her and which do not. If PMS symptoms do not respond to medication and are so severe that they interfere with her duties, which is rare, she should consider a job or even a career change.

Another target for the male Serial Sadist T.E. is the menopausal woman, some of whom, at certain times of the day, and for several months if not years, are simply not up to par.

San Fransican Shirley Krohn, a human resources supervisor at a major corporation, "was so outdone by her meno-pause that she took a medical leave. Now that she's back on the job, taking hormones, she's looking forward to the time when a woman can tell a male boss when she's either hav-ing or about to have a tough time with menopausal symp-toms, and that male colleague will suggest that they post-pone their meeting to a later time in the day."

For menopausal women, the best defense against the male Serial Sadist is a strong offense. But it should be based on solid knowledge. Menopause is highly idiosyn-cratic. Each should read the well-written best-seller *The Silent Passage* by Gail Sheehy.[16] After learning all she can about the physiology of her condition, shopping for a sym-pathetic gynecologist—multiple opinions are a must—learning which medications work for her and which do not, (there are some new transdermal hormonal patches on the market), after learning how to schedule her activity so that her periods of menopausal stress do not coincide with periods of high physical and psychological job stress, she should inform her boss of the fact of her condition, and ask for understanding. This should elicit a positive response. She should point out that many women "hit their stride" after menopause, after relief from the burdens of child-bearing and the prospect of it. They should remind their bosses that their PMS is gone—replaced, perhaps, by hot flashes now and then—but that only makes their cheeks pinker!

And the menopausal woman T.E.? Face it, she's out there too and there will be more and more like her as the glass ceilings are broken to shards and the female baby-boomers arrive at their new jobs and responsibilities coin-cident with the onset of menopause. The male Serial Sadist T.E.s will then have a field day as will all the male chauvinis-tic pigs that inhabit and inhibit American business. Manage-ment must be sensitive to them and should take drastic action to cut off sadistic behaviors by male executives in these circumstances. And watch out for the non-menopausal *female* Serial Sadist T.E.s as well.!

Just as they have had to learn how to get along with difficult people as part of their job, menopausal women must learn to control themselves. PMS and menopausal symptoms are still not an excuse for toxic behavior. Every woman executive has a bounden duty to try to control her behavior for her own good and that of her employer. Management itself must understand that even the best of their female executive corps will have *some* problems, *sometimes*, and they should allow for it in some planned manner. And don't believe for one moment that women will be more sympathetic than men. On the job, women can be just as competitive as men, and just as sadistic given the opportunity.

I had an executive secretary who was really "done in" by PMS. But she was smart and helpful and nice most of the time, but for a few days a month she turned bitchy and mean. There was no way that I could remember when her period came around. I said she was smart. She proved it by suggesting that she wear her red shoes when her period was about to happen. She'd come in the office, I'd see the red shoes and get up from my desk and cower in a corner begging her not to hit me. It would break us both up. It worked out great. It was our secret.

With female menopause, as opposed to PMS, it's a little more difficult. Only 5 to 15 percent of women have menopausal symptoms that send them to a doctor. Perhaps many more should go. Some menopausal women go really nuts. A menopausal neighbor of mine insisted that I got up in the middle of the night and dug up her yard (I used to own the land) looking for buried treasure! She also wandered the neighborhood telling people how to paint their houses, cut their grass, etc. When I was in high school, my girlfriend's mother used to run around outside and make faces through the window while we were playing bridge. I couldn't believe it. Mrs. Martin had always been such a nice person. Her husband explained to me what was going on, and I thought that I understood. But by the time my first wife was menopausal and nuttier than usual, I'd forgotten Mrs. Martin. (There should be a little treatise on menopausal symptoms and treatment written especially for ignorant [and busy] husbands, male bosses, work-mates, and, yes, *children*. Incredibly, there are still women in the workforce and personnel directors who don't know about PMS and menopause and their treatments. Worse, some don't seem to want to learn about them. One inter-viewee stated that "I would *never* talk to my boss about such a subject!")

Still under review is the supposed natural increase of the male hormone testosterone in women after menopause, which is supposed to make women more aggressive.[17] But the evidence is not all in yet and here again women don't seem to cotton to the idea which is holding up research on this interesting subject.[18]

"Male menopause," associated with gradual testos-terone loss with age in men can parallel the loss of estrogen in women in menopause. "There is a decrease in muscle mass, a loss of physical strength, a loss of bone density, loss of energy, loss of concentration, a build-up of body fat, lowered fertility, fading virility, depression, and mood swings."[19] Dr. Paul T. Costa, a psychologist at the National Institute on Aging, in speaking of the phenomenon, said, "Some older men may say their erections aren't as big as they recall them once being. But then their partner says, 'Well, dear, you overestimated them back then, too.'"[20]

This phenomenon, in men, is sometimes called the "midlife crisis," and parallels the physiological and behav-ioral changes that take place in the menopausal female. The effect has been much discussed and recently was the theme of a British play, the much worked over "The Holy Terror" by Simon Gray, which was transported to New York in the fall of 1992 and was the subject of a confused review of this confusing subject by Frank Rich in the *New York Times*. Though the physiological and psychological trauma are not as severe in men as they are in women, they can become targets for the female Serial Sadist T.E., who, herself, may be menopausal. When that happens, look out!

During World War II, I was working for a naval architectural design firm in New York City called Kindlund and Drake. They had taken over the design program that I had coordinated in Washington. Everything was rush-rush. I was desperate for office help.

It was nearly impossible to hire anyone with a good secretarial background that knew shipbuilding or ship-design. In desperation, we hired a former teacher, about forty-five years old. I was twenty-four. I had long since forgotten about Mrs. Martin, and it never occurred to me that Mrs. What's-Her-Name was menopausal. She was bitchy about everything. I mean like *everything!* I couldn't get work out of the secretarial pool because everyone disliked her. One day, during a meeting with government representatives, I asked her to bring me a file; in answer, she snapped her fingers at me as she pointed to the file cabinet. It was the last straw. I had never fired anyone and didn't know if I was allowed to. So I complained to Martin Kindlund. He immediately called her in. "Did you snap your fingers at Mr. Reed?" She said, "Yes." "While the people from the Maritime Commission were there?" Again she said "yes." Mr. Kindlund then asked, "Why?" I can still see her face, flushed bright pink, as she struggled to answer. She lost her job and I lost the help I needed. That situation must play out a thousand times a day all over the business world. Today, I would handle it by buying several books on menopause and its treatment and leave them on her desk. But then, I'm no longer twenty-four!

In addition to the menopausal woman and perhaps man, there are many people whose physiological problems are chemical. Some of that is outlined in the book *Body, Mind and Sugar.*[21]

Back in 1951, E. M. Abrahamson, M.D., and A. W. Pezet wrote that great book. It dealt with how the body used sugar. One example was the strange behavior of a brilliant pitcher, who from time to time "blew it" in mid- to late-afternoon in the seventh or eighth inning, including a no-hitter for no apparent reason. Studies of railroad accidents indicated that many of them happened in mid- and late-afternoon. The authors asked, why do so many industrial accidents take place in the afternoon?

Answer: The body's chemistry is such that, depending on a person's activity, metabolic rate, and what was eaten for breakfast and lunch, the body may have burned up all its sugar by three or four o'clock and torpor and lassitude took over. Dr. Abrahamson had a young executive patient with a very high heart rate that could only be controlled with morphine. The attacks continued, morphine cured temporarily but soon the patient was a candidate for junkie-land. One afternoon Abrahamson took a blood sample. Surprise! Instead of a normal 140 mg of sugar per 100cc of blood, it was like 55. Abrahamson immediately prescribed dextrose and in five minutes the patient's heart rate returned to normal. Was he cured? No. Because the dextrose turned on the body's insulin production which burned up the sugar at too high a rate. However, reducing the sugar intake eventually effected a permanent cure.

The British learned the importance of afternoon sugar replacement and conquered half the world from their little island due to their insistence on "afternoon tea," even in the midst of battle. Afternoon tea, with its jam and crumpets, not only replaces the body's sugar just as it's running out, but adds a mild shot of caffeine to boot.

In the office, without a "sugar fix," many people get cranky, nervous, and difficult, and become targets of opportunity for the serial sadist whose body chemistry and eating habits may also be similarly affected. Then it's war! I recommend that in any operation with high ambient stress, making afternoon tea a ritual will do much to reduce the toxic executive's toxicity, and help his or her peers, superiors, and subordinates to reduce theirs.

One of the mysterious "societal diseases" is "chronic fatigue syndrome" or CFS. Only recently have scientists at the National Institutes of Health made some progress that might lead to effective treatment. Primarily affecting young people, it has also been called "yuppie hypochondria," or "yuppie flu," and usually lasts for three to six months.[22] In one study it was traced to hormonal deficiencies, but investigators do not yet know if the deficiency is cause or effect. Another study noted that it was accompanied by an immune system dysfunction associated with the herpes virus.

CFS-prone people are targets of opportunity for Serial Sadists because they must always be involved in persecuting *someone!* The vagueness of the illness only reinforces the T.E.'s conviction of malingering.

The toxic executive will look for some physical or psychological problem in a subordinate and will make life miserable for him or her.

I knew one executive who insisted that his secretary pick him up at the airport even late at night. She had *nictophobia*—extreme fear of darkness. She even told him that she *hated* to drive at night. But he never let up. She *had* to pick him up or it meant her job!

There are people who hate flowers. They have *anthophobia*. Who cares why—they just do! Maybe it was a dear one's funeral. Or her father was an abusive horticulturist. Or maybe she choked on a flower she'd tried to eat when she was eight months old. No matter, the Serial Sadist T.E. makes her put fresh flowers on his *and her* desk every few days, *knowing that she hates to do it!* Because *he* doesn't hate flowers, he believes she's just stubborn or stupid and *he's* going to cure her!

Acrophobia is fear of heights. Some people get sick if they sit by one of those deep windows with five hundred feet down to the street. Yet I know a Serial Sadist T.E. who refuses to move his assistant's desk away from one of those awful windows in spite of her complaints.

There are many more phobias and manias that afflict people. No one is immune. So there are always plenty of targets for the Serial Sadist. (For a list of common manias and phobias get a copy of the *Home Medical Dictionary*.[23])

THE SUPER-PREJUDIST

An acquaintance of mine, a top executive at the American Association of Railroads, was a super-prejudist.

We both were guests of Admiral Ned Cowart, Commander of the Coast Guard, at his annual outdoor bash at the Coast Guard Station in Alexandria, Virginia. During the afternoon, my railroader friend made a series of gross ethnic comments about the Democrats and Jews who had put through Eisenhower's $40 billion highway program which had hurt the railroads. I said I was surprised to find that he was such a "prejudiced" person and suggested that it would not do his cause any good. He then said he knew that he was prejudiced and that it had taken him years to hone his prejudices to such a high point. Further, he was "teaching his children to be prejudiced."

In shock, I suggested to him that he was taking a chance on losing his children, for as they grew up and discovered how wrong he was, how immoral it was to be so prejudiced, they would sever the family relationship. He said he didn't care. If they were that stupid, he didn't want them around!

SEXUAL/RACIAL DISCRIMINATION

In a Washington, D.C., health club—where women daytime exercisers outnumber men 10-to-1—during repairs they allowed the women to use the men's locker room. The women went into shock. The men's locker room was *much* bigger, *much* lighter, *much* better equipped, with a jacuzzi you could float in! The ceilings were higher, the TV room bigger. Half the members were women. They paid the same as the men, but have half the number of lockers.

The women told the owners it would "take the National Guard to get them out of there. We'll chain ourselves to the lockers." They wanted equal space or they'd stay put. "Terrible," said Wendy Rudolph. "It's not fair. We're paying as much as the men and getting facilities that are clearly inferior."[24] (I understand that management has promised equal facilities.)

Some ten years ago the nation was first made aware of sexual discrimination by the case of Christine Craft, a TV newsperson in the Midwest who was fired for not being attractive enough. She sued and won a substantial award which was eventually thrown out on a procedural technicality by the Supreme Court of the United States. Since that time, the public has become more and more aware of active, malicious, unfair discrimination by executives in business, government—everywhere. There is no longer any doubt that women, blacks, Hispanics, and other minorities have been discriminated against in the American job market for many, many years, and still are. There is often confusion in separating sexual harassment from intolerance. Though they often go hand in hand, although as recently detailed in a report by the General Accounting Office on harassment of women at the nation's service academies, they are separated. (Sexual harassment is treated in the next chapter as a special case of addiction in the "Sexual Addiction" section.) Mistreatment of minorities in our society is endemic. For instance, women have as many heart attacks as men, but are not treated with the same celerity as are men.[25]

Even with the same education, job tenure, and work experience, "Female executives are far behind male managers in their climb up the corporate ladder," recites a report by Chicago's Institute of Human Resources and Industrial Relations. Even women who did not turn down geographic transfers were still not promoted.

The study used *Fortune 500* executives—223 women and 795 men. Men averaged thirty-seven years old and 86 percent were married. Women averaged thirty-four years old and 45 percent were married. All had bachelor degrees, some had graduate degrees. They were spread over the manufacturing and service industries. Men had relocated twice during their careers, as had women. The same job titles, salary, and bonus increases for men were 65 percent, for women 54 percent over a five-year period.

Women, both black and white, and especially black male executives are deflected from the career path to the top by some activity that has either "relations" or "affairs" in the job title. "These areas have little direct impact on the bottom line and offer scant opportunity for advancement," writes Richard G. Carter."[26] What he did not write is that these departments are the first to get cut back or cut off when times get tough, and since the economic causes are easily proven, these "parking" layoffs are not actionable. The discrimination took place at the first job assignment.

Roberta Spalter-Roth, of American University, observed that "Top management has a vision of the appropriate person to promote, and every study tells us it's someone who looks like them: middle aged, white, male and often with a stay-at-home wife. Women and minorities are not seen in the gut or subconscious as the appropriate candidate."[27] (Remember chapter 7's Doppelgänger effect.) But sexual and racial discrimination is getting to be expensive. Here are some recent damage awards.

After seven years of litigation, the U.S. Drug Enforcement Administration (DEA) has agreed to pay $275,000 to some Hispanic agents, and to promote them at the same rate as other agents. This settlement came only a few months after the FBI reached an agreement that would give six black FBI agents a total of $115,000 because of the racial discrimination they had suffered.[28]

One of academia's dirty little secrets is its discrimination against female faculty in granting tenure—the economic and sociological lifeblood of the faculty. In spite of being named "Faculty Member of the Year" by the University of Wisconsin's business school's advisory council, in spite of publishing her seventh article, in spite of her students' posting some of the highest scores in the nation on the CPA exam, Dr. Ceil Pillsbury was denied tenure. There were four up for tenure: three white male colleagues and Dr. Pillsbury. The other three made it. She did not. She complained and a grievance committee ruled in her favor in December 1990. But tenure was still denied because of a state law that prevented university regents from overriding a negative departmental tenure vote. She sued and made the cover of *On Campus,* a publication of the American Federation of Teachers.[29]

The University of Virginia has similar problems. At their prestigious Darden School of Business Administration, an outside committee ruled that a "hostile climate for women" flourishes among the faculty. The five-member group scored the tenure process and cited a 1990 tenure case at UVA that included allegations of sexual harassment.[30]

And Wall Street is rife with sexual discrimination. Women make up 40 percent of the work force but fill only 4 percent of the partnership and managing director jobs. Because women live, on average, nearly ten years longer than men, women control some 65 percent of all the investment wealth in the United States. Something is wrong that they do not use their power to right the wrongs of Wall Street in the matter of sexual discrimination.

Jolted by Anita Hill's testimony in the Senate's Judge Thomas confirmation hearings, firms like Merrill Lynch & Co. have taken a firm stand against sexism. "But there are still no women in Shearson's executive management group" says the *Wall Street Journal.*[31] One of the worst of the firms seems to be Goldman Sachs, one of the last firms still in partnership form. It has 146 partners, only four of them women. Joanne Flynn, a Goldman V.P., claims she was fired because of her sex and that males with equivalent duties were paid much more than she was. She sued and the judge in the case blasted Goldman for failure to produce documents Flynn needed, and for interposing "frivolous arguments." And another Goldman V.P., Rita M. Reid, was "reorganized" out of her job after fourteen years involvement with leveraged buyouts and mergers. She had earned a bonus of $375,000 in 1989. But in August of 1991, when Goldman reorganized her department, every male got a new job, but Rita did not. Rita was not only riffed, she was miffed. So she's suing Goldman for $12 million for loss of earnings and $6 million in punitive damages for emotional distress.[32]

Over at Kidder Peabody, Elizabeth Sobol, a former managing director, has filed suit in federal court because Kidder paid out skimpier bonuses to her than to male colleagues with similar responsibilities—she administered the work of eighteen investment banking professionals in her utility finance department, which was one of the most profitable divisions at Kidder.[33]

American Airlines got hit with a $7.1 million award to Barbara L. Sogg, who was reorganized out of her job as manager of flight services rather than promoted to general manager of AAL's LaGuardia office. It had gone to a male with considerably less tenure and even less experience.[34]

And right here in Fairfax County, Virginia, Irene Lugenbeel recently used the company's computer to prove that two male employees doing the same work that she was were paid $20,000 more per year. At age fifty-two, and coming up for retirement, she was afraid of filing a complaint—she didn't want to be fired. But she finally filed, and sure enough, she *was* fired by employer Iverson Technology Corporation of McLean. The EEOC took her case and early in 1992 she was awarded $125,000. Her boss, Jack Coon, was ready to testify *for*, not *against*, her, saying of her pay rate, "It was a great injustice." He further observed that she was "more qualified" than the others! She now has a new job with an Iverson competitor and makes much more money.[35]

But the biggie is the April 1992 $157 *million* paid by State Farm Insurance; the largest settlement ever paid in a civil rights case for sexual discrimination. Some 814 California women received an average of $193,000 each, and one, Muriel Kraszewski, longtime secretary to State Farm agents, and the person who initiated the suit, was awarded $431,000. Kraszewski had been passed over for an agent's job because she "had no college degree," but told State

Farm executives: "I've never worked for a man who *had* a college degree!" The court found that at State Farm, women were "lied to, and/or given false and misleading information . . . about educational requirements by State Farm executives." State Farm was recently described by *Fortune* magazine as "stunningly rich, with a surplus of $18 billion." The suit covered only their California operations and by the time the whole story plays out, that surplus is liable to shrink. Kraszewski now works for a competitor of State Farm and is earning in the six figures.[36]

Another major case was the $675,000 awarded in June 1992 to Sandra C. Shope, a top housing official in Louden County, Virginia. In addition, her boss, Timothy Krawczel, was fined $25,000 for his abusive conduct. Krawczel humiliated her by shouting at her in front of others, pounding on her desk, calling her names, including "a stupid woman." He told her "I'm the boss at home and I will be the boss here." Krawczel never treated the men in the office in the same humiliating way. Shope's complaints about Krawczel's behavior went on up the all-male line to the Board of Supervisors, but no one had taken any action.[37]

In a rather scary case, a federal appellate court has ruled that property owners are liable for the discriminatory acts of their employees *even when the owners have expressly forbidden the biased conduct.*

Darlene Walker won $5,000 in damages from the owner of a Falls Church appartment because the owner's property manager, Constance A. Crigler, refused to rent the unit to Walker because she was a woman. Crigler's action was in violation of the federal Fair Housing Act which prohibits bias against a person because of sex. The apartment was rented to two men for $20 per month less than Walker was willing to pay.

While the owner had specifically instructed Crigler against discrimination of any kind, Crigler declared bankruptcy after the judgment against her and the owner, who was held by the court to be "fully exonerated," nervertheless had to pay the judgment.

The EEOC recently filed a suit in Federal District Court in L.A. charging that Eiki International, Inc. violated the civil rights of an Indian-born employee, Rambhai Patel, when he was fired because of his accent. They cited a recent appeals court decision in Washington State upholding a $390,000 judgment against a Washington bank for refusing to promote a Cambodian-American because of his accent. The discrimination had triggered a post-traumatic stress disorder due to his seeing his family killed by the Khmer Rouge, according to medical experts retained by Phanna K. Xieng who won the award.[38] And Texaco, which should be used to large jury awards against it (Texas jurors don't like Texaco appropriating their state's name and then setting up corporate headquarters in White Plains, N.Y.), got banged with a $20.3 million jury verdict—which includes $15 million in punitive damages—in favor of Janella Sue Martin, a forty-nine-year-old Texaco credit supervisor who was passed over for advancement because of her gender. (The judge set the verdict aside but Martin is appealing.)[39]

Finally, Continental Airlines fired one of its agents at Boston's Logan International Airport for refusing to wear makeup. Officials said that Teresa Fischette's appearance was inconsistent with Continental's "new image."[40] (Many a time on airplanes I've wanted to say to over-made-up stewardi, "So, it's Halloween?" How much better most of them would look if they took most of that scary goop off their faces. That's why most of the kids are crying on airplanes, they've been scared to death.) Anyway, Fischette threatened suit, and after a *New York Times* scathing editorial,[41] and an appearance on the "Oprah Winfrey Show," Continental caved and she got an apology and her job back.[42]

Three Egyptian-American elevator operators in a Manhattan luxury condo sued and won $10,000 each for suffering "almost daily ethnic slurs" from a supervisor. They were called "camel jockeys" and their accents were imitated. The award was for "mental anguish, humiliation and outrage."[43]

RACIAL STEREOTYPING

Racial stereotyping goes on every day in every office in America. It is wrong. People who stereotype are weak, or at least lazy thinkers, and become toxic executives when they achieve positions of power. Stereotyping is typical of advertising executives who work hard at both creating and exploiting racial motifs.

Mark Green is Commissioner of Consumer Affairs for the City of New York. He is trying to document some of the more obvious instances of stereotyping in advertising.

Mark, an old friend, wrote a piece for the *Washington Post* pointing out the vast discrepancies in magazine depictions of African-Americans, Hispanics, and Asian-Americans as summarized in his department's study, "Invisible People."

His staff had reviewed some 30,000 ads in 27 general-circulation magazines and 156 catalogs. Though blacks were 11 percent of the readers, they were only used in 3 percent of the ads in magazines, and in 4.5 percent of the catalogs. While blacks have advanced in depiction from 0.5 percent in 1950 to 2 percent in 1970 and 3 percent in 1990, Mark made the point that at that rate it will be the year 2152 before readership and ad depiction approach unity!

Mark makes many good points, but the most important is this: None of the decision makers putting out the ads controls 100 percent of the stereotyping decisionmaking that so offends by omission. Each, therefore, claims zero accountability for the resulting painful statistics. These are toxic executives who need retraining.[44]

THE SUPER-POLITICALIST/RELIGIONIST T.E.

Also known as the Alter-Ego Executive, some T.E.s are super-political. Some are super-religious. They let external factors sway their judgments. They may not take it out on their subordinates, since they most often hire along party or religious lines, but they can make it rough on customers, suppliers, and even consultants who don't see things their way politically. This happened to me with a consulting client.

A pecan packager from Georgia had attended one of my merger seminars. He had a cold-storage warehouse which was unused eight months of the year. He had asked me what kind of a business he should enter that would utilize his excess cash, his people and his facilities, especially his cold-storage capacity. I knew one of the answers, as a few hundred miles away, in Savannah, was the Dromedary date importing operation with complementary seasonality, a cold-storage plant, and a marketing process quite similar to that for pecans. He asked me to come and run one of my in-house seminars.

Mr. Pecan picked me up at the airport in his new Jaguar, of which he complained bitterly on the way to his home, which was only a few miles from Plains, Georgia. I wondered out loud if I would have enough time to visit Plains. Without slowing the Jag he made a U-turn that nearly took my head off and headed back to the airport. No way was he going to pay in the five figures for an analysis of his problems by someone who was interested in visiting President Carter's hometown.

I reminded him that I had a contract and he'd have to pay me anyway, and I finally got him and the Jag turned around. But he kept shaking his head about his hiring a "Yankee Democrat." He only showed signs of normalcy when he and his son beat me and his V.P. of sales at tennis on the court at his home. We had a very successful seminar and, with his staff, planned to implement the program we came up with. But I never heard from him again, which is highly unusual for my clients.

Political perceptions can impact your business perceptions. This is bad for business. The same thing can happen with religionists.

Merkel Press, founded by Edgar Merkel, was the biggest printer in the Washington, D.C., area for some forty years. Mr. Merkel refused to bid on printing my *Mergers & Acquisitions* magazine at its inception without first learning my astrological sign! I didn't know my sign, but I gave him my birth date, discovered that I was a "Libra," and after a few more questions, he looked in some big books, and announced that *M&A* would make a lot of money for both of us if we started it in September. There were no more questions, no credit inquiry, none of the things normal to business. He gave me a generous credit line and took the contract. He turned out to be right about the success of *M&A*, but wrong about a lot of other things, as Merkel Press went in the tank a few years later.

Political or religious ideologues seldom make good businessmen or -women. Judging customers, suppliers, and employees by their political beliefs, religion, racial background, or astrological sign, is wrong. This same kind of thinking affects hiring decisions when judging a job-seeker by the schools he or she attended.

I remember a conversation I had with Dr. Vannevar Bush, retired president of M.I.T. and former head of the War Production Board during World War II. He was working at the Carnegie Institute's Department of Terrestrial Magnetism in Washington, D.C., and, in cooperation with my friend Dr. Ralph Shaw, the head librarian of the Department of Agriculture, was developing the "Memex," a machine that was eventually expected to store all of the world's knowledge photographically on a single disk, available for instant recall. I was negotiating to build some parts of the system.

It was a far-seeing idea, for with the invention of CD-ROM, Bush's vision is well on the way to reality, and while the storage medium at present is not photographic but magnetic, it is my belief that laser-driven microphotography will eventually beat out magnetics, proving Bush especially prescient. (AT&T recently announced the invention of a new magneto-optical system that could store information at a hundred times the amount on a CD-ROM disk.[45])

This brilliant man pointed out to me in one of our meetings that, of the twenty top people who had run the non-military effort in World War II, not one had attended a major educational institution for his or her undergraduate work. Each of them had found a mentor at the undergraduate level in a small college who had inspired them to accomplishment in later life. Compare this with the despair that many children and parents feel when their child does not "make Harvard," or Yale or Princeton or what have you. Most will be far better off finding an undergraduate institution where their issue will get some personal attention to help fulfill themselves intellectually and scholastically.

To make up one's mind as to the worth of persons based on their schools, religious, or political background and beliefs is wrong. In business it can be especially risky. Toxic executives latch on to popular criteria to create a set of easy values which they can employ in order to relieve themselves of the energy-consuming effort of *thinking*. My pecan man made bad judgments about people, politics, and cars.

Watch the film *Roger & Me*. It tells how the super-religious mayor of Flint, Michigan, after GM closed down local plants throwing some eight thousand people out of work, paid an evangelist, Robert Schuller, $20,000 to come to Flint and pray for a miracle. He also persuaded the city to back the building of an upscale hotel, a Hyatt Regency, to the tune of $14 million.

Next, with the help of God, Pat Boone, and a *real* kook, Anita Bryant, he decided that Flint, Michigan, could be made into a tourist's delight and spent $100 million to build the huge "Auto World," at something called the "Water Street Pavilion," which was opened with Donny and Marie Osmond performing. It closed in six months due to lack of visitors and the Hyatt went in the tank soon after.[46]

THE TOADY T.E.

Perhaps the most reprehensible of the toxic executive types are the toadies—those who grovel their way up the corporate ladder. Watch them at work. They go through a complete psychological change when the bosses show up. "Yes*sir*, J.B.," says the sycophantic junior executive toady to the CEO. The CEO could be wrong nine out of ten times, but this member of the toady troop will never criticize. He's got oil in his voice, oil on his hair, and greasy sweat on his hands has this "guido," as he slides and slithers his way to the top, sans talent, sans ideas, sans everything except his obsequiousness. Incredibly, with some executives it pays off.

For more about this fascinating trait, read Owen Edward's *Upward Nobility: How to Succeed in Business Without Losing Your Soul*.[47] He describes the "Toady Transformation," a metastasis that overtakes the professional sycophant whenever the boss enters the room: "Almost magically, the toady will manage to distance himself from his colleagues, however chummy he was just seconds before, and will somehow give the impression that he'd only been talking with these people to keep them from degenerating into the rebellious slackers they naturally are."

Jack Kemp, (otherwise a great guy), approached Toadyville's city limits by publicly swallowing his public criticism of the Bush budget, a performance quickly bested when Dan Quayle, "to the nation's horror, hopped into the spotlight to posit that our nation's leader had never taken the 'no new taxes pledge.'"[48] That was sure to make even the most dedicated Toadymeister gag.

THE T.E. AS DECISION MAKER—NOT!

Making decisions is what executives do. Given a set of facts with a series of possible outcomes, the executive sorts through the facts, the sources of information, and the various future scenarios that have been posited, and then makes a decision. The better the decision series, the higher the responsibilities, and, in most situations, the higher the rewards.

In a unitary business, one with only one basic product line, the company's culture is built around that product. Here, institutional memory is the scepter wielded by the decision-maker king and most decisions are easily made. But if there is a basic change in the business—such as aggressive foreign competition—as American automobile companies faced—there is no institutional memory to fall back on and non-decision makers and decision-avoiders take over. That's exactly what happened at General Motors and other automobile manufactories—to their sorrow.

The Toxic Executive will often delegate away his decisionmaking authority to others to protect him- or herself if things don't work out.

Another T.E. decision-avoidance ploy is to hire a consultant to come up with answers and then the consultant takes the blame when things don't work out.

In growing a business by acquisition, the Toxic Executive will acquire companies that will yield immediate profits by resorting to tax and accounting trickery rather than to searching out the operating and marketing synergies that can be cashed in over time. When the tax and accounting benefits run out, so does he or she—off to the next job. But there are other aspects to decisionmaking.

One important aspect is the toxic *non*-decision maker—really the decision-avoider.

I cannot imagine how any operation can stay in business that is run by someone who can't make decisions. I even knew one executive who claimed that *not* making a decision was, in fact, a decision!

The primary job of an executive is to make decisions—all the time, hour after hour, day after day. The T.E. doesn't know this and will delay and delay. It can destroy morale. In the M&A area, cutting off a loss stream by shutting down a failed acquisition is a tough decision to make—

especially if the T.E. had made or pushed for the acquisition in the first place.

Without getting too deeply into behavioral theory as to why many people—not only executives—avoid making hard decisions, every executive should sit down and make a list of all the decisions that he or she is avoiding, call in the staff, and put a time and a date next to every decision that must be made.

In business, the toxic decision-avoider fails to set standards for performance to serve as a quantitative base for such issues as promotion, pay, and firing.

Western Publishing, which printed my magazines for many years, had a long document that followed each printing right from manuscript, through typescript, through proofreading, camera, platemaking, printing, binding, and shipping. Every single glitch was reported on those sheets. All the reworks, mistakes, and late deliveries had a person's name next to it who'd been responsible, and each mistake was costed out. Sometimes we were at fault and we were charged for it. If it was their fault, we got a credit. As we accumulated data we plotted the frequency of each kind of error, who made it, and why. As the years went by, the list got shorter and shorter. That's what the phrase "institutional memory" is all about. The T.E. non-decisionmaker will refuse or at least fail to use such a system—too often it is discovered that the glitches are the T.E.'s!

10

THE ADDICTED
TOXIC EXECUTIVE

Just about every executive is addicted to something!

There are two kinds of addiction: substance and process. The most common executive substance addictions are alcohol, nicotine, caffeine, food, and soft-core drugs such as sleeping pills.

The most common executive process addictions are sex, gambling, money, work, and religion.

The subject of sexual discrimination in the workplace has been treated in the previous chapter. Discrimination is different from harassment, though they often go hand in hand.

SEXUAL ADDICTION AND HARASSMENT

One of the most notorious and disgusting examples of sexual addiction and harassment is the "Gantlet of Terror" experience of some twenty-six female servicewomen, fourteen of them of commissioned officer rank, who were assaulted at the Navy's Tailhook Association meeting in the Las Vegas Hilton in September 1991. Later investigation discovered that some seventy naval and marine officers, some of senior rank, were involved.[1]

After months of stonewalling by the participants in the

harassment, including Rear Admiral Jack Snyder, who was present but not active at the scene (and who later lost his job),[2] an aide to the admiral, Navy Lieutenant Paula Coughlin, told of the terror she experienced as a line of naval officers pushed her down a hallway, felt her breasts, pushed her to the floor, and tried to get her panties off. Her appeals for help to fellow officers not only went unheeded but resulted in even more physical or sexual assault. After biting one attacker on the arm she escaped, but two officers barred her way from the hallway. "It was the most frightening experience in my life," said Coughlin, whose father before her had been a Navy aviator. "I thought, 'I have no control over these guys, I'm going to be gang-raped.'" She said that a friend from flight school had witnessed the attack but had done nothing to prevent it. "He saw the crowd fall on me, he saw me go to the ground, he heard them yelling 'admiral's aide,' and he turned to get a drink. That one thing bothers me more than anything," said Coughlin.[3]

The Department of the Navy's subsequent investigation was frustrated by universal stonewalling of those present or engaging in the assaults, on orders of their superiors not to cooperate with the investigation. This department-wide resistance exacerbated the Navy's problems. "We now have investigators investigating investigators," said Senator Sam Nunn, the Georgia Democrat who headed the Senate Armed Services Committee which was holding up some forty-five hundred Navy and Marine Corps promotions until the officers were cleared of involvement in the Tailhook affair.[4]

(Barron Hilton, chairman of Hilton Hotels, said that the hotel had canceled the Tailhook organization's reservation for its 1993 convention there in Las Vegas, where they have convened annually since 1972. He said, "They are no longer welcome.")[5]

From now on, Navy and Marine Corps violators of its anti-harassment rules will automatically be kicked out of the service.[6] The Navy has completely changed its training methods to curb sexual harassment and to stick to its "core values."[7] Secretary of the Navy H. Lawrence Garrison, who was at the hotel at the time but failed to press for action against the harassers, resigned his job, taking full responsibility for the Naval Investigative Service's failure to take action. In fact, the investigating agent assigned to help Coughlin identify her assaulters tried to date her, called her "Sweet Cakes,"[8] and had been suspended a year earlier for similar unprofessional conduct.[9]

The new acting Navy secretary has issued a "stand-down" order so that all naval units can take a day off for sexual harassment sensitivity training.[10]

And the lesson has not yet sunk in. Even after the Navy cut its association with Tailhook (they had spent some $200,000 transporting the flyboys to Las Vegas for the party), one Marine general sent a cable to his commanders asking for nominations for the "Tailhooker of the Year"![11]

Nearly ten months after the Las Vegas gantlet affair, a large banner was hoisted in the officers' mess at Miramar Naval Air Station on June 18, 1992, at the "Tomcat Follies," with words about oral sex and U.S. Representative Patricia Schroeder of Colorado, a senior member of the Armed Services Committee, who had criticized the fliers' conduct and the Navy's failure to follow up and discipline those involved. Two senior officers were relieved of their commands as a result.[12] Later, two more were relieved for a tasteless skit whose nature was evidently too crude to report in the press.[13] A joke in circulation at the time: In the Navy, someone announces a visit by "an officer and a gentleman." The response, "Which one should I see first?"

And two admirals who had given their entire lives to the Navy lost their permanent promotions to flag rank because of two separate sexual happenings: bad jokes about women in service, and the failure to discipline cadets at the Naval Academy when male midshipmen handcuffed a female midshipman to a urinal.[14]

The only people who would act as did the Tailhook Association members, the general looking for nominations for "Tailhooker of the Year," the officers at Miramar, and the midshipmen at the Naval Academy, are those most likely unsure of their own masculinity. Lacking normal libido drives, they use surrogates. That's why they're so good at shooting off guns, because their own personal guns won't go off. They handcuff women to urinals, hang signs about oral sex about highly respected women, all as substitutes for their own actual or assumed inability to perform adequately sexually. The Tailhook Association members drank out of a large plastic model of a rhinoceros penis at Las Vegas before assaulting those twenty-six women, because, as one observer noted, "None of them could probably find their own weenies without a microscope." (To give you some indication of the mind-set of Navy investigative personnel, in reporting the gantlet run, they changed the phrase "rhinoceros penis" to "obscene drink dispenser" in attempting to lighten the effect of the sordid affair.)[15]

That the Navy is exceedingly tolerant of sexual harassment is proved by the recent relief from command of the captain of the Navy salvage ship *Safeguard*. There, Lieutenant Commander Donald J. Oswald failed to take aggressive action to improve the treatment of women on board his ship after allegations of fraternization and sexual harassment were made. This was the second time that a *Safeguard* captain got into trouble that was related to sexual harassment. Back in 1987, the then-captain was relieved of duty because he joked over the ship's audio system about "selling" female sailors and had pressured female sailors for sex.

Sexual addiction and its accompanying harassment are not confined to American companies and offices; they are widespread. In one of its first actions, the newly formed European Community firmly addressed the issue of sexual harassment. On July 3, 1991, the twelve-nation bloc adopted a code of practice aimed at "protecting the dignity of women and men at work." According to the code, sexual harassment is defined as "unwanted conduct of a sexual nature, or other conduct based on sex affecting the dignity of women and men at work, including unwelcome physical, verbal or nonverbal conduct."

Studying the issue, a special commission created for the purpose, had found that sexual harassment was a problem for millions of women (and some men) in the European Community nations, with a potential for "devastating effects upon health, confidence, morale and performance."

As a result, the French government has recently put some teeth in its sexual harassment laws, making it illegal "to solicit by order, constraint or pressure, favors of a sexual nature from a subordinate at the office. Infractions are punishable by a year in jail and/or a fine of up to $16,000."[16]

But government office seems to shelter harassers. Six complaints have been filed by female employees of the Alcohol, Tobacco, and Firearms Bureau against their male superiors who solicited them for sex for preferred assignments, promotions, and so on, according to the *New York Times*, January 12, 1993.

SEXUAL HARASSMENT AND THE TERRITORIAL IMPERATIVE

According to Desmond Morris, there are 193 living species of monkeys and apes. One hundred and ninety-two of them are covered with hair. The exception is the naked ape, *Homo sapiens*.[17] On average, 97 percent of its genetic material is identical with its hairy relatives. So is much of its behavior.

Instinct drives mammalian males of many species to mark out their territories with urine or with scent from special glands often around the eyes. Read Robert Ardrey's *The Territorial Imperative* to learn why this has, for the past twenty million years or so, reinforced the processes of natural selection that has made animals, including man, what they are today.

The remnants of these marking instincts—no matter

how tattered and torn by the civilizing of the species *Homo sapiens*—are still there in all of us.

Territorial defensive action specifics are generally confined to members of the same species or subspecies. A male baboon, after chasing off an interloper and thus establishing his dominance, immediately mounts the nearest female. She responds sexually to his territorial control. They thus pass on to their progeny, through their genes, the territorial dominance.

Baboons establish their constantly changing territories based on life threats—leopards, chimpanzees, lions—and the food supply, which varies by subspecies, geography, and other factors. While baboons do not seem to mark their territories, each group (or its leaders) seems to know where its territories begin and end, as do interlopers.

But a modern businessman may be confused. For example, a new office manager tours his territory but is not allowed to piss in the corners. He thus leaves no marks except a posted, pyramidal organization chart showing his dominance, which does turn on some females. But, given a same-sex aggressor, his instincts are still not only to repel the invader, but, after victory, to mount the nearest female. However, our office manager has five basic preventives against such instant gratification: first, our clothing gets in the way of open-office sex; second, office furniture is not designed to encourage the missionary-position coital processes; third, one female baboon looks pretty much like another, which is not true in the world of female *Homo sapiens*; fourth, 20 percent—perhaps more in the office environment—are not heterosexual, something so far unknown or unidentified in the other-than-man hominid world; fifth, modern office mores condemn such displays and the economic imperative gets in the way of the territorial imperative—he'll lose his fucking job.

But his libido may be such that he may not wait for such a same-sex invasion and the subsequent confrontation to become sexually aggressive and may engage in forced economic couching, as in Hollywood.

Esther Williams, film star of the forties and fifties, known for her choreography in bathing suits, said that sexual harassment was commonplace in Hollywood when she was making movies. She named Billy Rose and Morton Downey, Sr., father of the loudmouthed TV and radio talk show host, as career harassers. "We kept our mouths shut then, otherwise we couldn't get another job." She was a seventeen-year-old starlet when, standing next to Downey, he bragged about the size of his genitals and told her what he wanted to do to her in private. "I hated it, but I couldn't complain."[18]

ARENA BEHAVIOR

"Through the device of territory," writes Ardrey in *The Hunting Hypothesis*, "the competition for exclusive bits of real estate among competing males was matched in the female by sexual unresponsiveness to any but the landed gentry. Through the device of dominance in a species living in social groups, only those males reaching the highest rungs of the social [territorial] hierarchy might receive the sexual franchise."

The behavior of many species is often dictated by the display arena. Whether turkeys or turtles, monkeys or men, the parading of male characteristics to entice a female is common to thousands of species. The male, 99.9 percent of the time, is the more gaudy. It is therefore not understood how in recent times yuppies in Brooks Brothers' slope-shouldered suits have proved attractive to so many brightly clad, overdressed, over-cosmeticized females, except for his position on the pyramidal organization chart.

U.S. Senator Jesse Helms wants government to regulate not only what goes on between the sexes in their bedrooms, but what kind of art they should see. But most modern Americans feel that their sex lives are their own business and no one else's. But our society is beginning to condemn display and gratification of the aggressive male sexual instinct *outside* of the bedroom, specifically in the workplace. There, the two sexes are thrown together and must cohabit at work to preserve their economic life.

In order that your workplace discourages sexual harassment, make sure that management notifies its employees of the company's policy. The poster, "Sexual Harassment in Our Workplace: Your Legal Rights," is available for $2.50 from the Women's Legal Defense Fund, (202) 296-2600. Post it over the water cooler. And react fast if you're harassed: "Was that a remark you would have made to your mother, your sister, daughter, aunt, or wife?" And watch your body language. Make sure that you do not appear yielding and pleased when you are resentful and angry. If it's really offensive write the harasser a note asking him to cease and desist and keep a copy. (More hints later.)

Many, many, male (and a few female) executives do not yet fully understand how far the reaction to sexual aggression (read *harassment*) has come. Such harassment has proven personally, and in some cases financially embarrassing to many men and some few women. Lately, it has proved financially embarrassing to a few of our larger corporations.

THE FIRST SEXUAL HARASSMENT CLASS ACTION

In late 1991, after a preliminary hearing, we had the beginnings of the nation's first-ever sexual harassment class action. Instead of one woman complaining, the complaint stated that at least one hundred women had been subjected to a continuum of sexually based hostility in their work environment. The class action was approved for trial by a federal judge in Minneapolis.

Earlier, at a trial in May 1991, the plaintiffs had argued that there had been a pattern of sexual harassment at Eveleth Taconite Company a unit of Ogelbay Norton Company of Cleveland. The plaintiff's attorneys exhibited a book of about sixty nude photos, amateur cartoons, and graffiti appearing widely at the Eveleth facility and in supervisors' offices.

If the women win (the case is still in the courts as of this writing), it could be a major financial blow to Eveleth and will certainly result in more class-action suits being filed, perhaps by the hundreds if not the thousands across the United States.[19]

For instance, while not a class action, in Washington, D.C., a female bartender, Simone Locklear, working within shouting distance of the Capitol, won a $50,000 award in a sexual harassment case: $25,000 for "personal embarrassment, humiliation and indignity," and another $25,000 for her "anguish, pain and suffering." Punitive damages could also have been assessed in addition against the defendant, a Capitol Hill restaurant, Dubliner's, but were not. She had been sexually harassed by the general manager and other senior employees.

After she filed the complaint, the owners hired a detective to watch her and then fired her for "giving away drinks," but the court ruled that the action was retaliative.

Here are a few typical sexual harassment cases that confirm the widespread incidence of sexual harassment in the workplace and the growing cost to the companies that do not police it properly.

In *O'Dell v. Basabe*, an Idaho jury, under both common law and Idaho's Human Rights Act, ruled in favor of O'Dell, a personnel director at a J. R. Simplot Company unit. He was awarded $420,500 plus $1 million in punitive damages because he was fired for providing investigative support to a woman who had complained to him of sexual harassment by the company's president.

The K mart Corporation lost $3.2 million in a jury award. The Bank of America, United States Steel, the Black Clawson Company, New York Telephone, and many more companies have been found liable for the sexual harassment acts of their employees under the doctrine of *respondeat superior*, which makes the company responsible for the conduct of its employees as its agents even when the harassment contravened written policies and upper management was provably unaware of the harassment itself. In the Clawson case, it was found that the company's open-door policy was not sufficient to prevent harassment, that it was unreasonable to assume that lower-echelon women would automatically contact the company president with complaints of sexual harassment.

The U.S. Supreme Court recently struck a blow for justice in the case of a former Georgia high school student who was subject to continuous sexual harassment by a teacher and was eventually pressured into having sex. The school administrators and other teachers knew of the harassment but took no action; in fact, they tried to dissuade the girl from filing an action in federal court. The school board, supported by the Bush administration, argued that such victims were not entitled to money damages but were limited to obtaining orders prohibiting such conduct in the future. Lower courts had agreed, but the Supreme Court did not, opening the way to claims for money damages for acts of harassment against students of schools that receive Title IX federal funds.[20]

Thousands of women are subject to near-continuous sexual harassment. Only a very few ever get compensated for it. However, some have. If you are being harassed (man or woman), you should know the law. There are five books currently on the market that explain the rules. Here's how to collect damages:

Document the evidence. Keep a diary and record the offensive behavior, when it occurred, and who the aggressor was. Keep any notes, letters, or phone messages you receive.

Talk to co-workers to see if any have experienced similar behavior or have witnessed your problems. (Be careful here—it could lead to a suit for character defamation if names are named and the harassment is not proved. It can also lose you your job.)

Talk to the EEOC officer in your company or, if there is

none, to your supervisor. If the harasser is your boss, report it to his superior. If you must go outside the company, call the EEOC office in your area. (For information on all EEOC-enforced laws, call 800-USA-EEOC)

For general advice, try the 9-to-5 Job Problem Hotline, a service of the Cleveland-based 9-to-5 National Association of Working Women, at 800-522-0925.[21] And of five recent books on the subject which are reviewed by *Business Week*, *Sexual Harassment on the Job* is recommended as the best reference work, as it has a state-by-state run-down on harassment law.[22]

So-called "third-party harassment" actions are coming to the fore. Usually involving women being harrassed by customers, clients, suppliers and the like, women have been extremely reluctant to complain because of the economic effect on their employers and the threat to their careers. However some have taken too much and have taken action.

Catherine Holmes, an account supervisor at a New York advertising agency, was pursued by a senior vice president of Trans World Airlines, complained about it and as a result was fired at the behest of the harassing official. She has sued the agency, TWA, and the official for more than $2.2 million.

And Carol Powell, a blackjack dealer at a Hilton Hotel in Las Vegas, has sued because she was fired for complaining about sexual harassment by gamblers and resisting the advances of one gambler. Her superiors failed to take any action to ameliorate the situation.

We predict that there will be many more such suits.

THE CASANOVA COMPLEX

In a book called *The Casanova Complex*, Peter Trachtenberg writes of compulsive lovers, womanizers, those addicted to sex.

Trachtenberg breaks them down into different kinds of sexual addicts: Hitters, Drifters, Romantics, Nesters, Jugglers, and Tomcats. I've known them all, several in a mirror.

Borrowing Trachtenberg's topology, but not necessarily his descriptions, taking them each in turn, and moving them into the workplace, I make the following observations based on my own experiences:

The Hitters

I start with the worst, the most toxic (and the most common) of the lot, the "Hitters." They must "hit" on every "broad" that comes along. They are the lowest of the low, totally incapable of commitment or intimacy (and are often impotent unless stimulated by strange doings.) Hitters are the guerrillas of the war between the sexes. They're the ones who make crude remarks, tell crude jokes with sexual themes or at least overtones, all in the dissolved hope of sexual conquest. Women, for the Hitters, are solely sexual objects.

Hitters are cold-mannered, hoping to find someone who is into guilt and self-punishment. They are deliberate in their pursuits, like hyenas dogging herds of gazelles to take down injured waifs.

Like evangelists, the Hitters need witnesses. Each must parade his conquests before his fellow Hitters. They keep score. For women in the workplace, I issue a warning: These are dangerous men whose entire ego is wrapped up in the conquest. Beware of encouragement or acceptance which is followed by denial. Loss of control of a relationship is devastating to the Hitter. What is even more dangerous is the inevitable public breakup in a Hitter-derived relationship. With his ego shattered, the relationship can become violent. Be very careful with the office Hitter. He can turn into a hit man, if not for your life (which happens), at least for your job.

The Drifters

Drifters prey on the love-starved and sexually deprived. They use targets of opportunity such as love- and affection-starved divorcees. Their main talent is persistence, like wolves following a sleigh in the dead of winter. Into statistics, they know they'll get a lot of refusals but they get a lot of sex. To Drifters, the chase is important, the conquest not.

I once watched a disappointed wild-turkey hunter pay a farmer to let him shoot a tame peacock, which he promptly fed to his dog. That's what Drifters are like.

The Romantics

Like the opening to *Tale of Two Cities*, the Romantics are either the best of the lot or the worst of the lot.

The problem with most Romantics in the work environment is the brevity of the relationship. High on spirituality, their relationships are low on reality. Often growing out of chance proximity or shared endeavor, their hastily entered affairs are just as hastily terminated. Unfortunately, long-lasting, companionate love never develops, resentments are high, and office or plant rhythms are disturbed. This can really impact the bottom line. For this reason, and the growing number of sexual harassment cases against businesses, more and more companies are forbidding intra-office romance.

I disagree with Trachtenberg's thesis that romantic love begins in bed, that premature ejaculation or an episode of impotence can kill that love at its inception. On the contrary, to Romantics, all is forgivable. It is only when the lovers discover that they are stuck with a continuum of perfidy and deceit on one side or the other, or even both, that forgiveness ends as well. When this happens, the Romantics' very souls turn to mush, and *sploop*, it's over.

Romantics can never isolate themselves, nor even forgo their romanticism in keeping with Lord Byron's observation that "a true voluptuary will never abandon his mind to the grossness of reality." To an incurable Romantic, all the world's a Camelot, all men are Arthurs, all women Guineveres, and no Lancelots are ever about. Most Romantics, no matter how badly treated by time, by man, or by woman, would never forget or regret those grand and glorious moments with a mate of choice, who responded in eye and lip and body and mind.

To hell with the bottom line!

The Nesters

For the nesters, sex is not the driving element. It's the "cuddle-down" syndrome, in which one just wants a warm body next to one for reasons that are buried in the libido, in experiences in the womb, in genes, in growing up.

In the office, everyone recognizes the Hitter, the Drifter, and the Romantic, but the Nester is hard to identify. Besides, the male Nester is most women's dream man, as Dear Abbey discovered in her famous survey in which 60 percent of the women asked said they preferred a companionate over a sexual relationship. But the male nester wants to crawl inside the relationship, to return to the very womb from which he came, looking always for that so-comforting warmth so rudely disturbed by the trauma of birthing. It soon turns out not to be enough. Long-term relationships require more than just warmth.

The Jugglers

Dr. Herman Tarnower, author of *The Complete Scarsdale Medical Diet*, juggled many women. One woman didn't like it. I mean she *really* didn't like it. She shot him to death.

Tarnower kept two affairs going at once, with both women's clothes in his closets, each knowing of the other, and each knowing that he had still other affairs. Both served as bedmates and amanuenses as he alternated vacations with them. But one of them, Jean Harris, dean or headmistress of the chichi Madeira School, didn't like his failing attentions. She was being dumped for a younger woman, after a fifteen-year relationship with this nasty old man. She was especially hurt since she'd helped to make him rich.

An intellectual of some proportions, promised a marriage for which she had broken up her home, who only argued with Tarnower over the use of the subjunctive, Jean Harris bought a pistol in Virginia, drove to New York, and shot Tarnower. For what many consider to be a richly deserved death, Harris received a fifteen-year prison sentence and served twelve years of it before being pardoned by Governor Mario Cuomo.

Jugglers are seldom if ever monogamous. Constantly on the make, they rarely sleep alone. Jugglers seem to like complicated love affairs and, from my experience, complicated *business* affairs as well.

Unlike most jugglers, Tarnower had evidently talked marriage to both women. Jean Harris, regardless of her high position and accomplishments, evidently had very low self-esteem. She had humbled herself to someone who was obviously a womanizing old bastard who enjoyed his dominance.

Jugglers usually assure everyone that they do not believe in monogamy: "No way can one woman expect to satisfy me for my whole life." They are proudly polygynous. But in this Age of AIDS, their polygyny can no longer be flaunted, for the T.E. Juggler who brings home the bacon may also bring home Death.

Jugglers' targets in the office are usually shy, self-effacing women of low self-esteem. Those women must learn to identify the T.E. Juggler and stay away.

On his part, he'd better be careful. The National Rifle Association, buying the votes of cash-hungry congress-people and state legislators, panders to those millions of men whose own personal guns don't go off. These men have found a surrogate for their sexual impotence in rifle and pistol, which *do* go off for them. With huge amounts of money from these members, which include a number of past presidents of the United States, the NRA has made the purchase and transportation of deadly weapons through-out the land very, very easy. A discarded or deceived lover of either sex may react violently, as did Jean Harris. She, faced with the breakup of her personality, and sustained by prescription pills given by her lover-physician, finally snapped, just like that piece of Silly Putty when hit by a hammer, and bought a gun made easily purchaseable[22] by the National Rifle Association's lobbying and support of Virginia's state legislators.

The Tomcats

Frank Sinatra best fulfills the definition of a Tomcat. In spite of his active extramarital love life, which was well known to all, he always came back to his wife, Nancy, even after his marriage to Ava Gardner and its inevitable breakup.

Tomcats have homes and families. They have the best of both worlds—sexual variety and the comforts of domestic-ity—seemingly without suffering the guilt that is usually one of the chief consequences of leading a double life.

Tomcats are different from one-time or crisis adulterers. They are sexually addicted far more than some of the other candidates outlined here. Many can maintain long-term home relationships and still "cat-about" town. "He is a cautious man who nevertheless takes appalling risks with his marriage and career," writes Trachtenberg. Marion Barry, mayor of Washington, D.C., was of that kind.

In the Washington, D.C., area you see the suburbanite Tomcats in urban restaurants, and the urban Tomcats in suburban restaurants. And there are thousands of Tomcats who use their offices and corporate-maintained apart-ments for assignments with their maids-of-the-moment.

I used to play the piano and sing in a little restaurant out near Greenwich, Connecticut, called the Byram River Bea-gle Club. It was owned and run by Eddie White, the father of one of my high school friends, Betty White. I remember one Tomcat who showed up there at the Club on a Satur-day night who lived in Scarsdale. I used to caddie for him at the Scarsdale Golf Club. His name was Beasley. I said, "Hi, Mr. Beasley!" He was dumbfounded to see me way out there and didn't return my greeting, which rather surprised me.

I was only seventeen or so. But the redheaded bimbo he was nuzzling was also surprised, because she kept looking at him and repeating, "Beasley?" I did the best I could to dissemble, but the damage was done. I think he could have killed me. I think that Eddie White could have too. (Come to think of it, Eddie never had me back.)

It gets really complex when a married Tomcat is dating two different women in the same office. For some reason Tomcats think they can keep that a secret. But it's like your paycheck. Everybody knows how much it is. (It's also a good way to get fired.)

I knew one Tomcat T.E. who was always bragging about his in-office conquests, naming people I knew, something that no gentleman ever does. He also said that he could not have an orgasm with his wife unless he had slept earlier that day or evening with another woman.

Any way you slice it, fooling around in the office is toxic behavior for anyone, married or unmarried. But especially so for married people of either sex. Tomcat executives are toxic executives and can cause all kinds of trouble that impacts the bottom line.

Many athletes are Tomcats and are poor role models for youth. Mike Tyson's conviction for his rape of a Miss Black America candidate and Wilt Chamberlain's admission or bragging that he'd slept with twenty thousand women are only two conspicuous examples of the treatment accorded black women by black athletes. Haliford Fairchild, secretary of the general assembly of the Association of Black Psychologists, believes that many black men, symbolized in many ways by the black male athlete, have been brought into and have bought into a power system in which black women have been devalued. "That's because we have been disenfranchised for so many generations that we try harder to be like the dominant male model in American

society, and the dominant male model is the white male,"
he explains.[23]

OFFICE ROMANCES

Office romances can destroy an operation. I employed one
male office manager who, against company policy, was
dating his female assistant, who also had the job of handling the mail. For years my mail had been opened,
logged, and on my desk by 9:30 A.M. One day I noticed that
my mail wasn't getting to me until 11:00 A.M. or even later.
Why? I discovered that he let her open the mail by hand at
her desk rather than use the automatic letter opener in the
back room, or even use a common letter opener. He said
she was "afraid of them." I asked if he was dating her. He
said yes, but that he'd never even kissed her. But that was
the end of him and her, and the mail was soon on my desk
at 9:30 A.M. He went to work for the National Rifle Association, so his statement about never kissing her was probably
true.

THE WORKAHOLIC

The workaholic is as addicted to work as others are to sex,
alcohol, or drugs. Most workaholics are not productive.
They are of several types.

Type One workaholics are also insomniacs. They can't
sleep at night, so they work. They leave each evening with
a briefcase loaded with take-home work and make their
peers, subordinates, and some superiors look lazy by com-
parison. I learned not to trust them or their work because it
was often flawed. Why? Because in research or consulting
operations, access to complementary talents and to support talent such as mathematicians and statisticians is a
near-necessity. After one particularly bitter experience, I
said, "God, please deliver me from hardworking people."

The most productive people are those who work steadily during the day and then spend a relaxed evening with their family, who go camping or sailing (as I did) on weekends, and who arrive Monday morning rested and alert, rather than exhausted and brain-dead. I also discovered that when there *was* a rush job that did require long hours, they seemed to have the necessary energy reserves, where the workaholics did not.

Type Two workaholics are the task-oriented. Given an assignment, they're off and running without doing the necessary planning. They go at it hammer and tongs until it's done. Because they put their feet in gear before their brain, much of their output must be reworked. They exhaust their workmates and usually the funds. After completing the project, they are then no good for a month. In the long run they are inefficient.

Type Three workaholics goof off until the very last minute and then work twenty-four hours a day to finish the project. They give the boss and the company the vapors waiting for the results. This behavior may or may not be planned to gain attention. Most are Pollyannas. Some do bad work.

Type Four workaholics are the real phonies. They only *act* hardworking. I had one who came to my office about 6:30 P.M. one evening when most everybody else had left and said, "Mr. Reed, can (sic) I borrow your briefcase? I have some work to take home." Since he was in charge of the postage machine, petty cash, and the like, the next morning I had my head accountant start an audit. Sure enough, he'd been hitting the postage and petty cash accounts for about a hundred bucks a week.

The tragedy of the workaholics of all types is the price that their families pay. The male (and recently, the female workaholic) gets up early and comes home late.[24] He or she seldom if ever gets to see or play with the kids—one of the great joys of parenting. Their priorities are wrong. They provide for their kids economically while they deprive them parentally. More and more we are discovering that the workaholic parents' household is a de facto parentless household and a source of some of our vast social troubles.

THE SOBER ALCOHOLIC

There are two kinds of alcoholics: sober (not drinking) and active (drinking). Before talking about the second kind, here a few words about the first.

The finest man I ever knew in all my life was an alcoholic who came to work for me under the precondition that he join Alcoholics Anonymous, which he did that same day, and never took another drink. He wound up a wealthy man and a pillar of the community.

Emmet Deady knew poetry, philosophy, engineering, just about everything. Together, we built a business that had profits seventeen out of eighteen years. I knew him to be a genius at just about anything he attempted.

It is difficult for a heterosexual male to say that he loved another male, but I simply loved Emmet Deady. If pushed, I believe I could recall every moment of the eighteen years we spent together, reciting poetry, trading philosophies, discussing the people who were shaping our lives, and we theirs.

What a marvelous man. In eighteen years, as I like to say, "we never had an argument." No one believes me, so I make some up. But the truth is we never did. Strange.

I learned that his father before him was an alcoholic, and both of the kids from his first marriage were alcoholics.

I really wish that I believed in heaven so I could see Emmet again. I'd like to tell him how brilliant he was, how he always made me look good. And how, even when he disagreed with me as to a course of action, he cast aside his personal opinions and bought mine as I had bought his in the past.

For proud and gifted men, in that one trait alone, must be where greatness lies.

The stresses of modern business life are such that it creates alcoholism in even the best of us, and in the most unlikely circumstances. Some of the very best men and women in any organization are incipient alcoholics. It is a sickness that not only can be cured, but also can be prevented. Every organization of any size should have prevention as well as cure programs. Not infrequently the alcohol habit is set deeper by well-intentioned but naive disciplinary actions. Cure and prevention are work for trained people.

THE ACTIVE ALCOHOLIC

Active alcoholics are everywhere. Many of them are borderline cases whose sickness has not advanced to the point of detection. Nevertheless, even at this pre-alkie stage, they can ruin their own and others' lives.

Inside all of us are resentments that we suppress because of the economic imperative. Under the influence of alcohol, those resentments emerge. They must have targets. Many a secretary or junior executive, completely unaware of a boss's problems with the alcohol drug, has taken a continuum of unnecessary abuse, perhaps for years.

In seeking contracts from the Maritime Commission, I had to deal with a contracting officer who, I learned years later, was under the influence most of the day. I always wondered why he turned his face away when he talked to me and especially when he laughed. It was so I would not smell the liquor on his breath.

I thought it was *my* fault that he gave us such a hard time in negotiating the contracts. But it seems I was the only one that didn't know he was a drunk. The people who got contracts bought him lunch and drinks, lots of them. I guess I'm glad I never knew.

THE TOBACCOHOLIC

One of the worst offenders in the work environment today is the tobaccoholic. She or he is a user and is hooked on the tobacco drug in its various forms.

At Philadelphia's Hay Associates, after they bought my magazines, I had to meet with Hay's chief of personnel, an Australian woman, with several assistants jammed into a tiny office. She had hornswoggled a tiny, tiny, conference room with no windows and no ventilation. I was required to do business with her in that little tiny conference room, for the Hay rules said I could make no hires, clerical or otherwise, without getting them "tested," which meant I had to meet with her to discuss test scores.

Well, she smoked. Boy did she ever. I politely asked her to hold up the cigarettes at least in that little tiny conference room and she refused. She wouldn't meet in my office which was four times the size of her conference room and had windows and ventilation, even when I offered to suspend my no-smoking rules. So I had to meet in that stupid little room sometimes for hours, going over pre-hire test ratings and later performance ratings of some of my people and getting gassed.

I could never discover why such an unsympathetic person would be in charge of *personnel*! But I have gone back over our relationship and asked myself if my own behavior was responsible for hers. I now know that I could have handled it better. I could have offered to try to get her a larger office, for instance. I should not have argued with her about her dopey tests! Yeah. I could have done better!

Also at Hay Associates, Leonard Zweig, who took over the running of my *Mergers & Acquisitions* and *Directors & Boards* magazines, hired an outside consultant to plan a direct-mail campaign. Both Zweig and the consultant were sinks of ignorance when it came to knowledge of the merger marketplace and how to get subscriptions. I was forced to meet with Zweig—again in a windowless, airless conference room—along with this Madison Avenue hot-shot, who sucked on cigarettes the whole time, subjecting all of us to massive tobacco trauma. In spite of my informal understanding with Hay that I would not have to attend meetings with cigarette smokers, Zweig, himself a non-smoker, never made Mr. Madison Avenue quit. We also never got any significant subscription flow from him. They finally dumped the cigarette sucker and reverted to my promotional programs, which were three to four times as productive.

I had similar problems with some board meetings. It has always been an imposition on a nonsmoker for anyone to smoke during a board meeting. Today it is not as much of a problem. Twenty years ago, installation of desmoke appa-ratus in the board room or conference room was one of the costs of my service. Today, at least in the United States, boardroom smokers are a rarity and, bank on it, they're bound to be T.E.s!

The enormous cash flows available from a continuum of hundreds of millions of addicted users are funneled through firms like Henry Kravis's RJR Nabisco, Robert Preston Tisch's P. Lorillard, and Hamish Maxwell's Philip Morris Companies to create more addicts, many of whom will die an early and painful death—in the United States alone, four hundred thousand per year. The right to die that horrible death is promoted by advertising agencies targeting illiterate minorities and children[25] by fraud, said a recent U.S. Supreme Court decision.[26] "There's ample information that tobacco companies misrepresented them-selves, says the anti-smoking lobby. But lobbyists from the Tobacco Institute, buying votes of both liberal and conser-vative addicts in the legislatures at the local and national level, are continuing to fight.

The cash flows from ignorant addicts all over the world are awesome. Kravis, Tisch, Maxwell, and the like are using them to buy up prime companies all over the world. (It seems wrong that cash flows from tobacco sales, which kill 450,000 Americans annually, should allow people like

Robert Preston Tisch to buy up control, not only of CBS, but of the N.Y. Giants.)

Drawing on some fifty recent research reports on the effects of secondhand smoke, the Environmental Protection Agency recently reported that environmental tobacco smoke causes 3,000 lung cancer deaths per year, contributes to 150,000 to 300,000 respiratory infections in babies, triggers 8,000 to 26,000 new cases of asthma in previously unaffected kids, and exacerbates symptoms in 400,000 to 1 million asthmatic children. The report covers only the respiratory effects. Other sources report that heart attack, triggered by passive smoking, causes another 35,000 deaths per year.[27]

THE DRUGAHOLIC T.E.

There are several types of drugaholic T.E.s. The most common type, in the seventies and eighties, were the yuppie users of marijuana and cocaine. Dealing with an executive who gets high on cocaine once or twice a year may not be a problem except for him or her. But dealing with an executive taking three or four hits of cocaine a day can be a problem for subordinates, peers, and superiors alike. Only a skilled observer or another user can distinguish a drug-caused mood swing from one caused by psychological and/or physiological trauma. Early detection and therapeutic programs for all mood-altering drugs are getting to be more acceptable on the shop floor, in transportation, and in sports, but very little has been accomplished in the office environment.

For reasons that I have never understood, most labor unions are opposed to detection testing for drug use. Testing has not yet reached business, nor much of government, but I predict it will.

Like a Typhoid Mary, a drug user can infect others—especially if in a position of power or if unusually successful.

Marijuana is not supposed to be habit-forming, but can create psychological dependency. In musicians, it changes perceptions of the beat so that it seems to come to them more slowly. Therefore more notes can be played. It can work the same way in the office. Since it alters perceptions, it alters behavior. Any personality change of short duration is not only hard on the users but also on those with whom they interact—especially if they have no idea of the source of the mood change.

In our universe of users and abusers, we also have tens of thousands of Americans who live from pill to pill, whose medicine cabinets offer release from the reality of living.

Here again, such dependencies can be treated by those skilled in the field. IBM has estimated that to put a top-ranking executive in a top-ranking job costs between $150,000 to $350,000 in training costs. This is lost when drugs take over—even "soft" drugs such as sleeping pills.

Compounding the problem is the use of drugs or alcohol to enhance performance. Drummer Gene Krupa said after being jailed for marijuana abuse, that he could never have played as well as he did without the influence of marijuana. And most of Oscar Wilde's greatest works, along with those of Alexander Pope and Matthew Arnold were reportedly penned under the influence of laudanum, a derivative of opium, readily available in the eighteenth and nineteenth centuries.

But Alcoholics Anonymous claims that most clean and sober recovering addicts report that eventually—after a period of adjustment—they learn to perform as well or better than in their using days.

SECTION THREE

THE **TOXIC** EXECUTIVE AND *YOU*

11

GETTING ALONG WITH THE **TOXIC** EXECUTIVE

As Homo economicus, modern man has become near-completely dependent on the workplace for survival and has lost the skills necessary to survive in the little wilderness left on earth. Asphalt jungle survival techniques are ill-adapted to a bosky wilderness. The public assistance support system, at least now in the early to mid-nineties, is too overloaded to support everyone who quits his or her job out of pique with the boss. As a result, many people are stuck in the prison of a job they hate, because they hate their boss and don't know what to do about it.

So far in reading this book one might assume that supporting a case for quitting a job under a T.E. might be easy. But it is not. People who have job-related personal problems will probably have them in nearly any job. Learning how to get along with a truly nasty boss is as necessary a skill in a secretary as knowing how to run a word processor, in a draftsman as understanding a CAD system, in a junior financial executive as doing a discounted cash flow.

There is no magic to any of it. Learning to get along with a boss, especially a toxic boss, can, like most skills, be acquired. But it takes work. Hard work. And lots of it. In *Coping with an Intolerable Boss*, Lombardo and McCall of the Center for Creative Leadership (CCL) report that of seventy-three successful executives surveyed, some 26 percent reported that they had never had what they saw as an intolerable boss. But 74 percent said they had. Some had more than one.

Those numbers are similar to my own informal, random surveys conducted, for example, on trains, planes, buses, public and private golf courses, and at board meetings. About one in four in my survey said they could not remember any toxic bosses. However, *all* of the women I interviewed (CCL did not classify responses by sex) said they had. One woman said she never had anything *but* toxic bosses! And most employees (especially women) believed that confrontation was not the route to take, as it would only exacerbate the situation and could get them fired.

Very few of either sex had any notion of how to cope with an intolerable boss except to quit. No one mentioned that they had tried to look at their *own* behavior as triggering toxic behavior in their boss. When asked if they would or could do a self-analysis the next time they had an intolerable boss, most said they'd give it a try. Some admitted they had made serious mistakes in bitching about their bosses, which got back to the boss and led to the employees either being fired or transferred. None mentioned that the bitched-about boss called them in to discuss their disaffection. Only one mentioned that her boss was "just like my father, always checking up on me." (The problem of transference, projecting onto authority figures in business one's experiences with authority figures in youth, has not been dealt with in any detail in this book. In my informal research I noted that when I approached this area I generated a great deal of discomfort in the interviewee and, not wanting to complicate an already troubled life, I dropped both formal and informal inquiry. My own father worked for me and we had no problems, so I was not an appropriate person to get deeply involved in such an inquiry, in any event. In addition, it is much more a problem of the toxic worker rather than the toxic executive.)

How about getting the toxic boss fired? This works in

many organizations where mission fulfillment, as in the military, is the responsibility of the senior officers. It is very easy to contrive a failed mission and to bring down the wrath of the command on a supposedly toxic officer and get him or her transferred or even reduced in rank. (This also seems to work where jobs are protected by civil service or union contract.)

The CCL survey produced one important finding: Many intolerable bosses had redeeming qualities. They had "business brilliance" or, surprisingly, "very good manners." One who got high marks for instruction as "best teacher" was also described as a "total ass"!

This anomaly was only partially confirmed by my own surveys. I was looking for T.E.s, not genii. Some people were very angry and could find very little good in a boss who they considered was a T.E. When I heard this I sometimes wondered which one was the toxic.

I was also looking for universalities—behavioral traits common to all T.E.s—and was disappointed when I found none. It made the book much more difficult to write.

This leads to the first getting-along clue: Look for the good first, and then concentrate on the bad.

Your mirror is by far the best tool in your Getting-Along-with-the-Toxic-Executive Kit. Look in it. Frequently. Ask yourself how *your* behavior might have triggered toxic behavior in others—especially superiors. Be sure that they demonstrate toxic behaviors with others before classifying them as toxic executives.

One major caveat before going on. If you have trouble with a T.E. boss and need guidance in resolving your problems, take great care whom you pick to help you. While it is nice to have emotional support to get you through tough times, seek out people who are wise and won't project *their* frustrations on *your* boss. If you can afford it, use a professional. If not, be sure to use someone who has a background in counseling. Generally spouses are bad candidates. They are so personally affected by what happens to you emotionally and economically that their judgments are often fallible. Further, it has been my experience that few will suggest that you look at your *own* behavior, in fear of your taking that as criticism. You want usable advice, not merely emotional support. Probably the best person to ask, failing a professional, is an executive of equivalent rank to your boss. A retired executive is a good source of advice if you really want to learn how to get along with a toxic executive boss.

Absent completely neurotic behavior, which exists but is rare in career executives, it is frequently the unhappy employee's perceptions that are at fault. Under stressful conditions, miscommunication in business is quite common. In a recession, that which is perceived as unfairness and favoritism may have resulted from a frantic effort to survive. Insensitive and demanding behavior? Yes. But toxic? No. Look for the behavior-drivers in the company's economics.

In some fields, executives are less sensitive to the persona of employees than others. Filmmaking, publishing, advertising, and high-tech development, in which creative processes drive the bottom line, have very high rates of stress and high rates of turnover. Creative executives, themselves highly temperamental, are not trained to handle temperamental people. To get along with such an executive, one must learn what works and what doesn't. Many successful executives in those businesses have learned how to handle others and themselves. The late Steve Ross of Time Warner had no formal training in business, but with dedication to participative management and reward sharing, he operated very successfully for many years in a creativity-driven environment.

Performance appraisals of employees are frequent causes of conflict with toxic executives. T.E.s sometimes use the process to protect themselves. They "tend to grade down protégés who threaten to eclipse them," says Marilyn Moats Kennedy. She also says that "some bosses use reviews to remind even star performers that there's room to improve . . . it's a remarkably stupid demotivating tactic because all the employee thinks about is the lack of recognition and the permanence of the written word."[1]

Getting along with a toxic executive who misuses the evaluative process is necessary, as there are many of them around. Anyone getting a bad performance appraisal should quietly ask for a written statement of the behaviors that led to the poor appraisal. Then ask for time to respond. Document the actions that refute the evaluation's negatives and make sure that your response becomes a part of the permanent record. Confining the confrontation to the written record rather than in a verbal head-to-head conflictual battle is less threatening to the T.E.

There *is* inexcusable unfairness, favoritism, and harassment in the workplace along with all the other ills recited in the preceding chapters. For many ills, especially sexual harassment and age, gender, and racial prejudices and actions, legal means of redress are available. They *must* be pursued. Anita Hill's problem was her failure to confront Clarence Thomas with how his actions made her *feel*. If she had, chances are there would have been an apology and an end to the problem. As it is, Justice Thomas, not overly endowed with either learning or intellect, was confused. He knew how she *looked*, but never knew how she *felt*. Because of Hill's failure, his past, present, and future actions and acts will forever bear the color of her charges. That's not only bad for her, it's bad for him, bad for the Supreme Court, and bad for the nation.

The object of this chapter is to teach the mistreatee not only how to change the behavior of the mistreator, but to change the mistreatee's own behavior so as not to encourage continued mistreatment.

WORK AS THERAPY

Working, for me, has been 99 percent enjoyable. However, I don't believe it has always been so for the people who worked *for* me.

This chapter, then, is my mea culpa and is dedicated to all of those long-suffering people who worked for me when I was young and insensitive, driven, and, yes, even untrusting when I had a need to trust. For it took me many years in business to discover, and even more years to apply, the notion that if you give out love and respect and trust in the business environment, the chances are excellent that you will get back love and respect and trust—maybe not the same day or week or month, but it will come back in kind. But give out hate, disrespect, and mistrust, and chances are it will come back in kind—maybe swiftly and maybe not for years, but you'll get it back in kind.

Here are the four basic rules for getting along with the toxic executive.

RULE NUMBER ONE

Many T.E.s are completely unaware of the effect that their actions have on the people around them. They must be told.

As the injured party, your first inclination may be to fight back and hurt the T.E. the way you've been hurt. But if you set goals for the kinds of behavioral change you wish to effect in the T.E., some battles may not be worth waging.

For instance, be sure that the executive's behavior is consistently cruel and unfeeling and not the result of some transitory illness, a problem at home, or temporary pressure from above.

If convinced that your boss is in fact a toxic executive, you should not complain to your mate, your mother, your brother, your fellow workers, or your minister. This kind of catharsis is dangerous because it doesn't eliminate the toxic behavior. Rather, you should complain to the T.E., who may very well be completely unaware of the effect of his or her behavior on your morale and your common objectives.

How you go about making that complaint without being

classed as a career complainer is one of the purposes of this chapter.

Short of a confrontation, there are many ways to let the T.E. know of your annoyance. For instance, giving peremptory orders rather than polite requests is typical of the T.E. In response, a small frown, a set of pursed lips, a shake of the head may be all it takes to communicate your displeasure, but no flouncing, no pouting, no sulking, no long-term silences. You want him or her to ask you, "What's wrong?" And then you must tell him or her what's bothering you. The typical answer "Oh, nothing, nothing" is a lie and you deserve everything bad that will happen to you after that. You are *enjoying* your mistreatment and deserve no sympathy. (In addition, in the workplace, you are a liability—communication is the lifeblood of successful operations.)

If you still cannot evoke the question "What's wrong?" try a slowdown—unless, of course, you're already slow. Be careful about combining contrivances. For instance, don't combine a slowdown with a sullen and uncommunicative "attitude." This could, should, and probably will get you fired or transferred. The slowdown alone should get the T.E.'s attention.

If none of this works, confrontation is probably necessary and inevitable. So get it over with as soon as possible. This leads us to rule number two.

RULE NUMBER TWO

Do not let things go. Do not let your resentments build up while the T.E.'s memory fades. Whatever you're going to do, do it now!

There is a kind of statute of limitations involved. If you let things go and then, in a confrontation, mention things that the T.E. did two weeks ago, or months or years ago, you're in trouble. They won't be recalled, believed, or apologized for. You don't like what the T.E. did or said? Lay it on him or her as soon as you cool off.

Some people wait until the annual Christmas party to dump on their boss. It's the "liquor over logic" syndrome at work. That's as bad as his or her dumping on you in the first place. Besides, it's unfair and can ruin the party for both of you and maybe some other people. Every hour, day, week, month, or year you delay in expressing your resentments dilutes your case and decreases the chances for ameliorative behavior. Further, many a T.E. will not face up to problems with valued subordinates until he or she *does* invoke a confrontation.

RULE NUMBER THREE

Confrontations are often necessary. It may be the only way. But play it cool.

My first wife, Stella, was a cum laude graduate of George Washington University. While getting her masters in library science, she worked as a children's librarian and had to work for an impossibly difficult woman. A real T.E.

In the tiny Aurora Hills library in Arlington, Virginia, with her desk within talking distance, head librarian Miss Ruth Thomas repeatedly insisted on yelling for my wife to come to her office. In front of patrons and library aides, it was completely unnecessary and out of place in the quiet of that small place.

The yelling made my wife miserable. But instead of fighting back and laying a little misery back on Thomas by telling her how the yelling made her *feel*, my wife used me as a surrogate for her resentments. She made *my* life miserable by daily or nightly recounting all her Thomas resentments. She refused to say anything to Thomas. After two years of this, I'd had enough and insisted that we go for counseling. There she was finally convinced of the necessity for confronting Thomas. So, very quietly, which was her manner, she asked not to be yelled at any more. She said it bothered the *patrons*! She never told Thomas how bad it made *her* feel!

And she paid the price for her failure. Thomas, responding to the plea that the *patrons* were disturbed, installed a buzzer, which she spent half the day pushing. My wife resented the buzzer even more than the yelling. But again, she never complained to Thomas about it, only to me. She never told Thomas how bad the yelling and buzzing made her feel.

(The Arlington County library system seemed to have no means of dealing with these kinds of situations, which are common in all institutions. Their history of encouraging corrective behavioral modification from vertically upward complaints is miserable. It makes a whiner out of you, and that's a quick way to get fired. Worse, it will follow you to your next job—if you ever find one.)

Much of it was my fault. I should never have listened to her for those two unhappy years. I should have insisted on counseling much earlier. I should have insisted on a full-scale confrontation. Perhaps more than one.

My wife, for all her education, never learned how to deal with the toxics in the work environment. She never learned how to get along with them. Very few people do. She never did face up to the necessity for a confrontation.

RULE NUMBER FOUR

Confrontations with T.E.s are always planned!

If there are resentments, hurt feelings, and disappointments caused by a continuum of inconsiderate acts by a T.E., and hints of your displeasure have been ignored, a confrontation is probably necessary. But confrontations are serious business. They must be planned. If not, they turn out to be accusational and conflictual. They will be resented and will not result in behavior modification on the part of the T.E., and that is the object of the confrontation.

THE TWENTY STEPS IN A CONTROLLED
CONFRONTATION: A CASE

Let us assume that you are a mature woman and have advanced over the years to a top job. You are the head of a major department. One day you are called into your male boss's office along with all your staff and greeted with the announcement that he has decided on a major reorganization of duties, responsibilities, and assignments in your department, all without discussion or input from you or anyone in your department. At the meeting, he hands out a typed plan with a new pyramidal chart and position descriptions. "Here's the plan. Now, are there any questions?"

You recognize immediately that it is a well-thought-out plan and, if and when implemented, will bring improvements in operations. However, as the senior non-consulted person, you're furious. You've lost face. You and your people are obviously annoyed and discomfited at the suddenness and the crassness of moving all of you around without discussion and consultation.

It will be quite natural for you and your people to work out your resentments by immediately opposing the plan. The fact is, no matter how brilliantly conceived, with a disaffected staff any such unilaterally conceived plan has a low chance of being successfully implemented.

But if you blow up in that meeting, you're dead. If you complain to *his* boss, you're dead. If you continue to pick away at the plan itself, you're dead. If you leave the meeting and then grumble about it with your peers and subordinates, you're dead. What you should realize is that the T.E. may not be aware of the annoyance he has caused you and your people. He may think that he has done you a favor, because he had the moxie not only to think it through, but to get it through the higher-ups.

There will be dozens of questions about how the new organization will work, but the principal question does not get asked: "Why were we not consulted before you made the plan?"

As you trudge back to your office, you remember that this is the fifth time he's done something like this. As you recall them, your resentment grows. You're fed up. You're tired of keeping it inside. If you don't do something about it, you know that you're going to blow.

But you're not going to blow. You are going to seek a nonaccusational, nonconflictual, orderly confrontation.

Here, step by step, is the process for creating such a confrontation that you or anyone else can use in that kind of situation.

Step One. After you cool down and get your hair done, you make a resolve that, by hook or by crook, you are going to get along with this guy. Not only because he's brilliant, but because *getting along with difficult people is part of your job.* You must *feel* this commitment to getting along with him.

Step Two. Ask for a one-on-one, phones-off, closed-door meeting. Don't tell the T.E. the nature of the meeting, no matter how many times you're asked. Say only that it is very important to you and to the company.

Ask for at least one hour. *More if you think you'll need it.* Make it at a time and place when the T.E., not you, will be most comfortable, probably in the T.E.'s office near the end of the day. But no restaurants or bars or booze. This is serious business. (Don't bring anyone with you. That's ganging up, and the meeting will go nowhere.)

Step Three. Be prepared. Make sure you know exactly what you want out of the meeting. Make handwritten notes of what you intend to cover. Put down the gut facts that support the gut issues. Don't start with "Why was I not consulted?" but perhaps "How long have you been working on the plan?"

Step Four. Using your notes, role-play the coming meeting with someone not involved. Try to find someone not overly sympathetic and certainly not a fellow worker. Use a professional if at all possible. If you use an in-house professional, make sure you get a promise of confidentiality before you open up. Keep your notes and role-play program private. (Your plan will differ depending on whether you are a subordinate, a superior, or a co-worker. However, most problems involve toxic superiors dumping on you, their subordinate.)

Step Five. Always begin with the assumption that the T.E. is doing the best he can, that his toxic behavior has its origins in the distant past, perhaps from trauma-inducing actions of toxic parents. Bear in mind that most T.E.s have an extremely vulnerable self-image and a need for affection. You might even find out he believes you hate him!

Step Six. Always assume that you have a *mutual* problem. You are going to persuade him that he has made your job more difficult and that your disaffection and that of others may be instrumental not only in defeating the implementation of the plan itself, but the goals he has set for himself.

Once the meeting begins, be careful in broaching the subject. Ease into it and build carefully toward a finish. You will never get behavior modification with such a person by bulldozing him. And you must expect annoyance. But you must not become angry when he attempts to protect his carefully wrought personality. Try to remember that much of the action of the T.E. is probably unconscious, that he probably hasn't lain awake nights figuring ways to hurt you. Make no threats. (That's a different kind of meeting.)

Take into consideration that the T.E. might be so pressured from above for immediate actions and results that he may have no time for compassionate behavior or time to think about people's feelings. If so, ask him. "Were you pressured from above to effect this reorganization? Is that the reason I was not consulted?"

He might admit that he was. Also, he might get resentful and answer that the company has no time for mollycoddling. No time for whiners. No time for malingerers who won't implement orders. He must be made to realize that he's really saying that the company has no time for the human side of enterprise. No time for pleasantries. You must discover why you were not consulted, since it is the precipitating cause of the meeting request.

If he blames it on pressure from upstairs, empathize while you get the details. But, as you empathize, don't chicken out. Remember that the T.E. is provably inconsiderate, arrogant, demanding, rude, unpleasant, and devious. Remind yourself that *you* didn't make him that way, but that he must change because it is affecting you. Further, repeat that making the plan work impacts his own plans for the future.

Step Seven. Begin by outlining your observations of his actions, and your opinions of the reactions of others. *No personal criticisms.* (Remember that no one enjoys receiving criticism, only giving it.) If you find yourself slipping into the critical mode, be sure you are critical of the *behavior*, not the *person*.

Step Eight. Ask the T.E. how he thought others felt. Did they act the way he expected? Is that the result he wanted? If not, what might he have done differently? As his behavior is questioned and challenged, he may try to back out of the rest of the meeting. Don't let him. Remind him that you were promised an hour.

Step Nine. Make sure the T.E. knows that you are both dedicated to your jobs, that everyone is, but that different people see the same things differently. Now you must describe how *you* felt and how *you* now feel. Describe next how you believe others felt and how they now feel. Let him know the level of your annoyance and displeasure.

If this really is the fifth time he did something like this and you intend to remind him of all five, make sure you have the facts down cold—for instance, dates, times, and people, and what happened. Keep your notes confidential, except if you role-play or rehearse.

If he is a super-toxic T.E., remind him of especially deprecatory, hostile, and demeaning statements that he has made, or actions he has taken.

Describe the reactions that you felt or observed. Don't quote others to support your case—that's ganging up and will be resented. Make some reasonable (nonexaggerated) estimate of the frequency of the toxic behavior. If he says that time constraints make him act that way, ask him if you can help to relieve him of some of his more pressing obligations.

Step Ten. Listen. If your memory is faulty, write down what he says. Make sure you understand his side and repeat it back to him to make sure. Then repeat how you feel, and how you know, from your observations, how others feel. If the T.E. gets defensive, which is quite natural, don't try to be an amateur analyst and use psychobabble to point that out to him. Don't accuse him of being a "controlling person," or that he has a "persecution complex," or is "paranoid." (Any or all of that might be true, but you're not going to change his behavior with such observations.)

Step Eleven. Keep the T.E.'s attention focused on the issue—the reorganization plan. If he wanders away verbally or philosophically, bring him back. Don't let him off the hook. Bring him back by recalling the scenes that brought this meeting about. Remind him of your joint goals. Point out, if true, that it is not a *personal* thing with you. If it is, make sure that you lay that out. If you have had a nonbusiness, personal relationship, or felt one, it is important for him to know it. If you're not sure, don't mention it.

Step Twelve. If he gets combative, ask why. How will that get him what he wants? Why set up a win-lose situation? Point out that the world will not end if he apologizes for not consulting you and the others as long as he promises no more solo decisionmaking where your department is concerned. If at all possible, maintain the dispassionate mood. If it gets to a discussion of *your* failings, do not get drawn in. Gently, or even humorously, if you can manage it, remind him that you asked for the meeting to explain *his* behavior, and that if he wants to discuss your behavior, he should call and make an appointment. Do not assume that he has read this book. Just as only well people voluntarily seek help from a psychiatrist, most T.E.s don't read books like this. However, if for some reason the T.E. refuses to meet or kicks you out of his office, buy him a copy of this book, mark the proper places, and leave it on his desk. He just *might* read it. After all, he might not know that he's considered to be a T.E.

Step Thirteen. Work everything toward the notion of participative management. Point out the potential cost of a bypassed staff, a disappointed, disregarded, *permanently* angry work force. Direct the discussion toward work team empowerment.[2] Point out that there are four kinds of people that together make up good management work teams—innovators, analyzers, organizers, and managers. No one executive can be all these people at once. This is especially important in restructuring operations, as the innovator dreams up the ideas, the analyzer takes them apart, the organizer puts them back together again, and the manager or executive makes them work. Most problems must be attacked and solved in a series of steps and tasks, performed by a group with complementary skills. No way should any one person try to fulfill all those functions. Why? Because most managers are bad as innovators. Innovators are bad as managers. And analyzers will never finish analyzing unless they are pushed by the others. Organizers are generally bad as either innovators or managers.

Try to remember the T.E.'s past successes and point out, if true, that it was a *team* effort that made good things happen, something he may need to be reminded of.

Step Fourteen. While you should have decided, before the meeting, what you wanted out of it—the specific types and kinds of behavior modification you are after—and written it down, if, without chickening out, you can give effect to any of the T.E.'s defensive arguments, modify your objectives. But be sure that the boss knows what they are. Keep him focused on *your* objectives and *his* behavior.

Step Fifteen. Show respect. If he is older than you, make sure that you acknowledge his experience. If he deserves praise, give some. But no brownnosing. If the T.E. has been a mentor, make sure you express your gratitude. (If he was and you can't, *you* may be the one with the problem!) Have patience. The process is very painful for the T.E. But don't give up. Finish the discussion if you possibly can. Confrontational meetings should not be continued to another day.

Step Sixteen. Somewhere along the way point out that business should be fun. For you, for business to be enjoyable, it is necessary that you feel trusted and respected. And now you don't feel that way and something needs to be changed. Tell him that, under the present conditions, business is no longer fun for you, and perhaps for him. Ask how you can help to make business fun again for both of you. (You can always make this an early point if you wish, even point number one!)

Step Seventeen. If the T.E. still does not respond positively, be firm. Sum things up. Ask for a commitment to change. Beware of easy promises to change. It may be a ploy to terminate the meeting. Make sure that the T.E.

understands the nature of the required behavioral change. Repeat any understandings. Write them down if appropriate and read them back. But remember KISS: "Keep it simple, stupid." This is neither the time nor the place to exact a Magna Carta of behavior, but is the time and place for an agreement to modify behavior in the area targeted for discussion.

Step Eighteen. If agreement has been reached on some behavior-modifying details, don't hang around. Leave. If you felt you got nowhere, don't despair. If you haven't lost your temper, haven't gotten personal, haven't been critical but only observational, he may need a little time to save what's left of his persona. (Some T.E.s are devastated by such a reasoned confrontation. All they've experienced before are shouting matches.) Leave after making the point that much is at stake for you, and for him, and for the operation.

Step Nineteen. Make sure that the T.E. understands that you are dedicated to an improvement in your relationship with him no matter what. Make sure he knows that you are going to follow up. Make sure the T.E. understands that to continue in the old mode is not good for either of you. Your role-playing should be a big help here in avoiding your getting "preachy." And a final caveat. Never combine this attempt at behavior modification with a threat to quit. And another point: Don't confuse him by asking, for instance, for a raise, a new office, a new computer, or more help, unless they were the precipitating cause of the need for a confrontation in the first place.

Step Twenty. Changing behavior is tough. Since you started the process, you have bought yourself some commitments. If he changes, praise him. If he tries and fails, be kind and thank him for trying—it may be the most difficult thing he has ever done. *But don't give up!*

INVALIDATING THE INVALIDATOR

Psychologist Jay Carter, in his delightful little book *Nasty People: How to Stop Being Hurt by Them Without Becoming One of Them*, writes of the process of invalidation, "putting other people down in order to bring yourself up." He says that the way to handle the invalidator is either by humor, confrontation, or by being direct.[3]

A T.E. is a put-down artist. Carter points out how powerful the effects of put-downs are on the psyche. They last for years and can destroy self-esteem. A punch in the nose is understandable and can be returned in kind. But a rolling of the eyes, a bit of sharp sarcasm, an invalid criticism can be devastating to those with a brittle personality and are difficult to return in kind.

A friend will point out one fault at a time. The invalidator will recite a dozen. The invalidator's mission is to destroy self-esteem. A particular invalidator trick is to listen to you share a confidence, perhaps something you've done wrong, a fault, a compulsion you're trying to overcome. The invalidator then uses it against you.

Remember, in chapter 1, the secretary had a boss who was nice one day and rotten the next? The uncertainty destroyed her and she destroyed him by turning him in for tax-cheating. He was an invalidator. She became one. She never told him how she *felt*. The only defense against a career invalidator is to tell him or her how bad his or her *behavior* makes you *feel*.

The career invalidator T.E. uses generalizations to tear your persona apart. He or she makes sure you know that everybody agrees you're a jerk. You have no way to prove him or her wrong. If you already have low self-esteem, and it's your boss who tells you this, it can destroy you, which may be his or her intent. Your only defense is to insist that your detractors be named. If the T.E. can't or won't name them, they probably don't exist.

You should also ask the T.E. how the operation will ben-

efit from the invalidation. In business, for every toxic incident, ask the question, "How much money did that remark
(act, slight, rudeness) make the company?" *And don't be
afraid to repeat it. There's no way you can be fired for trying to
improve the bottom line!*

An invalidator is a manipulator: of facts, of people, of
situations. Like kids echoing insults in kindergarten, the
toxic invalidator tries to pull you down to his or her level
by getting you to reply in kind. Don't.

There is usually a kernel of truth in the invalidator's dis-
tortions, just enough so you can't deny it, just enough to
drive you nuts. Know that the career invalidator would not
be sensitive to *your* faults and failings if he or she were not
guilty of the same. Remember this and find a way, if possible without using the words, to point out that it takes one
to know one.

However, never forget the title of this chapter: "Getting
Along with the Toxic Executive." The career invalidator in
an executive role is a threat to the stability of any enterprise. But try to discover something *good* about the invalidator. If you can submerge your resentments long enough
to look, you may be rewarded with some insights into
human behavior that will stand you in good stead for
many years. Remember, the main object is to get along!

LEARNING TO RESIST BEING MANIPULATED

Many T.E.s are highly manipulative. The T.E. wants you to
do some unpleasant task, but he or she may not come right
out and tell you the "why" of it. Knowing that a direct
order may not be carried out, the request is tied to your fit-
ness report, a coming raise, a promotion, or it may excuse
you from past sins of omission or commission, for which
you "owe" the T.E. something. If none of this works, finally
come appeals to your "institutional fealty."

You can learn to resist this kind of manipulation. Instead

of going home at night and driving your spouse up the wall, learn to handle it immediately, right in the office. Here's how:

• Try to discover what is driving an unkind, inconsiderate, or inappropriate demand. Know that manipulative behavior is *learned* behavior. Where does it come from? Is it the T.E. or is it the corporate culture that's working this evil? Take the time to think this through. In the meantime, taking this breather might allow you to lose much of your anger. As a result, you may be better able to deal with the T.E.

• When asked or forced to do something that you are unsuited for, don't fully understand, or is very unpleasant, don't be steamrollered. Put your left palm over your right extended fingers in the classic time-out sign. What you need is a time-out for a "think-out." The T.E. might well realize that he or she is out of line during your think-out.

• If you feel imposed upon, react positively, not negatively. Break it down. Find something positive in it, something that you can agree with. Suppose you are asked to fire someone you didn't hire because the T.E. is afraid to. You don't want to do it. The T.E. says, "I want you to do it because she's a friend of yours." Heartily agree that she is a friend and that's precisely why you don't want anything to do with it. Thus you agree with the ends, but reject the means.

• Talk to the T.E. Tell him or her frankly of your concerns. Question the T.E. Why were *you* chosen for this unpleasant task? Is it because you are docile and uncomplaining? Does he or she expect that you will always be that way?

• Use humor to let the T.E. know of your displeasure. "I wouldn't do that for a million dollars! But I might do it if you say 'Please, pretty please, with sugar—lots of sugar—on it!'" Or, "I wouldn't do that if President Clinton himself asked me. But now, if it was Hillary . . . !'" Hopefully, the T.E. will get the point.

• If you lack assertiveness, there are many seminars and classes to help you. But be careful about a quick change in personality. One T.E. boss resented his secretary's new-found self-esteem and attacked: "Choose the course or your job!" Instead of getting mad, she told him how much more effective she would be in solving *his* problems! She then smashed the ball back into his court, "I'm not going to choose. *You* must choose. And I want it in writing." (The T.E. could never fire her for that. He and the company would be in court in a New York minute and the company would lose.) Now the tables are turned. He is now the victim of his own invalidation. So she isn't fired and she stays the course. And as she gains self-esteem, she gains his respect as well. That's the way the world works.

• Another kind of invalidator is the "pick-aparter." At the lowest intellectual level, the "things" level, these T.E.s are always trying to pick apart your clothes, cars, house, or personal appearance. Never, but never conjure with them. Unless you yourself are seeking abrasion (as is the invalidator), you must learn to ignore such remarks if you have a genuine desire to get along with the T.E. Difficult as it might be, act as though you don't hear the remarks and they may soon end.

• If they don't end, and the pick-aparter is your boss, write down each time he or she does a pick-apart. Write down what he or she said and when it was said. When you have a good list—say, ten items over a two-week period—type them up (on your own time, if possible) and hand them to him or her and ask why. Any humor you can add will help the T.E. to change.

• There are T.E.s who are people invalidators as well as idea and things invalidators. They can influence your behavior to your detriment. Borrow some logic from the law. In law there are two rules: In civil cases, guilt is established "by the preponderance of the evidence," and in criminal cases, "beyond a reasonable doubt." Use the latter in making judgments as to whether or not to trust someone, and not the former.

Remind yourself that no one is perfect. Trusting is better than not trusting every day of the week. Do a little mental

tallying before making a judgment and forcing a confrontation. Only when the list is long make a move.

Throughout this book I have advised anyone offended by
a toxic executive's behavior to inform him or her how that
behavior made you *feel*. I repeat, when asked what's wrong,
you *must* explain. If you answer "Oh, nothing," you have no
one to blame for continued mistreatment except yourself.
While I sympathize with some T.E. victims because they
could not express their feelings, they should at least learn
how to ask *themselves* how some act of a toxic executive made
them feel. "Advice to get in touch with your own feelings"
sounds like psychobabble, but when you discover that
you've been weeping when your boss criticizes you unjustly,
in order to avoid feeling anger, it's like seeing a rainbow during a downpour. In an intellectual defense, people use ratio-
nalization to make excuses for their behavior, which prevents
them from doing something about what's really bothering
them.[4] If you're unhappy with a T.E.'s behavior, let him or
her know it. Right then! Personally, I'm a great believer in
mirrors. To modify your own behavior, you should learn to
use them. Ask yourself in a mirror whether the T.E.'s behavior is stimulated or set off by toxic behavior on *your* part.

THE FOUR LIFE CURVES

In business, there are four life curves of accomplishment.
When young, the thrust is toward innovation. In middle
age, administrative and family responsibilities displace the
innovative drives, most often because the money is in
administrative jobs. In late middle age, the instructional
phase begins—the executive passes on to the next generation of executives the knowledges gained. Finally, with
retirement, the innovative juices start flowing again.

In order to fulfill any of those roles the executive needs
assistance from others. No man is an island. Even the
greatest violinist had a teacher. Remember, it takes two to
tango.

12

FROM **TOXIC** TO CARING IN TWELVE EASY STEPS

Each of us has inevitably hurt a great many people. We know who most of them are. We saw it in their eyes—the hurt, the pain, the surprise, the shock. It's tough to live with and can create real guilt. You don't sleep at night.

The behaviorists believe that the only way to effect behavioral change is to understand the forces that led you to toxic behavior in the first place. Shrink-time is not only expensive, it's time-consuming, and you might be dead before all the misery you caused is canceled out by the joy that you can bring to a relationship.

Don't worry that you cannot find all the people you wronged, insulted, worried, or dumped on, so that you can attempt to make things right with them. That's impossible. Most of them never told you how it made them *feel*. You can always take comfort in telling yourself that those who did not, may have gotten a charge out of being miserable!

Perhaps the most difficult part of living is trying to change someone's behavior, especially your own. One is not only faced with the inherited behaviors of the past five hundred million years, but one is personally faced with years of one's own conditioning by family, compeers, teachers, television, and various elements of the social and physical environment.

Every one of us has faults. Every one of us acts compulsively. Every one of us would like to learn how to modify his or her own behavior so as to make life easier on others and thus on ourselves. But how to bring this about?

There have been a dozen books on the subject of self-analysis, including one by the famed psychiatrist Karen Horney entitled *Self Analysis*.[1] It can be hard going, but can be helpful to some people. A new book, *Think Like a Shrink*, by psychiatrist Christ Zois, urges its readers to solve their problems themselves using "short-term therapy techniques" that force the reader to drop all defenses in order to face up quickly and honestly to troubling problems.[2] It is aimed not at psychotics—who are rarely encountered in the business world, contrary to the assertions of a popular but very bad book, *Crazy Bosses*, by someone who refuses to give his real name or the place where he works. (I am assuming it is a man because of the pseudonym).[3]

Before reading the twelve-step program that follows, remember that the object of this exercise is to change your own behavior. Just as you cannot control the behaviors of others without having control of yourself, you cannot change your own behavior without some self-knowledge of your own behaviors.

One fairly easy way to go about this without having recourse to psychobabble is to run through the classical Seven Deadly Sins. Are they running your life? Ask yourself about Lust, Avarice, Gluttony, Envy, Greed, Pride, and Anger. Are you handling their associated compulsions adequately? Do you watch yourself as you act out your compulsions? It's *very* hard to do. Further, without psycho-analysis—and I'm talking about *years* on the couch—you'll never find out where those drives came from. No matter—you can still change and make life easier for others and thus yourself. Try to rank-order your compulsions. If anger leads the list, you *may* need some therapy to get to its source in order to effect a change. And there are all kinds of behavior-modifying things you can do. One of the most important is to *take a time-out*. Visualize your left hand coming down repeatedly on the outstretched fingers of your right hand. If that doesn't work, make like you're the captain or the quarterback of a football team and actually make the motion. All you need is a little time to get control of yourself. *Take those time-outs*—even if they last overnight or even a weekend.

Here are the twelve easy steps from toxic to nurturing:

STEP ONE

Ask yourself if you are or are not a toxic executive.

This is a difficult task. If you ask your subordinates, it's a Catch-22. If they answer yes, they might feel they stand the chance of being fired, if you are, in fact, a T.E.!

You will probably never move from toxic to caring or nurturing until you are convinced that you are, in fact, a toxic executive; in any event, even the most caring of executives has *some* toxic behaviors that he or she would like to change. If you have read most of this book, you should by now have formed some opinions about yourself. If you have not yet taken the test for executive toxicity at the end of this book, take it now. If you've taken it before, compare the results. Then finish the book and take it again. See, you're already moving from toxic to caring!

Always preserve your answers in a safe place and continue to take the test as your behavior changes and you move toward caring. (I do advise you to keep test results to yourself unless you want to discuss them with a professional. The typesetting has been arranged so that it is easy to copy on the office or home copier, and I give you permission to copy it for your own purposes or for classroom use—but don't reproduce it for public distribution, or the publisher will be on top of you in a flash for the cash.)

One sure sign of a T.E. is his or her rejection of reality. If you are given to fudging answers to self-administered tests in order to preserve your ego, take the test several times and compare the numbers. See how it works!

STEP TWO

Get some idea as to how toxic you are area by area. While the test will give you some numbers, everyone in the world is different, and executive toxicity is a relative value and has geographic determinants. That which might be considered toxic in New York City may not be in Tokyo. You might have problems with peers and none with subordinates, problems with suppliers but not with customers, problems with fellow students but not with teachers. Toxicity can also be industry- and job-specific. So as you change jobs, take the test again.

Once you recognize that every executive in the world has *some* toxicity, you will graduate to discovering whether you are more or less toxic than others, given the same environment. There are hundreds of hints in this book to help you make up your mind as to just how toxic you are.

Don't make snap judgments and go on a guilt-trip if you discover that you are, for instance, a noncommunicating T.E. and decide to change by suddenly becoming voluble (and probably boring). Resist overnight change. If you're a mean old nonsmiling curmudgeon, please don't go on a massive guilt trip and confuse everyone by suddenly becoming affable and friendly. Chances are you'll frighten your people to death. You don't want to kill off your staff. Take it step by step.

Being toxic is not like being pregnant, when you either are or you're not; there are various kinds and degrees of toxicity. You should be looking to discover whether *on balance* you are a toxic, and then what *kind* of toxic traits you have. Step three will help you.

STEP THREE

Go through the book and write down all of the toxic things that you do habitually. Don't concentrate on something that happened twenty years ago that you regret. Think about what happened last week! Whom did you dump on, ridicule, make fun of, ignore, put down, mistrust, belittle, harass, bully, mock, lie about, criticize? Is there a pattern? Stand in front of a mirror and look yourself in the eye. And then ask yourself if, *on balance*, you have given more joy than sorrow to your peers and subordinates.

STEP FOUR

Rationalize your behavior in writing. Write down all the reasons why your toxic actions were justified. Then list why they were not. Weigh the lists against each other. Which one wins? If your answers were honest, and the actions were justified, give this book to someone else. If it's *mene, mene tekel upharsin* (you have been weighed in the balance and found wanting), read on.

STEP FIVE

Remember, you supervise more than jobs, you supervise people. You should learn to make your people feel important. And that is accomplished in these ways:

• Learn to listen to them. The sum total of usable information available from the people on a shop floor, a computer installation, a general office, or what have you is usually many times that of the executive in charge. That sum total can only be harnessed for the good of the company or operation if it is invoked. It is invoked by bonding, by making your people feel important, by involving them in your decisionmaking.

• Keep your people informed. If they don't know what's going on, they'll make something up and it's usually bad—especially in bad times. Make them a part of the information loop. Give out information and they will reciprocate.

• Treat them with respect. Any of them could be a

church elder managing a million-dollar annual budget, a father successfully putting four kids through college, a school board member with a $200 million budget, or a composer with a new symphony in the works—or a candidate for an Olympic gold!

• Remember that there are few universalities in human relations. It's different strokes for different folks. In rewarding good work, your own value system may not be the same as your subordinate's. While you may be money-driven, another will love you forever and work his butt off if he can have his own parking spot. Try to discover what is important to each of your people.

• Treat them as upscale people. That means upscale manners such as thank-yous, and requesting rather than demanding. It's going that extra mile or minute for them. It means that you stand up and greet them when they come into your office. It means that you treat them the same as the best or biggest customer or client. Even if you don't *feel* it, try it and you'll soon get the hang of it. The payoffs can be incredible—not only for them but for you!

STEP SIX

Show people that you care about them. Know their birthdays, their children's names. Feel their traumas. Share their troubles and remember that each one is an individual with his or her own particular set of demons. Learn what they are. Each of these people has problems with at least some or even all of the Seven Deadly Sins. And those problems are probably much different from yours.

In the process, try to forget about your own problems. Nothing is more boring or unproductive than for a subordinate to listen to the problems of a boss. The traumatized employee says, "I'm afraid of empty elevators"; in response, and in an attempt to empathize with the employee, you tell about some of your own fears. That's a no-no because you never get back to the employee's problems.

STEP SEVEN

Force yourself to behave differently from what you feel. When you feel angry and hurt and are about to lash out in a compulsive way that you fully know will hurt both of you, look in a mirror and try to smile back. This is hard to do—it is so much easier to stay hurt and angry than it is to smile. But remember that you are a boss. You are supposed to be a leader! People are shaping their lives around you. They may pattern their own behaviors after yours. You are a role model. Your conduct is important.

STEP EIGHT

Convince yourself that you *can* change.

Chris Argyris, Harvard Business School management behavior guru, says that teaching smart people how to learn is one of the world's most difficult tasks. But it can be done. (I'm assuming you're smart, or you wouldn't be reading this book!)

Two widely held myths—that after adolescence one's personality is pretty much set and can't be changed, and that there's a steady decline in the ability to learn in midlife and beyond—are just that, myths. With physiological survival needs assured, with safety and security needs met, with your need for belonging substantially satisfied, it is time to gain a feeling of self-worth, of self-esteem.

Remember back to how sensitive *you* were in the upward struggle. Think of how grateful you were for the attention, help, and encouragement you got from some caring boss who made you feel important.

When I was playing lots of golf at Washington Golf and Country Club, I frequently partnered with the club champion, Henry Kerfoot. I remember how much better I played with him than with anyone else. How come?

Because he praised my good shots and never criticized the bad. I knew when they were bad and didn't need to be reminded of them. He also showed me how to make the more difficult shots, including sand bunker play, and as a result I won a special "Stanley the Sand-Player Cup" one year. Henry was a nurturing partner. He made golf highly enjoyable. I am very grateful to him.

STEP NINE

Remember that the nurturing executive preserves the dignity of all of those around. Tell people they're slow and they'll get slower. Tell people they're dumb and they'll get dumber. *But* tell people they're fast and they'll get faster. Tell people they're smart and they'll get smarter. Make a vow that you will try to end every day with those around you a little happier, a little more confident, a little more satisfied. Every day of the week let each of them know that you trust them and that they are appreciated. Your subordinates will soon pick up on this and will learn from your own behavior. You and the whole place will be happier and more productive.

STEP TEN

Discover whether or not you like yourself. Many toxic executives do not like themselves. You cannot move from toxic to caring without liking yourself. In front of a mirror, tell yourself in a good clear voice that you like yourself. Do it just about every day. And the next time you dump on some person powerless to respond or defend himself or herself, try again to tell yourself how much you like yourself. When you find you can't, you're halfway home to caring.

STEP ELEVEN

Discover empowerment, letting the people who do the work decide how to do that work. It is management from within, not above. It is the old team-building techniques of the decade of participatory management that was the seventies, which included task diagnostics, skills analysis, work assignments, and work-sharing,[4] now brought up to date in the nineties by empowering the people who do the work to form self-managing work teams. (This includes people at every level of authority, staff, and line.) Let your people schedule their own work and decide for themselves the way it is to be done. Empowerment is a big deal because it shows respect for the individual. It gives them dignity and a feeling of self-worth. And it really works. There are side benefits, too. In one study, employees who felt they had the backing of the boss were ill only half as often as those who said they received little support.[5]

STEP TWELVE

Get rid of your arrogance. Think about the job to be done. Forget the perks, forget the title, forget the size of your office, forget about *things* and concentrate on people and their ideas. *People* make companies profitable, armies win, and governments work.

THE FORGIVING EXECUTIVE

The caring executive is a forgiving executive. He or she is consciously forgiving, continuously reminding himself or herself that all people are fallible, all make mistakes, all act compulsively at times, all are stressed either physiologically "by the thousand natural ills that men are heir to" or by peers, family, the economy. "The idea of forgiveness often seems abstract and 'religious' in an otherworldly kind of way," says Jim Wallis, editor of *Sojourners* magazine. "But in fact forgiveness is very practical and necessary for human life on the planet to survive . . . when we refuse to forgive, the cycle of vengeance, retaliation and violence just escalates." In *Hearts That We Broke Long Ago,* Merle Shain, a Canadian writer, analyzed the costs paid by the unforgiving person:

Until one forgives, life is governed by an endless cycle of resentments and retaliations and we spend our days scratching at the scabs of the wounds that we sustained long ago instead of letting them dry up and disappear. There is no way to hate another that does not cost the hater, no way to remain unforgiving without maiming yourself, because undissolved anger stutters through the body of the person who can't forgive.[6]

ONE FINAL NOTE

Try to remember to be *kind*—kindness costs you nothing except a few moments in time. Be *charitable*. Everyone has faults—some of them most likely remarkably like your own! Be *fair*—always get the facts before making judgments and watch out for your own prejudices. Be *honest*. Live up to your promises. Don't cheat—all you'll get is respect from cheaters who will in turn cheat you! Be *loyal*. This may be the hardest of all because your first loyalty should always be to the organization that pays you, rather than your fellow workers and employees. Finally, be *patient*. Rome was not built in a day, nor are companies and the human relationships on which they depend to survive and grow.

The accompanying toxicity table might help in determining where you might be in the toxic executive hierarchy.

The Toxic Executive Hierarchy

ATTRIBUTE	THE SUPER-TOXIC EXECUTIVE	THE TOXIC EXECUTIVE	THE SUB-TOXIC EXECUTIVE	THE TYRO-TOXIC EXECUTIVE	THE CARING EXECUTIVE
Personal trust	Conflictual	Accusational	Mistrusting	Suspicious	Trusting
Dealing with truth	Deceitful	Habitual liar	Situation-driven	Suspicious	Honest
Personal relationships	Put-downer	Invalidating	Insulting	Unfriendly	Friendly
Praise and credit	Steals ideas and takes all the credit	Discredits others and their ideas	No praise, no credit	Can't share credit, can't give praise	Shares, attributes
Meetings	Interrupter	Intentionally obtuse	Attempts domination	Nonlistener	Listener
Participation	None. A loner	Plays favorites	Team destroyer	Team disrupter	Team creator
Mentoring	No way. Never	Intentional misleader	Brown nosers only	Reluctantly	Loves teaching
Peer relationships	Trappist	Jealous	Hypercritical	Incommunicative	Helpful, sharing
Power relationships	Abuses power	Collects power	Misuses power	Has secret agenda	Uses carefully
Decisionmaking	Unilateral, abrupt	Self-Serving	Ill-considered	Indecisive	Analytical

13

HOW **TOXIC** AN EXECUTIVE ARE YOU?

SFR's Test for Executive Toxicity

TOXIC BEHAVIORS	NEVER	SOME TIMES	OFTEN	FRE-QUENTLY
1. Do you secretly listen in on others' telephone conversations?				
2. Do you habitually lock your desk when you go to lunch or to the john?				
3. Do you wake up grouchy and carry that to work?				
4. Do you look for things to criticize?				
5. Do you forget to tell people how to reach you when you're on a trip?				
6. Are you happy when competitors for your job fail?				
7. Do you forget to say "Thank you," "Good Morning," and use other generally accepted pleasantries?				
8. Are you late for your in-office appointments?				
9. Are you late for group meetings?				
10. Do you substitute the "self" words: *myself, himself, yourself,* for *me, him,* and *you?*				
11. Do the neighbors' kids annoy you?				
12. Do you read only parts of a newspaper?				

TOXIC BEHAVIORS	NEVER	SOME TIMES	OFTEN	FRE- QUENTLY
13. Do you get upset when it looks like you are wrong?				
14. Is your car unpolished?				
15. Have you been told you reject others' ideas and promote your own?				
16. Do you take credit you do not deserve?				
17. Do you blame others for your mistakes?				
18. Do you criticize acts of people who do not work for you?				
19. Do you target one particular person for your criticisms?				
20. Do you use aphorisms?				
21. Do you have secret agendas?				
22. Do you have problems with the truth?				
23. Do challengers to your authority annoy you?				
24. Do you shoot off guns just for the fun of it?				
25. Are you super-careful of your dress and appearance?				
26. Do you believe you should have been born 100 years or more ago?				
27. Do you think about your pay?				
28. Do you secretly "check up" on the work of your people?				
29. Do you stay away from problem solving?				
30. Do you have feelings of jealousy at others' success?				
31. Can one of your subordinates do your job better than you can?				
32. Do people tell you that you talk too much?				

TOXIC BEHAVIORS	NEVER	SOME TIMES	OFTEN	FRE- QUENTLY
33. Do you miss the gist of a discussion because you're thinking of what you're going to say next?				
34. Must most people go through your secretary to reach you?				
35. Have people stolen your ideas?				
36. When something new is proposed, is your first answer no?				
37. Do you feel people are watching you?				
38. On the job, do you buy things you don't really need?				
39. Do you use the company plane, car, copying machine, charge card, etc., for personal purposes?				
40. Do you bad-mouth former employees?				
41. Do you resist having your subordinates to dinner at your house?				
42. Are your subordinates stupid?				
43. Do you speak to your subordinates about their life-styles?				
44. Do you enforce dress rules in your "shop"?				
45. Do you quickly update a posted organization chart?				
46. Do you follow it?				
47. Do you update job descriptions?				
48. Do you use consultants and follow their advice?				
49. Do you follow a formal business plan?				
50. Do you fail to finish what you start?				
51. Have you been told that you make the simple complex?				

TOXIC BEHAVIORS	NEVER	SOME TIMES	OFTEN	FRE- QUENTLY
52. Do your people tell you that you nitpick?				
53. Do you adhere to standard operating procedures?				
54. Do you hire people who look, act, talk, or dress like you?				
55. Do you use foul language in ordinary conversations?				
56. Do you make promises you may not be able to keep?				
57. Do you file lawsuits you can't or shouldn't win?				
58. Has your pay been consistently more than "externally competitive and internally fair"?				
59. Do you get a charge out of spending the organization's money?				
60. Do you hire relatives because they *are* relatives?				
61. Do you have high turnover rates of your employees because of failure to run background checks?				
62. Do you hire more people than you really need?				
63. Do you frequent a country, city, or social club that discriminates?				
64. Do you fail to tell your subordinates how great they are?				
65. Do you hold to an opinion in spite of contrary evidence?				
66. Do you seek out targets for your aggressive feelings?				
67. Do you ever nix a proposed hire because of race, sex, or national origin?				
68. Do you keep people who stereotype?				

TOXIC BEHAVIORS	NEVER	SOME TIMES	OFTEN	FRE- QUENTLY
69. Have you ever, hired, fired, or promoted based on a person's political or religious convictions?				
70. Do your subordinates tell you that your behavior changes when your boss comes around?				
71. Have you been told that your decisionmaking is more reactive than proactive?				
72. Have you been accused of making sexually suggestive remarks in the workplace?				
73. Have you been accused of playing favorites?				
74. Do you aggressively try to be sexually attractive?				
75. Have you "hit" on people you are sexually attracted to in the workplace?				
76. Have you pursued them after getting a no?				
77. Have you had love affairs with others from the same workplace?				
78. Do you talk about these affairs?				
79. Do you take a briefcase (or its equivalent) home every night?				
80. Do you drink alcoholic beverages at lunch?				
81. Do you smoke in the workplace?				
82. Do you use drugs other than alcohol?				
83. Have you been told that you have failed to meet your commitments?				
84. Have you recently been told that you have put off making some important decisions?				

TOXIC BEHAVIORS	NEVER	SOME TIMES	OFTEN	FRE-QUENTLY
85. Have you had resistance to your performance evaluations (includes formal and informal methods).				
86. How often have you resisted being performance-rated by your subordinates?				
87. Have you been unprepared for meetings?				
88. Do you watch and like the TV show *Jeopardy?*				
89. Do you really *hate* to lose?				
90. Do you insist on having meetings with subordinates exclusively in your own office?				
91. Do you feel people you praise slack off or ask for a raise as a result?				
92. Do you check up on your people to be sure they're not goofing off?				
93. Do you force subordinates to do things they obviously do not want to do?				
94. Do you dislike hearing bad news that affects your job?				
95. How often were you mistreated in a former job?				
96. Do people gang up on you?				
97. Do you feel that people you hire owe you?				
98. Do you exclude your secretary or executive assistant from confidential meetings?				
99. Do you use your boss's authority rather than your own to get something done?				

TOXIC BEHAVIORS	NEVER	SOME TIMES	OFTEN	FRE- QUENTLY
100. Will you disbelieve the results of this test because most people lie to themselves?				

Total of all columns _____.

This is not a "scientific" test. It is intended only to show relative progress from toxic to nurturing.

Score yourself 0 points for entries in the "Never" column, 1 point for entries in the "Sometimes" column, 2 points for entries in the "Often" column, and 3 points for entries in the "Frequently" column.

A total of 100 points or over probably means you are a **super-toxic executive**. From 75 to 99 means you're just an ordinary, mean, and rotten toxic executive, or at least a sub-toxic or a tyro-toxic. Any total below 75 means you should thank your parents, teachers, family, and perhaps genes that you most likely put more back into your job, society, and relationships than you take out.

NOTES

CHAPTER 1

1. David Campbell, *If I'm in Charge Here Why Is Everybody Laughing?* (Greensboro, NC: Center for Creative Leadership).

2. James A. Autry, *Love & Profit.* (New York: Morrow, 1991).

3. Stephen R. Covey, *Principle-Centered Leadership* (New York: Summit Books, 1991); and *The Habits of Highly Effective People: Powerful Lessons in Personal Change* (New York: Simon & Schuster, 1990).

4. *General Electric Company 1991 Annual Report* (Fairfield, CT: General Electric).

5. Mark Potts, "Seeking A Better Idea: With Cutting Management Tool, GE's Chief Aims to Forge a Boundaryless Firm," (*Washington Post,* October 7, 1990).

6. "GE Told to Toughen Fraud Case Penalties," (*Washington Post,* June 3, 1992).

7. Philip H. Jos, et al., "In Praise of Difficult People: A Portrait of the Committed Whistleblower" (*Public Administration Review,* November–December 1989).

8. "GE's Drive to Purge Fraud Is Hampered by Workers' Mistrust: Some Fear Getting the Ax if They Follow Directive to Report Wrongdoing" (*Wall Street Journal,* July 22, 1992).

9. "GE Is Expected To Admit Guilt In Dotan Case" (*Wall Street Journal,* July 10, 1992); and "General Electric Pleads Guilty, Pays $69 Million to Settle Whistleblower Suit," (*Wall Street Journal,* July 23, 1992).

10. "Israel Eases Stance in Arms Aid Probe." (*Washington Post,* July 29, 1992).

11. "Israeli Military Aid Scandal Jolts GE: Company to

Settle Fraud Charges, Defends Ethics Program" (*Washington Post*, July 20, 1992).

12. "Chief of GE Says It Should Have Found Fraud Tied to Gear Purchases by Israel" (*Wall Street Journal*, July 30, 1992).

13. "Remember Big Brother? Now He's a Company Man." (Ideas & Trends, *New York Times*, March 31, 1991).

14. Harry Levinson, "The Abrasive Personality at the Office" (*Psychology Today*, May 1978); and Harry Levinson, "The Abrasive Personality" (*Harvard Business Review*, May–June, 1978).

15. "Managers Are Sent to 'Charm Schools' to Learn about Polishing Up Their Acts" (*Wall Street Journal*, December 14, 1990).

16. Bruce H. Mayhew and Roger L. Levinger, "On the Emergence of Oligarchy in Human Interaction" (*American Journal of Sociology*, March 1977, 1017–49.

17. Newt Gingrich, "Language: A Key Mechanism of Control." Gopac.

18. *Moore Cadillac Brochure* (Vienna, VA: Spring 1992.

19. "Independent Inventors Find Frustration in Selling Ideas: Some Manufacturers Seem to Suffer from 'Not Invented Here' Syndrome" (*Wall Street Journal*, August 21, 1991).

20. Stanley Foster Reed, "A Dialogue with Buckminster Fuller" (*Mergers & Acquisitions*, Fall 1965).

21. "McDonald's Pickle: He Began Fast Food But Gets No Credit" (*Wall Street Journal*, July 15, 1991).

22. "The Checkoff" (*Wall Street Journal*, July 21, 1992).

23. "Gender Gap: Do Women Sell Themselves Short in Performance Reviews?" (*Wall Street Journal*, July 21, 1992).

24. "Chief Reads Riot Act At I.B.M." (*New York Times*, May 29, 1991).

25. Charles I. Gragg, "Whose Fault Was It?" (*Harvard Business Review*).

26. David Rieff, "Victims All? Recovery, Co-Dependency, and the Art of Blaming Somebody Else" (*Harper's*, October, 1991).

27. John Bradshaw, *Homecoming: Reclaiming and Championing Your Inner Child* (New York: Bantam Books, 1990).

28. "To the Rescue of Recovery." (Letters, *Harper's*, January 1992).

29. Wendy Kaminer, "I'm Dysfunctional, You're Dysfunctional" (Reading, MA: Addison-Wesley, 1992).

30. Suzanne Slesin, "I Need You, You Need Me." (The Sexes, *New York Times*, July 12, 1992).

31. "Est Founder Is Ordered to Pay $380,000 for Fraud" (*Washington Post*, July 16, 1992).

32. Robert M. Hochheiser, *How to Work for a Jerk* (New York: Vintage Books, 1987).

33. Hendrie Weisinger, "How Tough Critics May Be Mentors in Disguise" (*Working Woman*, June 4, 1988).

34. "Disgruntled Workers Intent on Revenge Increasingly Harm Colleagues and Bosses" (*Wall Street Journal*, September 15, 1992).

35. "Shades of Gloom" (*American Health*, May 1991).

36. Thomas J. Peters and Robert H. Waterman, Jr., *In Search of Excellence: Lessons from America's Best-Run Companies*. New York: Warner Books, 1984).

CHAPTER 2

1. Manfred F. R. Kets de Vries and Danny Miller, *The Neurotic Organization: Diagnosing and Revitalizing Unhealthy Companies*. (New York: HarperBusiness, 1984).

2. Donald L. Bartlett and James B. Steele, *America: What Went Wrong?* (Kansas City, MO: Andrews and McMeel, 1992).

3. "Middle-Management Spread Hits Corporate America" (*Washington Post*, May 26, 1991).

4. "Number of U.S. Millionaires Soars" (*Washington Post*, July 11, 1992).

5. "U.S. Helps Firms Push Arms Sales" (*Washington Post*, May 8, 1992).

6. "White House Girds to Promote Huge Arms Sales to Many Nations" (*Wall Street Journal*, July 24, 1992).

7. "Selling Arms to Keep Jobs: The Signals It Sends Abroad" (*New York Times*, September 20, 1992).

8. "Study Says Research Centers Waste Millions" (*Washington Post*, July 10, 1992).

9. "Plagiarists Take Note: Machine's on Guard" (*New York Times*, January 7, 1992).

10. "Chrysler Told to Pay Inventor $11.3 Million" (*New York Times*, June 12, 1992).

11. "Filing of Criminal Charges Likely in Probe of Coal Firms" (*Washington Post*, October 21, 1991).

12. "Rockwell, Two Workers Indicted" (*New York Times*, November 11, 1991).

13. Marya Mannes, "Let's Stop Exalting Jerks: It's Time We Knocked Our Shabby Idols Off Their Pedestals" (*Saturday Evening Post*, October 6, 1962).

CHAPTER 3

1. Abraham H. Maslow, *Motivation and Personality* (New York: Harper & Row, 1954).

2. Gary Portnoy and Judy Hart Angelo, "Theme from Cheers: Where Everybody Knows Your Name" (Miami: Addax Music, 1983).

3. Robert Ardrey, *The Territorial Imperative: A Personal Inquiry into the Animal Origins of Property & Nations* (New York: Athenaeum, 1966).

4. Susan Forward, *Toxic Parents: Overcoming Their Hurtful Legacy, and Reclaiming Your Life* (New York: Bantam Books, 1990).

5. Stephen Arterburn and Jack Felton, *Toxic Faith: Understanding and Overcoming Religious Addiction* (Nashville: Olivier-Nelson Books, 1991).

6. Gloria Steinem, *Revolution from Within: A Book of Self-Esteem.* (Boston: Little, Brown, 1992).

7. "Hey, I'm Terrific" (*Newsweek*, February 17, 1992).

8. "Novelist Updike Sees a Nation Frustrated by Its Own Dreams" (*Wall Street Journal*, September 16, 1992).

9. Norman Cousins, *Anatomy of an Illness as Perceived by the Patient: Reflections on Healing & Regeneration* (New York: Norton, 1979).

10. Barbara Brown, *New Mind, New Body. Bio-Feedback: New Directions for the Mind* (New York: Bantam Books, 1974).

11. David Harold Fink, *Release from Nervous Tension* (New York: Simon & Schuster, 1943).

CHAPTER 5

1. Masaaki Imai, *Kaizen: The Key to Japan's Competitive Success* (New York: Random House, 1986).

2. Redford Williams, *The Trusting Heart: Great News about Type A Behavior* (New York: Random House, 1989).

3. Douglas McGregor, *The Human Side of Enterprise* Austin, TX: Pro.-Ed., 1985, Twenty-fifth annual printing).

CHAPTER 6

1. "$30 Million Loss Seen at Salomon" (*New York Times*, January 18, 1992).

2. "Levine Is Involved in Questionable Deal, CBS Show Reports" (*Wall Street Journal*, September 24, 1991).

3. Walter Kiechel III, "The Self-Absorbed Executive" (*Fortune*, December 13, 1982).

4. Stanley Foster Reed, "On the Dynamics of Group Decisionmaking in High Places" (*Directors & Boards*, Winter 1978).

5. "Justices Extend Trademark Shield to 'Trade Dress'" (*Wall Street Journal*, June 29, 1992); and "Texas Tortilla Flap Widens Trademark Law's Reach" (*Washington Post*, June 27, 1992).

6. Muriel Solomon, *Working with Difficult People* (Englewood Cliffs, NJ: Prentice-Hall, 1990).

7. "Anatomy of a Rumor" (*New York Times*, June 4, 1991).

8. Michael Schrage, "American Companies Need to Improve Listening Skills" (*Washington Post*, June 21, 1991).

9. Fernando Bartolomé, "Nobody Trusts the Boss Completely—Now What?" (*Harvard Business Review*, March–April 1989).

10. Stanley Foster Reed, "Psychological Factors Affecting the Retention of Misfits and Losers in Segmental Operations" (*Mergers & Acquisitions*, January–February 1969).

11. "A Board Room Coup at Rexene" (*New York Times*, March 3, 1992).

12. Tom Wicker, "A Predictable Demise" (*New York Times*, December 5, 1991).

13. Rowland Evans and Robert Novak (Column, *Washington Post*, December 4, 1991).

14. David S. Broder, "Presidential Staff Changes, Signaling Trouble, Rarely Deliver Cure" (*Washington Post*, December 4, 1991).

15. "Sununu Sayonara: He Broke 7 Cardinal Rules" (*New York Times*, December 5, 1991).

16. "Sununu and the Jews" (*Newsweek*, July 8, 1991); and William Safire, "Sununu Blames the Jews: Agnew Lives" (Column, *Washington Post*, June 27, 1991).

17. "John Sununu Taken for a Ride" (*Washington Post*, January 30, 1992).

18. "Skinner's Frequent Flights Reported" (*Washington Post*, May 4, 1992); and "Skinner Took Flight Lessons at U.S. Expense" (*Washington Post*, July 3, 1991).

19. "Skinner Pays for $6,000 in gifts, Quits Club Board" (*Washington Post*, June 17, 1992).

20. "Digital Cites Expense Account Abuse Tab of $30 Million" (*Washington Post*, March 25, 1992).

21. "Alabama Governor on Spot Over Flying to His Sermons" (*New York Times*, October 6, 1991).

22. "Governor Hunt's Record Sent to Jury" (*Washington Post*, July 17, 1992).

23. "Northrop Agrees to Pay $4.2 Million to Settle Whistleblower Suit" (*Wall Street Journal*, May 29, 1992).

24. Scott Shuger, "Stopping the Next Sununu" (*Newsweek*, July 8, 1992).

25. "Fishing for the Workplace Imposter" (*New York Times*, April 14, 1991).

26. "Briefs" (*Wall Street Journal*, May 23, 1991).

CHAPTER 7

1. "Hard Times Increase Intolerance in Workplace" (*Washington Business Journal*, November 18, 1991).

2. "Smokers' Bill of Rights Brings Out Big Guns" (*Washington Post*, February 8, 1992).

3. "Purex Tries to Outgun Clorox" (*Business Week*, March 23, 1974).

4. Theodore Levitt, "Creativity Is Not Enough" (*Harvard Business Review*, March–April 1964.

5. Stanley Foster Reed, "From the Thoughtful Businessman" (*Harvard Business Review*, March–April 1964).

6. Doron P. Levin, "Irreconcilable Differences: Ross Perot versus General Motors" (Boston: Little, Brown, 1989).

7. Todd Mason, *Perot: An Unauthorized Biography*. (Homewood, IL: Dow Jones-Irwin, 1990).

8. "Perot Drops Out of Presidential Race" (*Washington Post*, July 17, 1992).

9. John Mintz, "Walking Away from Fights He Cannot Win Is Perot's Pattern" (*Washington Post*, July 17, 1992).

10. Warren Bennis, *Why Leaders Can't Lead* (San Francisco: Jossey-Bass, 1989).

11. Terry L. Leap and Michael D. Crino, "How to Deal with Bizarre Employee Behavior" (*Harvard Business Review*, May–June 1986).

12. Haynes Johnson, "The Price of Political Promises" (*Washington Post*, December 22, 1991).

CHAPTER 8

1. James A. Brussel, M. D. Cantzlaar and George L. Cantzlaar, *The Layman's Dictionary of Psychiatry* (New York: Barnes & Nobel, 1967).

2. "Silencing the Opposition Gets Harder" (*New York Times*, July 2, 1992).

3. "Quayle Charges Some Lawyers Are 'Ripping Off' the System" (*Washington Post*, September 7, 1991).

4. "Guilty! Too Many Lawyers and Too Much Litigation. Here's a Better Way" (*Business Week*, April 13, 1992).

5. "Securities Arbitration: How Investors Fare"(GAO/GGD-92-74, Gaithersberg, MD: General Accounting Office).

6. "Board Room Back-Scratching?" (*New York Times*, June 2, 1992).

7. "CEOs Get a Bigger Piece of the Pie" (*Washington Post*, July 15, 1991).

8. "Executive Pay Rises, as Profits Fall" (*Washington Post*, April 25, 1992).

9. "Stock Option Windfalls Fuel Debate on Corporate Pay" (*Washington Post*, January 31, 1992).

10. "Top Dollar Survey: Some Disparity Between Executive Pay and Performance" (*Washington Post*, June 29, 1992).

11. "A Most Unusual Executive Bonus Plan, at General Dynamics, Top Managers Receive a Windfall after Talking Up the Stock" (*Washington Post*, October 21, 1991).

12. "Notice of Offer to Purchase for Cash" (Tombstone ad in *Wall Street Journal*, June 10, 1992).

13. Peter Carlson, "Chairmen of the Bucks" (*Washington Post Magazine*, April 5, 1992).

14. "Suit Charging General Dynamics with Fraud Finally Goes to Trial" (*Wall Street Journal*, December 19, 1991).

15. "ITT Will Sell Stake in Alcatel To Its Partner" (*Wall Street Journal*, March 4, 1992).

16. "ITT's Stock Jumps On Asset-Sale Talk" (*Washington Post*, February 27, 1992).

17. "ITT Chairman's Compensation Dropped in '91" (*Wall Street Journal*, March 27, 1992).

18. "Araskog, Confronted by ITT Holders, Defends $11.4 Million '90 Compensation" (*Wall Street Journal*, May 8, 1991).

19. "The Challenge to Champion's Chief" (*Washington Post*, April 10, 1992).

20. "California Pension Funds Target Champion International's Executive Pay" (*Washington Post*, March 6, 1992).

21. "SEC Report Attacks Big Drexel Bonuses" (*New York Times*, October 4, 1991).

22. "Goldman Chiefs Made Over $15 Million Each" (*Wall Street Journal*, July 22, 1992).

23. "Top Officers' Pay Can be Hard to Figure without a Calculator and Lots of Sifting" (*Wall Street Journal*, June 21, 1991).

24. "Executive-pay Issue Spurs Some Reforms" (*USA Today*, May 28, 1992).

25. Graef S. Crystal, *In Search of Excess: The Overcompensation of American Executives* (New York: Norton, 1991).

26. "Trying to Decode Proxies? Read Very, Very Carefully" (*New York Times*, April 13, 1992).

27. "The Abused Executive Stock Option" (*New York Times*, June 7, 1992).

28. "If CEO Pay Makes You Sick, Don't Look at the Stock Options" (*Business Week*, April 13, 1992).

29. "Stock Options Soften Bite of Executive Pay Cuts" (*Washington Post*, March 11, 1992).

30. "CEO Pay: Disclosure Is the Best Policy" (*Business Week*, July 6, 1992).

31. *Executive Compensation/Share Ownership*. (Business Roundtable, Undated Report).

32. "The SEC's CEO-Pay Plan: No Panacea" (*Business Week*, July 6, 1992).

33. "Sending Less Than Our Best to Japan: Below-Average Firms Represented" (*Washington Post*, January 11, 1992).

34. Bryan Burrough, *Vendetta: American Express and the*

Smearing of Edmond Safra (New York: HarperCollins, 1992).

35. "Compensation Gap: High Pay of CEOs Traveling with Bush Touches Nerve in Asia. Japanese, Who Earn Less, Ask Why the Executives Make So Much in Tough Times" (*Wall Street Journal*, December 29, 1991).

36. "Compensation and Accountability" (Review & Outlook, *Wall Street Journal*, May 22, 1991).

37. "Bush Contingent Takes Heat over CEO Pay" (*USA Today*, December 8, 1992).

38. "Time CEO Takes Heat for Salary" (*Washington Post*, September 26, 1991).

39. "Herman Miller Links Worker-CEO Pay" (*Wall Street Journal*, May 8, 1992).

40. "Writer Quits Fortune, Citing Meddling by Time Warner" (*Wall Street Journal*, June 26, 1991).

41. "Magazine to Drop Column by Expert on Executive Pay" (*New York Times*, February 25, 1992).

42. "Executive Pay Hits New Highs" (*New York Times*, May 11, 1992).

43. "Firms Rethink Lucrative Severance Pacts for Top Executives as Criticism Swells." (*Wall Street Journal* November 11, 1991).

44. "Time Warner's Ousted Co-Chief Got $18.7 Million in Severance and Salary," (*Wall Street Journal*, May 1, 1992).

45. "Macy's Creditors Challenge 'Golden Parachute'" (*Washington Post*, June 20, 1992).

46. "Philip Morris's Ex-chairman Maxwell Gets $24 Million Compensation Package" (*Wall Street Journal*, March 20, 1992).

47. "Ex Bank Chairman Finds Higher Pay As a Consultant" (*Wall Street Journal*, March 5, 1992).

48. Hyman, Michael, et. al. "Ethical Codes Are Not Enough" (*Business Horizons*, March–April, 1990).

49. "Wang Is Running Out of Running Room: Endless Missteps Have Brought the Computer Maker to Its Knees" (*Business Week*, July 27, 1992).

50. Andrew Grove, "Close Friend, Tough Hire" (*Washington Post*, April 22, 1991).

CHAPTER 9

1. Doron P. Levin, "Irreconcilable Differences: Ross Perot Versus General Motors" (Boston: Little Brown & Company, 1989).

2. Gerald Rafshoon, "Why I left Perot" (*Washington Post*, July 16, 1992).

3. Anne M. Russell, "The End of the Big Bad Boss" (*Working Woman*, March 1990).

4. *Ibid.*

5. James J. Kilpatrick, "Monster Man of the FBI" (*Washington Post*, March 23, 1992).

6. "Real-Life L.A. Law." (Editorial, *New York Times*, July 11, 1991).

7. Robert Reinhold, "Study of Los Angeles Police Finds Violence and Racism Are Routine" (*New York Times*, July 10, 1991).

8. "Citizens Panel Limits Powers of Chief Gates" (*Washington Post*, July 17, 1991).

9. Thomas A. Reppetto, "He Did It His Way" (Book Review of *Chief* by Daryl F. Gates, *New York Times*, June 21, 1992).

10. "Gates Bids Farewell to LAPD, Leaving a Legacy of Controversy" (*Washington Post*, June 27, 1992).

11. Francis Russel, *A City in Terror: 1919—The Boston Police Strike* (New York: Viking, 1975).

12. "New L.A Police Chief Probes Organized Crime Unit for Spying" (*Washington Post*, July 11, 1992).

13. "L.A. Deputy Chief Has Troubles, Too" (*USA Today*, May 28, 1991).

14. "Ready, Boss? One, Two, Three, Fire!" (Bob Levey's Washington, *Washington Post*, May 10, 1991).

15. *Information Please Almanac.* (Boston: Houghton Mifflin, 1991).

16. Gail Sheehy, *The Silent Passage—Menopause* (New York: Random House, 1991).

17. David Campbell, *If I'm in Charge Here Why Is Everybody Laughing?* (Center for Creative Leadership, Greensboro, N.C.).

18. James A. Autry, *Love & Profit* (New York: William Morrow and Company, Inc., 1991).

19. "Male Menopause? Jury Is Still Out" (*New York Times*, May 20, 1992).

20. "Overheard" (*Newsweek*, June 1, 1992).

21. E. M. Abrahamson and A. W. Pezet, *Body, Mind, and Sugar*. (New York: Henry Holt, 1951).

22. "Scientists Find Hormonal Deficit in Chronic Fatigue Sufferers" (*New York Times*, November 2, 1992).

23. *The Home Medical Dictionary*. (Miami: P.S.I. & Associates, 1991).

24. "Fit . . . to Be Tied at Posh Health Club: Women Flex Muscle Over Locker Room" (*Washington Post*, February 28, 1992).

25. "Medical Sexism" (*ABC's 20-20*, June 12, 1992).

26. "Escaping Corporate Ghettoes" (*New York Times*, June 28, 1992).

27. "'All the Right Stuff' Often Goes Wrong for Female Managers" (*Washington Post*, January 12, 1992).

28. "DEA, Hispanic Agents Settle Bias Lawsuit" (*Washington Post*, June 10, 1992).

29. Judy Mann, "Academia's Dirty Little Secret" (*Washington Post*, February 19, 1992).

30. "U-Va. School Called 'Hostile' to Women: Outside Committee Cites Harassment Against Business Faculty Members" (*Washington Post*, May 27, 1992).

31. "Financial Firms Act to Curb Office Sexism, with Mixed Results: Despite Monetary Rewards, Vestiges of Locker Room Remain in the Workplace" (*Wall Street Journal*, November 5, 1991).

32. "Goldman Sachs Is Dogged by Charges of Discriminating Against Two Women" (*Wall Street Journal*, November 20, 1991).

33. "A Senior Wall Street Woman Asks: Why Is My Bonus Thinner Than His?" (*Wall Street Journal*, January 3, 1992).

34. "Woman Gets $7 Million in Airline Discrimination Suit" (*New York Times*, January 25, 1992).

35. "In Fairfax, Pay Bias Suit Exacts a Personal Price" (*Washington Post*, January 21, 1992).

36. "Women Win $157 Million in Bias Suit" (*Washington Post*, April 29, 1992).

37. "$675,000 Awarded in Va. Sex Bias Case" (*Washington Post*, June 20, 1992).

38. "U.S. Sues Over Dismissal for Accent" (*New York Times*, January 18, 1992).

39. "Texaco Gets New Trial in Sexual Discrimination Case" (*Wall Street Journal*, July 22, 1992).

40. "Airline Removes Agent for Not Using Makeup" (AP story, May 11, 1991).

41. "Continental's New Face Is Red" (*New York Times*, May 14, 1991).

42. "Continental Airlines Makes Over Rules on Use of Makeup" (*Wall Street Journal*, May 16, 1991).

43. "Three Elevator Men Win Bias Case on Ethnic Slurs" (*New York Times*, July 10, 1991).

44. Mark Green, "Warning: Some Ads Are a Serious Risk to Us All" (*Washington Post*, January 12, 1992).

45. "New Way to Store More Data" (*New York Times*, August 6, 1992).

46. Michael Moore, *Roger & Me: The Story of a Rebel and His Mike* (91-minute Videocassette; Warner Home Video, 1990).

47. Owen Edwards, *Upward Nobility* (New York: Crown, 1991).

48. ———, *Upward Nobility: How to Succeed in Business Without Losing Your Soul* (New York: Crown).

CHAPTER 10

1. "Navy Probe Faults at Least 70 Officers" (*Washington Post*, June 3, 1992).

2. "Navy Relieves Commander in Harassment Case" (*Washington Post*, December 22, 1991).

3. "A Gantlet of Terror, Frustration: Navy Pilot Recounts Tailhook Incident" (*Washington Post*, June 24, 1992).

4. "Navy Investigations: A Raft of Failures" (*New York Times*, June 28, 1992).

5. "Hilton Bars Aviator Group Tied to Scandal" (*New York Times*, August 5, 1992).

6. "Navy Toughens Policies on Sexual Harassment" (*Washington Post*, February 20, 1992).

7. "Navy Changes Its Training to Curb Sexual Harassment" (*New York Times*, June 22, 1992).

8. "Tailhook Investigator Removed after Complaint" (*Washington Post*, July 9, 1992).

9. "Navy Agent Removed from Tailhook Probe Had Been Suspended in 1990" (*Washington Post*, July 11, 1992).

10. "Navy Chief Seeks Anti-Harassment Law" (*New York Times*, July 3, 1992).

11. "Tailhook: Scandal Time" (*Newsweek*, July 6, 1992).

12. "Navy Punishes Two Top Officers over Lewd Banner at a Banquet" (*New York Times*, July 3, 1992).

13. "Navy Relieves 2 More Over Lewd Sketches" (*New York Times*, July 7, 1992).

14. "Harassment Questions Kill 2 Admirals' Promotions" (*New York Times*, July 18, 1992).

15. "Officials Say Navy Tried to Soften Report" (*New York Times*, July 8, 1992).

16. "Sexual Harassment Abroad" (*Parade*, January 12, 1992).

17. Desmond Morris, *The Naked Ape* (New York: McGraw-Hill, 1967).

18. "Hollywood and Harassment" (*Washington Post*, October 26, 1992).

19. "Judge Approves First Sex-Bias Class Action" (*New York Times*, December 18, 1991).

20. "Harassment Damages Approved" (*Washington Post*, February 27, 1992).

21. Laura Goldstein, "Hands off at Work" (*Self*, November 1991).

22. "Sexual Harassment: The Age of Anxiety" (*Business Week*, July 6, 1992).

23. "Beyond Innocence and Guilt Lies Sexism" (*New York Times*, February 15, 1992).

24. Marguerite Kelly, "A Workaholic Spouse" (*Washington Post*, January 23, 1992).

25. "I'd Toddle a Mile For a Camel" (*Business Week*, December 23, 1991); "R. J. Reynolds Battles the AMA, Defending Joe Camel Cartoon Ad" (*Wall Street Journal*, February 5, 1992); and "Judge Cites Possible Fraud in Tobacco Research" (*New York Times*, February 8, 1992).

26. "This Decision May Be Hazardous to Tobacco's Health: The High Court Leaves the Industry Open to Suits Charging Concealment" (*Business Week*, July 6, 1992).

27. "Poison at Home and at Work: A New Report Calls Secondhand Smoke a Killer" (*Newsweek*, June 29, 1992).

CHAPTER 11

1. "Persuading Bosses to Revise Reviews" (*Wall Street Journal*, May 22, 1992).

2. Collin Siedor, *Hidden Assets: Empowering America's Workers* (Videocassette; Atlanta: Dystar Television, 1991); *Secrets of Executive Success: How Anyone Can Handle the Human Side of Work and Grow Their Career.* (Emmaus, PA: Rodale Press, 1991); and Richard S. Wellins, William C. Byham and Jeanne M. Wilson, *Empowered Teams: Creating Self-directed Work Groups That Improve Quality, Productivity and Participation.* (San Francisco: Jossey-Bass, 1991).

3. Jay Carter, *Nasty People: How to Stop Being Hurt by Them Without Becoming One of Them.* (Chicago: Contemporary Books, 1989).

4. "How Did That Make Me Feel?" (Book review of *Think Life a Shrink* by Christ Zois, *Newsweek*, June 15, 1992).

CHAPTER 12

1. Karen Horney, *Self Analysis* (New York: Norton, 1968).

2. "How Did That Make Me Feel?" (Book review of *Think Like a Shrink* by Christ Zois, *Newsweek*, June 15, 1992).

3. Stanley Bing, *Crazy Bosses: Spotting Them, Serving Them, Surviving Them* (New York: Morris, 1992).

4. Charles G. Burck, "What Happens When Workers Manage Themselves: A Decade of Participative Management on the Factory Floor Provides Answers About What Works, What Doesn't, and Why" (*Fortune*, July 27, 1981, 63–69).

5. Morty Lefkoe, "Corporate Culture and Worker Health" (*New York Times*, May 24, 1992).

6. Coleman McCarthy, "Forgiveness: Human and Practical" (*Washington Post*, January 20, 1992).

INDEX